Palgrave Histories of Policing, Punishment and Justice

Series Editor
David G. Barrie
University of Western Australia
Crawley, Australia

Since the 1960s, studies of police, punishment and the courts have been an integral and popular part of historical scholarship, and have followed in the historical trajectory of a more expansive criminal justice apparatus around the world. This international book series aims to examine and debate some of the most pressing issues and problems in the field, and to stimulate new directions in research. It will showcase the work of both emerging and leading scholars of the social, cultural and institutional histories of police, punishment and the judicial sphere, and welcomes work grounded in various disciplines including criminology, sociology, history, law, legal history and political science.

More information about this series at
http://www.palgrave.com/gp/series/15080

Steven Anderson

A History of Capital Punishment in the Australian Colonies, 1788 to 1900

palgrave
macmillan

Steven Anderson
The Department of History
The University of Adelaide
Adelaide, SA, Australia

Palgrave Histories of Policing, Punishment and Justice
ISBN 978-3-030-53766-1 ISBN 978-3-030-53767-8 (eBook)
https://doi.org/10.1007/978-3-030-53767-8

Cover illustration: f8 archive/Alamy Stock Photo

This Palgrave Macmillan imprint is published by the registered company Springer Nature Switzerland AG
The registered company address is: Gewerbestrasse 11, 6330 Cham, Switzerland

Dedicated to the memory of
Glenn Anderson
(1954–2011)

Contents

List of Illustrations

Preface

For guilty criminals being sentenced in an Australian courtroom today, the words 'you are to be hanged by the neck until dead' is not a turn of phrase they need to worry about hearing. In fact, there is a whole range of punishments that have now become extinct on the continent. Prisons and fines have colonised a penal infrastructure that once condoned sanctions like transportation, the pillory and the lash as a criminal's 'just desserts'. While it existed on the statute books, capital punishment was the law's most feared punishment but it too changed dramatically. In the early days of settlement public executions could attract spectators in the thousands; children were occasionally lifted up higher so they could better see the consequences of a life of crime. Criminals might choose to ignore the counsel of the God-fearing clergymen over their shoulder and shock the crowd with their bravado in the face of eternity. Nervous and sometimes inebriated executioners, usually one-time criminals themselves, often fumbled the job. For a time the criminal's body was liable to be 'hung in chains' afterwards—a rotting carcass blowing in the wind left to underscore the hangman's example. And all this could be carried out on a criminal guilty of a crime less than that of murder; property offences were enough to see a person hang in the first decades of British settlement. For those living today who are old enough to hold a personal memory of Australia's last execution—that of Ronald Ryan in 1967—there is no doubt that their recollections of his death are a world away from the type of colonial executions evoked above.

This book gives a comprehensive overview of capital punishment in the Australian colonial period (1788–1900) for the very first time. Many of the basic facts about each colony are outlined in an early chapter on Australia's 'hanging years'—execution numbers, the frequency of mercy and the changing nature of capital crimes. It shows how the 'settings' of capital punishment were slightly different for each jurisdiction but always shifting in the same direction. The middle chapters provide an overview of the practice of executions broken down into three components: the realities of execution procedure, the behaviour of the dying criminal and the nature of the crowd gathered below the drop. It reveals the perceived problems with the way executions were being conducted and how they were corrected in each case. The reason for the abolition of public executions, and their partial reintroduction for Indigenous Australian offenders, is discussed after that. Depending on the race of the condemned criminal, Australia was simultaneously a leader and a straggler when it came to this issue in the context of the British Empire. The push for the total abolition of the death penalty concerns the final chapter so that a well-rounded perspective on the punishment can be achieved. In the end, the death penalty survived to Federation in each of the Australian colonies but it emerged in a sanitised, professionalised and institutionalised form.

Running through the entirety of the book is a quest to understand not just how, but why, capital punishment changed in the direction it did over the course of the colonial period. I argue that the 'lesson' of the gallows, something that those in positions of authority held dear, was threatened by the way executions were being carried out. Colonial authorities went about removing these distractions one-by-one to ensure that the didactic intention of an execution could remain intact. Crucially, any change the punishment underwent had to accord with the unique and ever-changing cultural norms and popular memory of Australian colonists. This argument could not have been formulated without reference to the more sociologically-minded literature on culture and punishment which I pay my respects to in the Introduction. I also justify this approach against other candidates of analysis (i.e. Foucault, Marx, Elias or more traditional accounts of penal 'progress') that also have the potential to explain penal change.

The transformation of the Australian death penalty has many international analogues. Comparative and transnationally-minded scholars of punishment are sure to find this book useful—there is nowhere else that so many facts and figures about the Australian situation are compiled in one place. Those interested in ongoing debates about penal change active in fields like sociology, criminology, penology and history will also find the practical application of a conceptual position instructive. For those with a penchant for Australian history alone, the gallows wove its way into some of its most notorious chapters: the bushranging epidemic, convict mutinies, frontier conflicts and crimes of lasting notoriety (think of the 'cannibal convict' Alexander Pearce, for example). From examining the contours of the death penalty much can be learnt about different features of colonial society as a whole. Although this book is focused on the colonial period (1788–1900), it was the era when the vast majority (over 90%) of the approximately two thousand executions in Australian history took place. To know how the gallows operated prior to Federation on 1 January 1901 is necessary if anyone is to make sense to what happened after it.

The history of capital punishment in Australia is yet to be given the full scholarly attention it deserves. It lacks a comprehensive study that has been to the benefit of the historical debate in places like England, Germany, France, the Netherlands, the United States of America and Canada. This is the first monograph of comparable size and scope to be published about capital punishment in Australia. The existing body of academic literature on the topic has proved useful but is most often limited by jurisdiction, timeframe or a specific feature of the penalty. An extensive web of primary sources collected over many years was mustered from all six colonies to accomplish the task. To categorise them broadly it utilises: parliamentary material; government reports; trial accounts; gaol records; published memoirs; travel accounts; newspaper articles;

visual sources; private correspondence; and abolitionist pamphlets. A wide variety of colonists are also heard from—some not often given a voice in existing histories. Legislators, judges, lawyers, sheriffs, journalists and clergymen exist alongside criminals, executioners, women, travelling writers, pioneering residents and Indigenous Australians. All have a unique perspective on the issues that emerge when discussing something as emotive as capital punishment.

Documenting the history of capital punishment in six separate jurisdictions over a 112-year time-span was a challenging task to say the least—one that took me a full decade to complete. I am thankful for the financial assistance granted to me from the following institutions during that time to conduct this research: The Australian Commonwealth Government; The University of Adelaide; The Australian Historical Association; and The National Library of Australia. The University of Adelaide has proved to be a stimulating and supportive research environment throughout this process. I am grateful to the Series Editor (Associate Professor David Barrie) as well as the team at Palgrave Macmillan (Josie Taylor and Liam Inscoe-Jones in particular) for their show of faith in the latest iteration of this project. The assistance of Kayalvizhi Saravanakumar was also appreciated. It should be acknowledged that portions of Chapter 7 have appeared in the following publication: Steven Anderson, 'Punishment as Pacification: The Role of Indigenous Executions on the South Australian Frontier, 1836–1862', *Aboriginal History*, vol. 39, 2015, pp. 3–26.

If I listed everyone by name that I have shared this journey with I would soon run out of space. So to all of the friends, colleagues and postgraduates who have supported and advised me—rest easy knowing that you have helped in ways that 12-point Times New Roman cannot express. There are, however, a handful of people who were crucial in making this book all it could be. If it has a godfather the most likely candidate is Associate Professor Paul Sendziuk. As my PhD supervisor he has helped nurture this project from infancy and it has benefited extensively from his wise counsel. Gay Anderson always had her eye out for any errors in punctuation, syntax and spelling along the way. To Emma: there is no other smile I look forward to seeing more than yours. To Gay, Martyn, Kathryn, Amanda, Nima, Layla, Arya, Mila, Alice and Charlotte—I am lucky to have been brought up in such a supportive family environment. Finally, I dedicate this work to my late father, Glenn Anderson, who is still remembered nine years on by his adoring widow, children and now—through old photographs—by his five young grandchildren.

Adelaide, Australia Steven Anderson

1

Introduction: Thinking About Punishment Over Time

Consider the execution of John Knatchbull in 1844 outside Sydney's Darlinghurst Gaol (Illustration 1.1) compared to that of Ned Kelly in 1880 at the Old Melbourne Gaol (Illustration 1.2). Both were notorious figures in Australian criminal history during their lifetime except that the former was sentenced to a public execution while the latter underwent a private execution. The sketch of Knatchbull, a convicted murderer of aristocratic birth, does well to capture the atmosphere of public executions.[1] To the far right, horses mounted with late spectators are in full stride, rushing to join the throng of an estimated 10,000 Sydneysiders present. In the foreground male, female, and child spectators are all visible in a crowd that swells the closer it comes to the towering image of the scaffold. A dozen mounted military personnel stand guard at the base of the structure. Following the steps upward are two clergymen attending to Knatchbull while the executioner makes the

[1] For newspaper accounts of Knatchbull's execution, see *The Sydney Morning Herald*, 14 February 1844, pp. 2–3; *The Australian*, 15 February 1844, p. 3; *Morning Chronicle*, 14 February 1844, p. 2. For a secondary account of his crime, execution, and aristocratic background, see Colin Roderick, *John Knatchbull: From Quarterdeck to Gallows*, Sydney: Angus & Robertson, 1963.

S. Anderson, *A History of Capital Punishment in the Australian Colonies, 1788 to 1900*,
Palgrave Histories of Policing, Punishment and Justice,
https://doi.org/10.1007/978-3-030-53767-8_1

Illustration 1.1 The execution of John Knatchbull outside Sydney's Darlinghurst Gaol on 13 February 1844 (*Source* 'Woolloomooloo Gaol, Execution of John Knatchbull', Government Printing Office, Glass Negative 1–21799, held by State Archives and Records Authority of NSW)

final adjustments to the rope around his neck. The jutting architecture of Darlinghurst Gaol informs the background of the work but the drama is soon to be played out on the tongue of the entrance gate. One imagines that, as Knatchbull fell into the cavity below, the static image of the prison was secondary to the screams, gasps and jolts of Sydneysiders gathered shoulder to shoulder.

The image of Ned Kelly's hanging gives the opposing perspective of a private execution. The ten thousand itching, impatient spectators at Knatchbull's feet are exchanged for the cold interior walls of Melbourne Gaol. In the absence of the distracting public, legal functionaries and religious advisors enclose him while the symbol of the cross is held steadily over his head. The white cap would soon be pulled over Kelly's face, hiding the grotesque contortions that always occur the moment the noose jabs at the neck. Though not depicted in the sketch, contemporary newspaper reports attest to the fact that there was a small crowd watching the hanging in the cellblock itself but not one was a curious onlooker. Each of the twenty-three spectators was

Illustration 1.2 The execution of Ned Kelly inside Melbourne Gaol on 11 November 1880 (*Source* 'Sketch of Ned Kelly at the Gallows, Melbourne Gaol, 11 November 1888', copied and digitised from an image appearing in the *Australasian Sketcher*, 20 November 1880, p. 185, John Oxley Library, State Library of Queensland, record number: 187795)

present in a professional capacity—mostly journalists and government officials. They recorded their names and occupations as a matter of legal necessity.[2] To the newspapermen who would publish their accounts, the powerful architecture of the prison was all around them, inhabited by

[2]'Witnesses to Kelly's Execution, 11 October 1880', Public Record Office Victoria, VPRS 4969/2/78.

them, inescapable no matter where their eyes looked. From the perspective of Ned Kelly, looking outwards from the drop at Melbourne Gaol, the distractions had been removed; all that was staring back at him was the blank faces of officialdom and the dreary walls of the prison block.

Between the execution of John Knatchbull in 1844 and Ned Kelly in 1880 the Australian colonial parliaments—commencing with New South Wales in 1853—passed legislation to abolish public executions. It irrevocably changed the way hangings were carried out on the continent. However, a closer look at the subject of capital punishment in the Australian colonies reveals a host of other, subtler shifts occurring—not all strictly related to the practice of executions. To begin with the number of available capital crimes were being whittled down. When European settlement took hold at Sydney Cove, a dizzying array of offences could see a person hang—its early penal regime was, after all, a child of England's notorious 'bloody code'. Yet, at the conclusion of the nineteenth century no colony had more than a dozen capital offences on their statute books. Mercy appeared to be dispensed more freely as the years passed. For those sentenced to death in New South Wales between 1788 and 1798 only 28% were extended mercy, compared to a commutation rate of 67.1% between 1890 and 1900.[3] Moreover, after spiking around the highpoint of the convict era in the 1820s and 1830s, execution numbers in Australia steadily declined in proportion to a growing population. Eventually only criminals of the deepest dye were considered a problem for the hangman to solve—the rest were usually left for the prison warden to sort out. When all things are considered, a forensic examination of the Australian death penalty reveals a punishment never settled or fixed, but one subject to constant debate and revision.

The history of the Australian continent was transformed the moment the British decided to colonize the land to ease the congestion of its own penal system. New South Wales, intended first as a penal settlement, was

[3]These numbers are adapted from two separate sources, see Ken Macnab, Tim Castle, Amanda Kaladelfos, 'NSW Capital Convictions Database', *Frances Forbes Society for Australian Legal History* 2013, http://research.forbessociety.org.au/, viewed 13 August 2015; Carolyn Strange, 'Discretionary Justice: Political Culture and the Death Penalty in New South Wales and Ontario, 1890–1920', in C. Strange (ed.), *Qualities of Mercy: Justice, Punishment, and Discretion*, Vancouver: UBC Press, 1996, p. 143. Note that in the period 1788–1798 only fully confirmed executions and commutations from that period were included in the final calculation.

the first colony established by Britain in 1788. The legal fiction of *Terra Nullius*, meanwhile, was invoked to deprive traditional owners the control of land occupied by their forefathers. The eastern colonies of Tasmania (formerly known as Van Diemen's Land), Victoria and Queensland were carved out from the vast tract originally designated for New South Wales. Western Australia and South Australia were established from the outset as separate colonies. It is easy to look back at the six Australian colonies as a homogenous whole but it is important to remember that each one eventually developed its own administration, judiciary and legal system. As such each individual colony's experience of capital punishment, though evolving in a similar direction, often moved to slightly different time signatures. This similar but separate trajectory was continued even after the six colonies federated to form the new nation of Australia on 1 January 1901. Capital punishment itself was first abolished in Queensland in 1922 while the remaining jurisdictions waited until the latter half of the twentieth century to do the same.[4]

Throughout the nineteenth century, the 'lesson' of the gallows was a phrase used often in the Australian colonies. It alludes to the idea that communication is essential to the practice of punishment. Embedded within any execution was a host of messages, the most obvious being strictly penal in nature. In the words of Samuel Frederick Milford in 1866, Judge of the Supreme Court of New South Wales: 'The object of capital punishment is to alarm and deter persons predisposed to crime from committing it'.[5] Those administering punishment always looked for strategies to best communicate that fact to the onlooker. For instance, some Australian jurisdictions thought it necessary to hang Indigenous offenders on a gallows mounted at the very spot where their crime was committed, preferably in front of the wrongdoer's own people. Only then, the authorities believed, could the consequences of transgressing settler law be fully understood. However, the intended lesson of the gallows was often subject to a number of unwanted and unforeseen

[4]Sam Garkawe, 'The Reintroduction of the Death Penalty in Australia?—Political and Legal Considerations', *Criminal Law Journal*, vol. 24, no. 2, 2002, pp. 101–108.

[5]United Kingdom, 'Report of the Capital Punishment Commission: Together with the Minutes of Evidence and Appendix', London: Printed by George E. Eyre and William Spottiswoode, 1866, p. 588.

distractions—even at run-of-the-mill executions of European criminals. An unruly scaffold crowd, a botched hanging, the misbehaving criminal, a punishment too severe for the crime—all of these factors had the potential to derail the example. In the blink of an eye, a just punishment could morph into an unruly exhibition that meant all the wrong things. It is no consequence then that all of these distractions, slowly but surely, were removed by the time of Federation. Hangings were hidden inside the prison, the list of capital crimes was narrowed and the post of hangman was professionalised. Executions became, for most people, only accessible through the reportage of journalists. I argue throughout this monograph that safeguarding the lesson of an execution in the midst of changing cultural beliefs and popular memory is what shaped the evolution of capital punishment over time in Australia.

Chapter 2 sets the scene by providing an overview of Australia's 'hanging years'. The colonial period was, after all, where the vast majority of executions took place. It expands upon the existing historiography of capital punishment in Australia to give a basic picture in each of the six colonies of execution numbers, the frequency of mercy and the type of offences that were capital. A variety of factors extrinsic to the penal system ended up intersecting with the operation of the gallows. For example, norms around gender, race and age impacted decisions around mercy. As for what crimes should remain capital, the gender imbalance, the bushranger problem and the isolation of the frontier all had a role to play in the decisions made. There were small but consistent alterations allowing for the parameters of capital punishment to sit comfortably within colonial society over time. In the end it is clear that capital punishment was not a penalty on the rise but one slowly receding in prominence. As Federation neared, it was a punishment used mostly as a last resort—there only to check crimes of the severest type.

Chapter 3 explores the execution procedure in colonial Australia between 1788 and 1900 from sentencing all the way through to when the hanged body was examined by medical professionals. A set of circulars sent out by the Colonial Office in England to the Australian colonies in 1880 are used for this purpose and demonstrate the gap between the ideal and the reality of execution procedure in the colonial period. What becomes apparent is that there was an evergrowing sensitivity among colonists towards the sight of unnecessary pain and suffering in criminals. The constant bungling of the execution procedure, both major and minor, distracted from the example of the punishment. In the name of 'decency' and 'humanity' the execution was transformed from an amateur undertaking to a standardised and professionalised practice by the time of Federation. Though aware of other modes of execution developing abroad—like electrocution in America or the guillotine in France—hanging remained the only official means through which death was meted out.

The ability for the condemned criminal to actively shape the meaning of their punishment in his or her final moments is the subject of Chapter 4. A penitent criminal underlined the justice of the sentence but a misbehaving one left open the possibility of other interpretations. When the criminal mounted the scaffold there was the popular cultural expectation that they 'die game' or, in other words, with a degree of courage, pluckiness and bravado. It encouraged many criminals to misbehave and hide away any feelings of contrition for the crime that had been committed. The role of the executioner, clergymen and sheriff was to shepherd criminals into thinking that penitence was the only option available to them. However, the case of Ned Kelly is invoked to demonstrate just how difficult it was for the state to control the narrative of an execution—even when everything went exactly according to plan.

Chapter 5 deals with the changing way that onlookers interacted with executions in the colonies. The perception was that the lower classes were attracted to the foot of the public scaffold while it was also troubling that women and children were known to attend. This concerned middle and upper class colonists who were convinced that witnessing the gory spectacle of hangings only served to demoralise the onlooker and acclimatise them to violence. It also conflicted with the idealised role of these groups that existed within the colonial culture—as disciplined workers, moral guardians of the home or the virtuous next generation. When public executions were abolished colonial sheriffs were put in charge of determining who was able to view the private hanging. At these new executions an exceedingly small and select number of citizens were admitted into the gaol on the day of the hanging, complemented by the usual number of prison officials, journalists and medical men. The crowd, once seen as guardians of due process in earlier epochs, was now considered a distraction from the execution itself.

Nothing did more to change the character of capital punishment in the colonial period than the abolition of public executions. Chapter 6 focuses on the practical measures that were necessary to introduce private executions in colonial Australia. The contents of the various Private Execution Acts are examined as are the lengthy processes that New South Wales and Victoria went through to have the legislation approved by England. The parliamentary debates and the reaction of the colonial newspapers underline the long-term issues regarding public executions, especially surrounding the behaviour of the crowd and the attitude of the dying criminal. It is argued that the trigger for the transition to private executions was the cultural legacy of convictism and a desire for the older penal colonies to appear 'civilised' to the outside world. It was a unique trigger that caused them to enact this penal reform comparatively early in the context of the British Empire.

Indigenous executions in South Australia and Western Australia were an exception to the trend to greater seclusion when hanging criminals but one that makes sense when properly contextualised. Chapter 7 demonstrates how these two jurisdictions reprised public executions for Indigenous Australian offenders only a handful of years after they had abolished the practice completely. It was grounded in a disparaging cultural construction of Indigenous intellect, temperament and habit as rendered by the colonial authorities. Despite their partial reinstatement, the public execution of an Indigenous offender was a rare occurrence after the amendments were passed. The experience of New South Wales, Tasmania, Victoria and Queensland in regards to Indigenous executions is also touched upon. Just as it influenced many other areas of colonial life and governance, ideas of race intersected with the operation of the Australian gallows in fascinating ways.

Though capital punishment always enjoyed the majority support of colonial lawmakers, Chapter 8 documents the vocal minority pushing for the abolition of capital punishment altogether. Prominent abolitionist voices emerged after the middle of the nineteenth century. They brought arguments from religion and jurisprudence but also expressed a want to keep pace with the 'civilized' world abroad. Colonial parliaments witnessed a series of abolitionist bills, particularly in New South Wales, but none were ever passed into law. Abolitionists never united to form a coherent movement to exact prolonged pressure for change. It was an idea pursued intermittently with only short bursts of coherent agitation. Australian abolitionists are to be credited with creating a political and cultural environment where reform was feasible. Yet, in the end, an explanation for the changes the gallows underwent in the colonial period must go deeper than an examination of these attempts at abolition.

The move away from the public, deliberately painful, bodily punishment towards private, sanitised and institutionalised forms of punishment was one replicated many times over in the west—albeit on different timelines. The impact this trend had upon capital punishment (particularly in the nineteenth century) is a feature of impressive book-length historical studies found in prominent jurisdictions like England, Germany, France, the Netherlands and The United States.[6] More recently, there has been a welcome shift to round out our understanding of the history of the death penalty in jurisdictions once considered 'peripheral'—like Canada and Scotland for example—which also contain references to this pattern.[7] The sociology of punishment is a field that has emerged in part to better understand transforming penal systems—the death penalty included. In fact, anyone acquainted with this sociological literature might already find some of the conceptual points made above familiar. David Garland and Philip Smith are two scholars in particular whom many, myself included, owe a large

---

[6]Stuart Banner, *The Death Penalty: An American History*, Cambridge, MA: Harvard University Press, 2002; Richard J. Evans, *Rituals of Retribution: Capital Punishment in Germany, 1600–1987*, Oxford: Oxford University Press, 1996; Paul Friedland, *Seeing Justice Done: The Age of Spectacular Capital Punishment in France*, Oxford: Oxford University Press, 2012; David Garland, *Peculiar Institution: America's Death Penalty in an Age of Abolition*, Oxford: Oxford University Press, 2010; V.A.C. Gatrell, *The Hanging Tree: Execution and the English People 1770–1868*, Oxford: Oxford University Press, 1994; Louis P. Masur, *Rites of Execution: Capital Punishment and the Transformation of American Culture, 1776–1865*, Oxford: Oxford University Press, 1989, p. 7; Pieter Spierenburg, *The Spectacle of Suffering: Executions and the Evolution of Repression; From a Preindustrial Metropolis to the European Experience*, Cambridge: Cambridge University Press, 1984.

[7]Rachel E. Bennett, *Capital Punishment and the Criminal Corpse in Scotland, 1740–1834*, Basingstoke: Palgrave Macmillan, 2018; Ken Leyton-Brown, *The Practice of Execution in Canada*, Vancouver: UBC Press, 2010.

debt for systematically theorising the relationship between punishment and culture in recent times. The usefulness of their ideas comes in the ability for a historical study such as this one to be produced. Still, to justify the importance of culture and communication against other possible candidates, it is necessary to briefly explore some of the foundational touchstones for understanding punishment—from 'traditional' approaches of penal change to Foucault, the Marxists and those following the example of Norbert Elias. It is a tour that will force us to leave the safety of Australian shores for just a moment, but a necessary journey should we desire to know why punishment changes over time.

What might be labelled a 'traditional' approach to understanding the evolution of punishment will often privilege the agency of individual figures, groups of reformers, or intellectuals who were close to the levers of government. Leon Radzinowicz's monumental five volume *History of the English Criminal Law and Its Administration from 1750* (published between 1948 and 1986) is often pointed to as an example of such an approach.[8] Present in his work is a belief in progress, a trust in the benevolence of humanitarians and the confidence that British penal reform arrived at a noble terminus. Many have noted the tone of a Whig history looming over Radzinowicz's analysis of the criminal law. In the opening lines of Volume 1 he confirms his belief that: 'Lord Macaulay's generalisation that the history of England is the history of progress is as true of the criminal law of this country as of the other social institutions of which it is a part'.[9] For Radzinowicz, the flowering nineteenth-century humanitarian impulse left an indelible mark upon capital punishment in England. His opinion expressed in Volume 4 of his *History* was that public executions were abolished because of 'the improvement of morals and manners [and] the growth of humanity'.[10] As for the aggravated penalties that accompanied death in earlier ages—torture, dissection,

[8]Leon Radzinowicz, *A History of the English Criminal Law and Its Administration from 1750*, vols. 1–4, London: Stevens and Sons Limited, 1948–1968; Leon Radzinowicz and Roger Hood, *A History of the English Criminal Law and Its Administration from 1750*, vol. 5, London: Stevens and Sons Limited, 1986.

[9]Radzinowicz, vol. 1, 1948, p. ix.

[10]Radzinowicz, vol. 4, 1968, pp. 343–353, quote on p. 352.

hanging in chains, drawing and quartering—these too were abandoned because a 'growing sense of humanity had made them increasingly repugnant'.[11] Yet, the willingness of scholars like Radzinowicz to alloy freewheeling individual agency with ideas of penal 'progress' was troublesome to the critical evaluation of penal history that gathered pace in the 1970s.

The French thinker Michel Foucault has proved to be the most dominant theoretical touchstone for studies of punishment since the publication of his book *Discipline and Punish: The Birth of the Prison* in 1975 (translated into English in 1977). To understand the intricacies of Foucault's argument, one must first recognise his idea that punishment in every age is about the accumulation of power and control. Underneath the outward justifications of benevolent reformers, power was his 'timeless origin' that organised human behaviour.[12] For Foucault the reason for the evolution of punishment through time was simple—the punishing authority found better ways to punish which rendered public and violent penalties directed at the body obsolete. In earlier times (like France's *Ancien Régime*) punishment was spectacle—the body wore the penalty, it was public, the extent of the punishment was unlimited and arbitrarily applied to the offender who was seen as a personal enemy of the sovereign. Foucault is quick to observe that the nature of the punishing authority's power was both temporal and explicit, an 'irregular terrorism' enacted top-down by the King onto his subjects.[13] All this changed in the late eighteenth and early nineteenth century when the state learnt to punish more effectively by hijacking the technologies of modernity and adopting the omnipresent tools of discipline and surveillance. Thus conceived, the hidden rationale of penal evolution is a restless authority seeking to maximise its control over society: '[N]ot to punish less but to punish better; to punish with an attenuated severity perhaps, but in order to punish with more universality and necessity;

[11] Radzinowicz, vol. 4, 1968, p. 344.

[12] Richard Rorty, *Contingency, Irony, Solidarity*, Cambridge: Cambridge University Press, 1989, pp. 61–62.

[13] David Garland, *Punishment and Modern Society: A Study in Social Theory*, Oxford: Clarendon Press, 1990, p. 142.

to insert the power to punish more deeply into the social body'.[14] The panopticon prison design was, famously, the purest physical manifestation of modern state power according to Foucault. It made visible a set of disciplinary mechanisms that were not only forced upon captive prison populations but upon civil society more generally: in schools, workshops, monasteries and hospitals.

Karl Marx himself had little to say about punishment but many historians have since drawn upon the nexus of class, labour and changing modes of production to explain why punishment took on various forms across the centuries.[15] Georg Rusche and Otto Kirchheimer, both connected to the Frankfurt School, showed how the economic base directly impacted upon choices of punishment over the long term.[16] They called it 'self-evident' that 'enslavement as a form of punishment is impossible without a slave economy, that prison labor is impossible without manufacture or industry, that monetary fines for all classes of society are impossible without a money economy'.[17] Beyond studying the influence of the mode of production on penal choices, class dynamics came into focus during the 1970s for those working on English history. E.P. Thompson demonstrated in *Whigs and Hunters* (1975) that definitions of criminality (such as the capital offences labelled in the 'Black Act' of 1723) were intimately linked to broader class and economic interests.[18] In Douglas Hay's famous essay, published in *Albion's Fatal Tree* (1975), the eighteenth-century criminal law was deemed to be the 'chief ideological instrument' of the ruling class.[19] The drama of the courtroom and the paternalism of judges were crucial while the execution itself was the 'climactic emotional point of the criminal law – the moment of terror

---

[14] Michel Foucault, *Discipline and Punish: The Birth of the Prison* [1975], Alan Sheridan (trans), second Vintage Books edition, New York: Vintage Books, 1995, p. 82.

[15] References to punishment by Marx in *Das Kapital* are explored in, Dario Melossi, 'The Penal Question in *Capital*', *Crime and Social Justice*, vol. 5, 1976, pp. 26–33.

[16] Georg Rusche and Otto Kirchheimer, *Punishment and Social Structure* [1939], New Brunswick: Transaction Publishers, 2003.

[17] Rusche and Kirchheimer, 2003, p. 6.

[18] E.P. Thompson, *Whigs and Hunters: The Origin of the Black Act*, London: Allen Lane, 1975.

[19] Douglas Hay, 'Property, Authority and the Criminal Law', in *Albion's Fatal Tree: Crime and Society in Eighteenth-Century England* [1975], revised edition, London: Verso, 2011, pp. 17–64, quote on p. 26.

around which the system revolved'.[20] Similarly, Peter Linebaugh stated in *The London Hanged* (2003) that if hangings are to be considered theatre, executions teach a simple lesson: 'Respect Private Property'.[21]

From the 1980s, the ideas of the German-born sociologist Norbert Elias, as presented in *The Civilizing Process* (1939), had started to enter the fray. For Elias, the 'motor of civilization' was the growing interdependency of the upper classes—something he tied to the increasingly complex way that state functions (say, tax collection or servicing an army) were being administered.[22] In Elias' words, these interdependent social structures encouraged 'a constraint on the affects, a self-discipline and self-control, a peculiarly courtly rationality' that gave the 'common stamp' to Western civilisation.[23] Given Elias did not address the issue of penal evolution in his analysis, Pieter Spierenburg was the first to realise its explanatory potential with the publication of *The Spectacle of Suffering* (1984).[24] Tighter webs of social interdependence present in emergent social structures like the nation-state fostered a growth in empathy towards the dying criminal. This upshot in 'mutual identification', as Spierenburg called it, made many onlookers uncomfortable with the violence of more arcane forms of punishment.[25] Thus, the gradual abolition of public punishments in Amsterdam (the focus of his study) was the 'political conclusion' to a much longer term change in the 'sensibilities' of Dutch elites.[26] Moreover, Spierenburg contends that spectacular and cruel punishments were no longer necessary in jurisdictions where the monopoly on violence had been secured by the sovereign—authorities could 'afford to show a milder and more liberal

---

[20] Hay, 2011, p. 28.

[21] Peter Linebaugh, *The London Hanged: Crime and Civil Society in the Eighteenth Century*, London: Verso, 2003, pp. xxii–xxiii.

[22] Norbert Elias, *The Civilizing Process* [1939], second revised edition, E. Dunning, J. Goudsblom, and S. Mennell (eds), E. Jephcott (trans), Oxford: Blackwell, 2000, p. 129.

[23] Elias, 2000, pp. 190–191.

[24] Spierenburg, 1984, p. x.

[25] 'Mutual identification' basically means humanism when stated in less abstract terms, see Spierenburg, 1984, p. 185. For a passing discussion on the concept elsewhere, see Stephen Mennell, 'Decivilising Processes: Theoretical Significance and Some Lines of Research', *International Sociology*, vol. 5, no. 2, 1990, pp. 209–210.

[26] Spierenburg, 1984, p. 183.

face' under such circumstances he writes.[27] John Pratt and John McGuire are two others who have recently utilised Elias framework in a penal context.[28] The latter even called Elias' concepts a 'useful explanatory tool' when applied to the history of capital punishment in Australia.[29]

By the 1990s many criticisms had built up within and between these existing schools of thought. Radzinowicz's history and others like it were instructive and comprehensive but ultimately naïve. To someone like Foucault the progress of modernity was questionable, the freedoms of the Enlightenment suspect and the motivations of humanitarian reformers duplicitous. Meanwhile, Marxists were perplexed that the rational accumulation of power and control in Foucault's world appeared detached from any sort of coherent social goal. One Marxist historian used to making class the fulcrum of his analysis, labelled it 'bizarre' that there is power everywhere but apparently concentrated nowhere and, by extension, put to no greater purpose.[30] In turn, many well worn criticisms of material histories were levelled at Marxist penal analyses—concerns about individual agency being subsumed by economic structures or that intellectual developments were being ignored. For example, where does the work of key Enlightenment thinkers, like Cesare Beccaria's revolutionary ideas on proportionality and certainty, fit into Marxist discussions on penal change? As for Elias, many have wondered about the validity of making assumptions about 'unobservable' psychic restraints and emotional dispositions of historical actors considering these types of investigations are hard enough to accomplish in the modern laboratory.[31] Tying patterns of state formation and interdependence to penal reform also had its issues regarding the timing of reform. Take the fact that the sparsely populated Australian colonies had abolished public executions

27Spierenburg, 1984, p. 205.

28John Pratt, *Punishment and Civilization: Penal Tolerance and Intolerance in Modern Society*, London: Sage, 2002; John McGuire, 'Judicial Violence and the "Civilizing Process": Race and the Transition from Public to Private Executions in Colonial Australia', *Australian Historical Studies*, vol. 29, no. 111, 1998, pp. 187–209.

29McGuire, 1998, p. 190.

30Hay, 2011, p. xxxiii.

31Garland, 1990, p. 229.

in the 1850s while France (a model of the Civilizing Process to Elias) still had public guillotining on the streets of Paris as late as 1939.

David Garland's masterly *Punishment and Modern Society* (1990) was vital in surveying the different analyses on punishment that then existed. It was also a work that helped establish cultural approaches as a viable way to solve some of the shortcomings that had built up in existing schools of thought. He recognised that choices of punishment which may appear on the surface to be the result of economic efficiencies, bureaucratic prerogatives or the objectives of crime control are first predicated upon a normative judgement of what is acceptable or unacceptable within a given social context. Put another way, possible candidates of action are always vetted by the values and norms operating from outside of the strict parameters of the penal sphere.[32] He also articulates the active role punishment has to help organise meaning within culture—to make intelligible to the onlooker the nature of state authority or the role of an individual within society, for example. More subtly, ideas about race, gender and age can be understood by the way they are treated in the penal space.[33] Punishment, for Garland in this work, is a 'complex cultural artefact' of a specific time and place.[34] It is an account that favoured local contingencies as agents of causal import rather than large, and sometimes ahistorical, structural forces.

When the technical vocabulary of sociologists about the relationship between punishment and culture is put to one side it is clear that historians were also noticing this connection around the same time as Garland. A buttoned-up historical study like Louis P. Masur's *Rites of Execution* (1989) is a good example. For Masur, America's antebellum executions could be studied like a 'text' to provide a 'window onto ideological assumptions, social relations, and collective fictions'.[35] Religiosity, republican values and middle-class sensibilities were some of the cultural beliefs coded into the very design of public executions to form a coherent message that could be 'viewed, heard and read' by the throng of

[32] Garland, 1990, p. 241.
[33] Garland, 1990, pp. 265–273.
[34] Garland, 1990, p. 198.
[35] Masur, 1989, p. 7.

onlookers.[36] An offshoot of cultural history—the history of emotions—started to gather momentum as well. V.A.C. Gatrell's *The Hanging Tree* (1994) did much to push emotions, or at least a far more nuanced understanding of them, into the debate around capital punishment in England. For instance, the squeamishness of English elites towards the gallows was judged not to be a form of sympathy but of cowardice—a means to psychologically distance and avoid confronting the reality of another's pain.[37] More recently, emotions, culture and punishment have all been pollinating in new ways across different international contexts.[38]

To return to the sociological literature, Philip Smith provided a welcome foray into the debate with *Punishment and Culture* (2008), a work that expanded upon many of Garland's earlier thoughts. It also provides much of the conceptual scaffolding for the ideas around penal change presented here. Smith takes punishment to be a kind of 'speech act' encoded by the authorities in material signs and symbols, which is then sent out and decoded by the onlooker.[39] The problem for authorities is that their carefully designed punishments can 'take on new, unsavoury meanings' due to their interaction with culture.[40] As just one example, Smith describes how the prison chain gang working on the side of the road in the American South came irksomely close to the 'poisoned iconography of slavery', eventually leading to its reduced usage.[41] He uses terms like 'genre-shift' or 're-narration' to describe when the official meaning of punishment has been unhelpfully contaminated by wider cultural norms. If the message is not being received appropriately then the punishment becomes vulnerable to alteration. Penal reform is simply 'repair work' by the authorities so that the troublesome punishment can

---

[36] Masur, 1989, p. 26.

[37] Gatrell, 1994, pp. 266–271. McGowen reflects on this distinction in his extended review of *The Hanging Tree,* see Randall McGowen, 'Revisiting the Hanging Tree: Gatrell on Emotion and History', *British Journal of Criminology*, vol. 40, 2000, pp. 1–13.

[38] For example, Paul Friedland, as part of a book-length work, traced the oscillating emotional distance the spectator felt with the suffering figure on the French scaffold, Friedland, 2012, pp. 119–191.

[39] Philip Smith, *Punishment and Culture*, Chicago: University of Chicago Press, 2008, p. 16.

[40] Smith, 2008, p. 26.

[41] Smith, 2008, pp. 86–89 and 173.

match up with the existing conceptions of 'appropriate' punishment that pre-exist within the civil discourse.[42]

So why is punishment 'misread' by the onlooker? What makes one particular punishment sit better than another within the prevailing cultural setting? For Smith there are clear bedrocks for cultural meaning and production that should never be transgressed. The work of Émile Durkheim and his followers are of special relevance in this regard. The sacred—profane divide, purity—pollution divide and ideas of the 'left sacred' all come in and out of Smith's analysis to explain why punishment is read in counterproductive ways. As an example of how this works in practice, Bentham's panopticon is reimagined by Smith as a purifying machine that aligns with Durkheimian boundaries—not the site emblematic of social control as Foucault would posit. Regulating bodily functions, sanitising bad smells, keeping clean the inmates and their cells, these were Bentham's real aims for the panopticon as interpreted by Smith.[43] Though Smith's ideas on the production and reception of penal messages are central to the framework of penal change pursued in this book, I do not follow him down this path. Doing so would get in the way of producing a truly localised study, nimble enough to respond to the spontaneous combustions of local cultural forces found in the Australian colonies.[44]

The source of developing cultural norms and memory that came to interfere with capital punishment in Australia should always be closely linked to the historical contingencies of settlement. Take, just as a starting point, the fact that Britain established penal settlements all over the continent to accommodate its bulging convict population. There was, it should be noted, a profoundly English tone to the standards of

---

[42] Smith, 2008, p. 46.

[43] Smith, 2008, pp. 99–107.

[44] As an aside, Garland was reluctant to close off the interpretive possibilities of other social theorists—those who have been criticised for not considering cultural forces enough. Foucault, Elias and Durkheim are all kept in mind during *Peculiar Institution* (2010), his extended analysis of capital punishment in American history. Garland also came out the other end of writing in *Punishment and Modern Society* reluctant to reduce punishment to a single causal relationship or transposable rule that can be observed in all societies across time and place, see David Garland, *Peculiar Institution: America's Death Penalty in an Age of Abolition*, Oxford: Oxford University Press, 2010; Garland, 1990, p. 282.

conduct and mental outlook in the colonial period. Yet, these influences were constantly being filtered through the practical necessities of living a new life on the other side of the world.[45] Aspects of colonial culture may be comparable to other societies around the globe but their unique blend on the continent is, naturally, one of a kind. The core mechanism of penal messaging and reception driving penal change is still a dynamic that ought to be justified by reference to other candidates of analysis like those presented by Foucault, Elias, the Marxists and more conventional accounts of 'penal progress' found elsewhere. It encourages the historian to look upon capital punishment in Australia with fresh eyes, alert to the impact that culture and popular memory can have on penal practice. In fact, sometimes the most random of factors could align on the gallows stage to be made visible for all to see.

[45]Penny Russell's work on colonial Australian etiquette also observes this dynamic in action, see Penny Russell, *Savage or Civilised? Manners in Colonial Australia*, Sydney: New South, 2010.

2

Australia's Hanging Years

William Blackstone's monumental *Commentaries on the Laws of England* (1765–1769) was barely two decades old when it was carried with the First Fleet to Sydney Cove.[1] Habitually taken to new colonial outposts, it assisted legal practitioners and administrators on the intricacies of law in a settlement originally conceived to alleviate the overcrowded penal infrastructure of England. At the beginning of the fourth book, *Of Public Wrongs* (1769), New South Wales' administrators could read of how all punishments fell into three different 'species' according to Blackstone: those that aimed to reform the individual offender; those that sought to deter others; and those that totally prevented any further wrong-doing. All punishments, including the death penalty, intersected with these principles to varying degrees. In a statement that echoed Enlightenment penal ideals, Blackstone opined that 'atonement or expiation' for crime was a divine responsibility; for mere humans 'preventing future

[1] Bruce Kercher, *An Unruly Child: A History of Law in Australia*, Sydney: Allen and Unwin, 1995, p. xii.

S. Anderson, *A History of Capital Punishment in the Australian Colonies, 1788 to 1900*,
Palgrave Histories of Policing, Punishment and Justice,
https://doi.org/10.1007/978-3-030-53767-8_2

crimes' was the sole end of punishment.[2] Blackstone also makes a quiet plea for governments to show greater leniency when handling criminal wrongs—too often, he thought, the English gallows resembled 'a wanton effusion of human blood'.[3] It was, however, an opinion that took a while to take hold in Britain's newest colony. Once the gallows arrived on the Australian continent, capital punishment was meted out to wrong-doers by colonial authorities in ways familiar to new settlers, albeit for much the same reasons as Blackstone pointed out. This chapter provides an overview of Australia's 'hanging years' given the colonial period was where the majority of executions took place. It discusses the numbers of those executed, how mercy was applied in individual cases and the reduction of capital crimes on the statute books.

Capital Crimes in the Colonies

As scholars like Bruce Kercher and Alex Castles have noted, the early legal history of Australia was often a case of melding English principles with the limitations and novelties of local conditions.[4] When the British colonization of Australia began in 1788, New South Wales inherited English law except where it was neither practical nor necessary. Punishment was, to use the words of the colony's first Judge Advocate, to be 'inflicted according to the laws of England as nearly as may be, considering and allowing for the circumstances and situation of the settlement and its inhabitants'.[5] When Western Australia and South Australia were proclaimed colonies (in 1829 and 1836, respectively) each adopted the bulk of English law as it then stood at the time. However, there was a slight variation for the colonies that separated from New South Wales—that is, Van Diemen's Land in 1825, Victoria in 1851 and Queensland in 1859. These colonies took a snapshot of New South Wales' law,

---

[2]William Blackstone, *Commentaries on the Laws of England: Book the Fourth* [1769], in W. Prest and R. Paley (eds), Oxford: Oxford University Press, 2016, pp. 7–8.

[3]Blackstone, 2016, p. 6.

[4]Alex Castles, *An Australian Legal History*, Sydney: The Law Book Company Limited, 1982; Kercher, 1995.

[5]David Collins as quoted in, Castles, 1982, p. 61.

rather than inheriting that of England's directly.[6] Thus, reforms to capital punishment in England throughout the nineteenth century, and also to New South Wales earlier on, are of special importance to understanding the evolution of capital offences in the Australian colonies more broadly.

At the time New South Wales was proclaimed a colony in 1788, England had a famously excessive capital code. Serious crimes like murder and rape were represented but so too were infringements like hunting in disguise and tree cutting for profit. Many have considered the expansion of the capital code in England (through legislation like the 'Black Act' of 1723) as an attempt by the propertied classes to secure their possessions and livelihoods in a quickly industrializing world.[7] Yet, despite England's 'bloody code' promising over two-hundred capital crimes, in practice, only the commission of twenty-five or so of them might actually earn the offender a trip to Tyburn's hanging tree.[8] Early in the nineteenth century reform-minded MPs in the British Parliament—headlined by men like Samuel Romilly, William Ewart, James Makintosh and Robert Peel—sought to temper England's penal code. Their job was mostly completed by 1837 at which point there was a wholesale reduction of capital crimes. From 1861 until the end of the nineteenth century, only five crimes could warrant the death penalty in England: murder; high treason; espionage; piracy with violence; and arson in the royal dockyards.[9] Once criticised for being more akin to a lottery than justice, the capital code in England was reduced, narrowed and far more considered by 1900.

To turn to the situation in New South Wales, it adopted many of the reforms related to capital punishment as they were passed in England.

[6]For a brief explanation of the intricacies of the legal standing of each jurisdiction when they were proclaimed a colony, see Kercher, 1995, pp. xi–xii.

[7]E.P. Thompson, *Whigs and Hunters: The Origin of the Black Act*, London: Allen Lane, 1975; Douglas Hay, Peter Linebaugh, John G. Rule, E.P. Thompson, and Cal Winslow, *Albion's Fatal Tree: Crime and Society in Eighteenth-Century England* [1975], revised edition, London: Verso, 2011; Peter Linebaugh, *The London Hanged: Crime and Civil Society in the Eighteenth Century*, London: Verso, 2003.

[8]Castles, 1982, p. 56.

[9]John Briggs, Christopher Harrison, Angus McInnes, and David Vincent, *Crime and Punishment in England: An Introductory History*, London: UCL Press, 1996, p. 134; Jo Lennan and George Williams, 'The Death Penalty in Australian Law', *Sydney Law Review*, vol. 34, 2012, p. 666.

G. D. Woods has usefully identified the years 1828, 1833, 1837 and 1838 as key markers for the retreat of the death penalty in the colony.[10] Taken alone, 1828 is an important landmark owing to the passage of the *Australian Courts Act*. The Act ended any speculation that the laws operating in England as of 25 July 1828 (the precise date chosen) were enforceable in Australian jurisdictions. By extension, alterations to capital statutes made in England prior to that date were automatically received into the criminal law of New South Wales. Thereafter, it was at the individual discretion of lawmakers to adopt or ignore English legislation as they saw fit. 1828 also marked the year that many forms of simple larceny were officially made non-capital while petit treason was to be prosecuted simply as murder. In 1833, lesser cases of forgery, yet more forms of larceny as well as the theft of specific livestock (cattle, sheep, horses, etc.) were no longer a problem for the hangman. The changes for 1837 in the colony were comparatively modest and did not reduce the number of capital crimes per se—both hanging in chains and dissection of the body after execution was abolished.

1838 was an important year for the capital statutes in New South Wales. By adopting a raft of English statutes passed the previous year, the tone of the criminal law in the colony was substantially altered. Many forms of property-related crimes like housebreaking, burglary, robbery, pickpocketing, smuggling, shipwrecking and arson were made non-capital so long as (to speak in the broadest terms about it) no one was harmed or threatened during its commission. However, if there was any intent to murder while committing many of the aforementioned crimes (i.e. not just harm the victim) then death was sometimes kept as a possibility. Extortion, riot, incitement to mutiny and some offences relating to slavery were similarly downgraded. Various forms of attempted murder were made non-capital but in sometimes confusing ways. For instance, strangling or suffocating with intent to murder was made non-capital but poisoning, stabbing, cutting or bodily injury with similar murderous intent was still visited with death. For the most part,

---

[10]Gregory D. Woods, *A History of Criminal Law in New South Wales: The Colonial Period, 1788–1900*, Sydney: The Federation Press, 2002, pp. 112–128.

longer terms of transportation took up the void for many of these one-time capital crimes.[11]

The extensive set of English capital crimes reproduced in New South Wales in 1788 was eventually whittled down. In fact, on the eve of Federation in 1901 only eleven crimes remained capital in New South Wales. Nine of them were defined by the *Criminal Law Amendment Act of 1883*:

> [M]urder (including murder committed recklessly, but not manslaughter) (s 9); attempted murder (s 16); acts done to property with like intent (s 17); rape (s 39); carnally knowing a girl under ten (s 41); burglary with intent to murder or cause grievous bodily harm (s 103); setting fire to a church or dwelling knowing a person to be inside (s 177); setting fire to or destroying a ship or vessel carrying persons (s 212); and exhibiting a false light or signal with intent to bring a vessel into danger (s 215).[12]

The remaining two capital crimes, treason and arson in the royal dockyards, were still applicable in New South Wales owing to English law that was adopted earlier on in the settlement's history.[13] A study by Jo Lennan and George Williams attests to the fact that, by the conclusion of the nineteenth century, each Australian jurisdiction had a relatively modest capital code. In fact, all were less voluminous than that of New South Wales. The number of capital crimes in each colonial jurisdiction at the time the colonies' federated in 1901, in order from most to least, was as follows: New South Wales (11); Victoria (9); Tasmania (8); Queensland (5); Western Australia (5) and South Australia (2).[14] South Australia, the jurisdiction with the least capital crimes by the close of the century, decided that only murder (including petit treason) and piracy with an attempt to murder should warrant the death penalty. This arrangement was agreed upon as far back as 1876 with the passage of the *Criminal Law*

---

[11] Woods, 2002, pp. 128–136.

[12] Lennan and Williams, 2012, p. 668.

[13] Lennan and Williams, 2012, p. 668.

[14] For a complete list of every capital crime in each jurisdiction at the time of Federation in 1901, see Lennan and Williams, 2012, pp. 667–668.

Consolidation Act.[15] Not one jurisdiction took the initiative to abolish capital punishment until the twentieth century.

As each Australian colony was maturing there were mechanisms available to shape the use of capital punishment to local conditions rather than just blindly follow the English example. That said, forms of colonial governance prior to the 1850s had, for the most part, the appointed governor of each colony intimately involved in the initiation and review of any new legislation. It was only until responsible government was granted to the majority of the Australian colonies in the 1850s (Western Australia waited until 1890) that the balance of power shifted dramatically in favour of elected lawmakers. Open parliamentary deliberation gave colonies a new-found freedom to tailor the capital code to their own needs and desires. Major milestones for the penal laws in each jurisdiction—perhaps the creation of a criminal code or a comprehensive consolidation of its criminal law—were key markers of change and endorsement for a colony's own capital code. As seen in the case of New South Wales though, the adoption of English statutes was the most common way to keep pace with reform abroad. Capital crimes in Australian jurisdictions, in terms of sheer numbers, trended downwards in the colonial period from the time of settlement onwards. However, no two colonies had a completely identical set of capital offences. Some jurisdictions only partially adopted statutes passed by the British Parliament while others expanded their capital statutes in new ways owing to local concerns. Working backwards from the situation at Federation, there were clearly areas of criminal activity in which colonial lawmakers resisted reform. This was mostly for various sexual crimes, aggravated robberies, attempted murder, and security and defence—all areas which will now be investigated further.

To start with sexual crimes, the Australian colonies were slow to remove the death penalty for rape and carnal knowledge of a minor. While Britain had abolished rape as a capital sentence in 1841, Victoria, Western Australia and New South Wales still retained it as a capital

[15] South Australia, no. 38 of 1876, *Criminal Law Consolidation Act*, s5 and s227.

offence as of 1900.[16] Queensland was another colony that delayed following the English example until 1899 with the passage of their *Criminal Code Act*.[17] As scholars like Kaladelfos and Barber have noted, lawmakers believed that the 'purity' of colonial females (particularly the isolated women of the interior) needed additional protection in thinly populated districts from two perceived threats—namely, the Indigenous male and the immoral white bushman.[18] Consider this statement from John Bramson to Queensland's Legislative Assembly in 1865 in support of maintaining rape as a capital offence:

> Capital punishment will be kept for rape because the women in this colony are in a more defenceless position than at home, from our limited population and scattered habitation, and, consequently they are very liable to violence in the absence of their natural protections; and they are also liable to assaults by the Aboriginals. For the Aboriginals, I believe, hanging is the only thing that brings home to them the terror of the law.[19]

Another sexual crime that was still capital in Victoria and New South Wales in 1900 was carnal knowledge of girls under ten.[20] Although Tasmania had removed it as a capital offence before 1900, it was another

[16]Lennan and Williams, 2012, pp. 667–668. It should be noted that, despite rape being a capital offence there in 1900, Victoria had earlier introduced the non-capital crime of 'rape with mitigating circumstances' in 1888, see Kathy Laster and Roger Douglas, 'A Matter of Life and Death: The Victorian Executive and the Decision to Execute 1842–1967', *The Australian and New Zealand Journal of Criminology*, vol. 24, no. 2, 1991, p. 146.

[17]Despite Queensland's Criminal Code being passed in 1899, it did not come into force until the start of 1901, see Ross Barber, 'The Labor Party and the Abolition of Capital Punishment in Queensland, 1899–1922', *Queensland Heritage*, vol. 1, no. 9, 1968, p. 3.

[18]A. Kaladelfos, 'The Politics of Punishment: Rape and the Death Penalty in Colonial Australia, 1841–1901', *History Australia*, vol. 9, no. 1, 2012, pp. 155–175; Ross Barber, 'Rape as a Capital Offence in Nineteenth Century Queensland', *Australian Journal of Politics and History*, vol. 21, no. 1, 1975, pp. 31–41. See also Carmel Harris, 'The Terror of the Law as Applied to Black Rapists in Colonial Queensland', *Hecate*, vol. 8, no. 2, 1982, pp. 22–48.

[19]John Bramson said this in relation to an 'Offences Against the Person Bill', see Ross Barber, 'Capital Punishment in Queensland', unpublished BA (Hons) thesis, The University of Queensland, 1967, p. 57.

[20]Lennan and Williams, 2012, pp. 667–668.

jurisdiction that made criminals liable to execution for carnal knowledge of minors for a large portion of the nineteenth century.[21] The same offence was made non-capital in England as of 1841, incidentally by the same legislation that had abolished rape as a capital crime.[22] Like with rape, one Victorian MP pointed out that there was 'no such thing as consent' in cases involving people so young.[23] When discussing the clauses around carnal knowledge in New South Wales' *Criminal Law Amendment Act of 1883* MPs remarked in similar terms about the differences between England and their colony. The 'temptations' to commit such a crime, one New South Wales MP suggested, 'were greater here than in England, because people were more isolated'.[24]

Buggery was a sexual act that remained a capital offence for a long time in the Australian colonies. In England the crime of buggery (inclusive of bestiality), remained a capital offence until 1861; the last recorded hanging for the crime took place there in 1836.[25] By 1900, however, Victoria and Tasmania held onto sodomy as a capital crime.[26] Richard Davis has speculated that its longevity as a capital offence in Tasmania was owing to a heavy gender imbalance in the colony. In the first decades of settlement, the island's males could outnumber its female population by as much as three to one depending upon the year selected.[27] Davis suggests that successive convict era governors thought sodomy needed to be treated severely because 'leniency would suggest to the convict population that the government condoned unnatural crimes'.[28] A fear that homosexual activity was rampant in Australia's penal settlements was

[21] Richard Davis, *The Tasmanian Gallows: A Study of Capital Punishment*, Hobart: Cat and Fiddle Press, 1974, p. 31.

[22] United Kingdom, Chapter 56 of 1841, *An Act for Taking Away the Punishment of Death in Certain Cases, and Substituting Other Punishments in Lieu Thereof*, s3.

[23] H. Cuthbert as quoted in, *Victorian Hansard*, Legislative Council, 2 September 1890 p. 1334.

[24] H.C. Dangar as quoted in, *New South Wales Parliamentary Hansard*, Legislative Assembly, 14 September 1882, p. 412.

[25] Michael Kirby, 'The Sodomy Offence: England's Least Lovely Criminal Law Export?', in C. Lennox and M. Waites, *Human Rights, Sexual Orientation and Gender Identity in The Commonwealth*, London: School of Advanced Study University of London, pp. 62–63.

[26] Victoria, no. 1079 of 1890, *The Crimes Act*, s58; Tasmania, no. 5 of 1863, *An Act to Consolidate and Amend the Legislative Enactments Relating to Offences Against the Person*, s59.

[27] Castles, 1982, p. 261.

[28] Davis, 1974, p. 31.

raised in William Molesworth's widely circulated 1837 report into the convict system.[29] Moreover, preventing sexual activity among convicts was taken into account when modifying their physical sleeping quarters and managing day-to-day discipline.[30] Victoria had more caveats than Tasmania on its definition of sodomy as defined by its *Crimes Act of 1890*. There, death was only warranted in instances that involved anyone under fourteen, or for persons of any age should violence and a lack of consent accompany its commission.[31] Although colonial authorities were technically executing men for sodomy into the 1860s, the victim's age was a key consideration as to whether or not the punishment would actually be carried out.[32]

Aggravated forms of robbery were treated harshly by colonial statute books for a long time. Robbery accompanied with wounding, violence or similar bodily harm, was still considered a capital offence in Victoria and Western Australia by the end of the nineteenth century. The same crime remained capital in New South Wales as well, though it needed to be accompanied by an intent to murder. This is something of a hangover from an earlier period when successive colonial administrations were trying to suppress bushranging. For instance, various laws passed in Sydney during the 1830s affirmed the death penalty for people who harboured a known robber and for anyone fraudulently receiving mail—both crimes known to sustain convicts on the run.[33] Tasmania unequivocally refused for much of the 1830s to adopt an English statute that made the theft or killing of livestock non-capital.[34] Moreover, it

---

[29]Zachary Thompson, 'Destroying Sodom in the South Pacific: How the Terror of Sodomy was Invoked to End Convict Transportation to New South Wales c.1837', unpublished BA (Hons) thesis, The University of Sydney, 2013.

[30]C. Gilchrist, 'Space, Sexuality and Convict Resistance in Van Diemen's Land: The Limits of Repression?', *Eras Journal*, vol. 6, 2004.

[31]Victoria, no. 1079 of 1890, *The Crimes Act*, s58.

[32]For two cases, one of Thomas Ross in Tasmania and another of John Kelly in Victoria, that the newspapers reported as sodomy in 1861, see *Launceston Examiner*, 5 January 1861, p. 5; *Launceston Examiner*, 31 January 1861, p. 3; *Ovens and Murray Advertiser*, 23 May 1867, p. 4.

[33]New South Wales, no. 3 of 1832, *Offenders Punishment and Justices Summary Jurisdiction*, 1832, s13; New South Wales, no. 24 of 1835, *An Act to Provide for the Conveyance and Postage of Letters*, s26.

[34]For the original English Act, see United Kingdom, Chapter 62 of 1832, *An Act for Abolishing the Punishment of Death in Certain Cases, and Substituting a Lesser Punishment in Lieu Thereof*.

expanded its capital code in 1835 when it determined that any escaped convict in Tasmania who used firearms or committed a felony while at large was liable to suffer death.[35] Western Australia was the last penal outpost on the continent and similarly expanded its capital code with an eye to control escaped transportees. In 1854 an Act made it a capital offence for convicts illegally at large to commit robbery with violence, enter a dwelling and intend to commit a felony, or attempt to wound anyone with a weapon. The legislation's preamble explained that 'more stringent laws than now exist' were needed to suppress crime by absconded convicts and guarantee the safety of officials trying to capture them.[36] Though the majority of these convict-era capital offences were abolished by 1900, it does demonstrate how colonial administrators looked to the gallows as a means to combat perceived threats to public safety.

While murder itself was a capital crime in all six colonies at Federation, the lesser crime of attempted murder remained capital in New South Wales, Victoria, Western Australia and Tasmania. Wounding, poisoning and drowning were some of the different methods explicitly referred too by the relevant statutes. Some colonies also had the death penalty in place for crimes that involved destroying dwellings or ships by setting them

For the Tasmanian legislation that exempted sections of it from being ratified in the colony, see Tasmania, no. 6 of 1834, *An Act to extend to Van Diemen's Land Certain Statutes Passed in England for Amending the Laws Relating to Forgeries—to Embezzlements by Public Officers—and to Offences Against the Coin—and for Abolishing Capital Punishments in Certain Cases.* For the Tasmanian legislation that brought the colony back in line with English standards, see Tasmania, no. 17 of 1836, *An Act for the Prevention of Sheep and Cattle Stealing, and for Abolishing the Punishment of Death in Such Cases.*

[35]Tasmania, no. 2 of 1835, *An Act to Consolidate and Amend Certain of the Laws Relating to the Courts of General Quarter Sessions and to the More Effectual Punishment and Control of Transported and Other Offenders*, s59. See also Tasmania, no. 14 of 1838, *An Act for the More Perfect Constitution of Courts of General Quarter Sessions and to Provide for the More Effectual Punishment and Control of Transported and other Offenders*, s54. Later in the convict period, Tasmanian legislation affirmed that violent robberies and setting fire to crops would also earn the offender a death sentence, see Tasmania, no. 5 of 1840, *An Act to Amend the Laws of This Colony Relating to Robbery and Stealing from the Person*, s2; Tasmania, no. 1 of 1845, *An Act to Remove Doubts in Certain Cases of Arson.*

[36]Western Australia, no. 7 of 1854, *An Ordinance for the Suppression of Violent Crimes Committed by Convicts Illegally at Large*, preamble and s2–4. An 1868 Act clarified the provisions of section 4 related to attempting to wounding someone with a weapon, see Western Australia, no. 9 of 1868, *An Ordinance to Make Better Provision for the Suppression of Violent Crimes Committed by Convicts.*

alight. Although it may seem frivolous by modern standards, such crimes were also in place to prevent the endangerment of life. New South Wales, Victoria and Tasmania all had provisions that, should the intent be to kill people located inside the structure, such damage should be considered a capital offence. The same rationale was in place for New South Wales, the only colony that considered the display of false signals to ships with such severity. Or for Tasmania which placed the casting off of a ship on the same terms as setting fire to it.[37] England, meanwhile, only treated murder capitally after 1861, other violent crimes short of taking human life was a job for the prison warden.

The last area of crime where capital offences still persisted in the colonies at the time of Federation is that of security and defence. New South Wales, Queensland and Western Australia all thought treason should be met with death. Interestingly, Tasmania's *Defence Act of 1885* made members of its own defence force liable to capital punishment should a soldier desert to the enemy or traitorously surrender a fortification.[38] By 1900 New South Wales was the only colony that retained arson in the royal dockyards as an offence punishable by death while forms of piracy accompanied with violence were made capital only in Tasmania, Queensland and South Australia.[39] As late as 1899 one Queensland MP affirmed his position that the death penalty for piracy was 'very proper for the offence' since the perpetrators of such a crime 'needed no more consideration than wild beasts'.[40] Fears over inadequate defence capabilities were one of the major reasons for Federation while shipping was the means by which the colonies connected with other markets within the British Empire. However, given high treason, espionage and arson in the royal dockyards were still capital offences in England as of 1900, the Australian colonies were not alone in taking a tough stance towards these matters.

---

[37]Lennan and Williams, 2012, pp. 667–668.

[38]Tasmania, no. 16 of 1885, *The Defence Act*, s75.

[39]Lennan and Williams, 2012, pp. 667–668.

[40]Arthur Rutledge as quoted in, *The Week*, 13 October 1899, p. 26.

When comparing the English capital code to that of the Australian colonies—and, for that matter, the colonies to each other—there were points of divergence and convergence. Though the trajectory was to reduce the number of capital offences, the unique factors of Australia settlement led to the occasionally tardy adoption of English standards. The gender imbalance within the colonies, an isolated frontier, the presence of convicts and a desire to safeguard the 'purity' of women and children were all invoked in different circumstances to keep an offence capital after England had downgraded it. Yet, as any historian of the gallows knows, it is one thing for a capital crime to exist on the statute books but quite another for hanging to be actually carried out to the letter of the law. Both members of the executive and the judiciary had means available to guarantee that only those criminals they thought deserving would actually shake hands with the hangman. First though we need to reach an estimation of how many criminals were actually executed in Australian history.

Keeping Count: Australian Execution Numbers

One of the most pressing—but hitherto unanswered—questions about the history of capital punishment in Australia is a basic one: how many people were executed? Given the size of the task, spanning six jurisdictions and over a century, counting executions in Australia is a challenging exercise. Separate gaol registers, court records, government statistical returns and published accounts all need to be collected, verified and corroborated to get close to an accurate picture. Although caveats must still be placed on the final estimation, the published accounts of both local and academic historians to this point make it possible to piece together the number of executions that were carried out in all of Australian history.[41] Certainly, the earliest instance of a European

[41] It is worth noting that a continent-wide estimation of execution numbers was conducted in the 1980s by Satyanshu Mukherjee et al. It put the number of executions carried out in Australia after 1820 at 1648 people. Although Mukherjee's estimation was restricted to the

execution in what is now Australian territory was in 1629 following the wrecking of the *Batavia*, a Dutch trading ship engaged by the East India Company. When the ship's Captain, Francisco Pelsaert, sailed for help a mutiny took place among survivors who were left stranded on an island off the west coast of the mainland. Upon return Pelsaert captured the leaders of the coup, then tried and executed them accordingly.[42] Though the *Batavia* is a fascinating tale of the Dutch in Australia, these are not the types of executions that are tallied below. Nor are any fatal punishments known to traditional Indigenous Australian societies, or, for that matter, any unchecked killing meted out on the nineteenth-century frontier. Rather, this analysis concerns those who were executed in Australia pursuant to a judicial sentence following British settlement in 1788. That said, there are some important information about the courts, crimes and criminals worth pointing out as the picture of execution numbers is being pieced together in each individual colony.

New South Wales is not only the oldest colony but also the place where the most hangings were carried out. A dataset created by Macnab, Castle and Kaladelfos provides a picture of execution numbers for the jurisdiction. It lists 964 confirmed executions in New South Wales between 1788 and 1954 while another 35 were likely to have been carried out. All but 21 of the total confirmed executions were administered prior to Federation in 1901.[43] This final count does, however, overlap with some of the executions counted by other scholars in Queensland, Victoria, Tasmania and Norfolk Island since many of their earliest capital cases were technically conducted under the authority of the New South Wales judiciary as explained below. The New South Wales Court of Criminal Jurisdiction was established from the outset

---

period after 1820, there has also been a wealth of research published since that time which allows for a more complete picture to be arrived at. See Satyanshu K. Mukherjee, John R. Walker, and Evelyn N. Jacobsen (eds), *Crime and Punishment in the Colonies: A Statistical Profile*, Historical Statistics Monograph no. 6, Sydney: History Project Inc., 1986.

[42] Helen Doyle, 'Batavia', in G. Davison, J. Hirst, and S. Macintyre (eds), *The Oxford Companion to Australian History*, revised edition, Melbourne: Oxford University Press, 2001, pp. 62–63.

[43] K. Macnab, T. Castle, and A. Kaladelfos, 'NSW Capital Convictions Database', *Frances Forbes Society for Australian Legal History* 2013, http://research.forbessociety.org.au/, viewed 13 August 2015.

when Governor Arthur Phillip arrived in 1788 and, though it operated like a military tribunal for much of its history, it handled capital cases until 1824. Cases were tried in front of six military officers and a Judge Advocate with a majority verdict of five needed for a successful capital conviction. The old Court of Criminal Jurisdiction gave way to the New South Wales Supreme Court from 1824 which handled capital cases thereafter.[44] The highpoint for executions in New South Wales was in the decade 1826–1836 under Governors Darling and Bourke where 363 hangings took place.[45] Tim Castles has noted how popular support for harsh penalties was rooted in fears of growing crime rates and a desire for the administration to assert control in a settlement with a high concentration of convicts.[46] Outside of execution numbers, the types of crimes for which people were executed changed dramatically. In the first ten years of settlement, property-related crimes like stealing and robbery were the main reason for execution. Of the 36 confirmed hangings between 1788 and 1798 only three were murderers.[47] Yet, by the final decade of the colonial period, executed criminals in New South Wales were almost always convicted murderers—21 of the 25 criminals to be exact between the years 1890 and 1900.[48]

Given Tasmania was administered first by New South Wales for over two decades, serious crimes like murder needed to be heard in Sydney prior to the 1820s. From 1821 though, the New South Wales Court of Criminal Jurisdiction travelled to hear capital cases (alongside others) on the island. The Tasmanian Supreme Court was established in 1824 a few years later.[49] Despite being the colony with the smallest landmass, Tasmania hosted the second-most executions of any Australian jurisdiction. Mark Finnane and Chris Leppard have recently concluded that 545 executions were carried out in Tasmanian history with all but three of

---

[44] 'New South Wales Courts', *The Prosecution Project* 2019, https://prosecutionproject.griffith.edu.au/other-resources/new-south-wales-courts/, viewed 22 December 2019.

[45] Tim Castle, 'Constructing Death: Newspaper Reports of Executions in Colonial New South Wales, 1826–1837', *Journal of Australian Colonial History*, vol. 9, 2007, p. 51.

[46] Castles, 2007, p. 51.

[47] Macnab, Castle, and Kaladelfos, 2013.

[48] Macnab, Castle, and Kaladelfos, 2013.

[49] 'Tasmanian Courts', *The Prosecution Project* 2019, https://prosecutionproject.griffith.edu.au/other-resources/tasmanian-courts/, viewed 2 December 2019.

them taking place in the colonial period.[50] Their numbers include those tried in Sydney but executed in Tasmania before the establishment of its Supreme Court (at least 15) as well as 37 people hanged on Norfolk Island. Tasmania also treated property crimes seriously in the early days. For example, prior to 1837 an executed criminal was more likely to be guilty of a property offence (stealing, receiving, robbery, bushranging etc.) than a homicide-related one.[51] The high point for executions was during Governor Arthur's administration from 1824 to 1836—in fact, 103 executions came in the years 1826 and 1827 alone.[52] Like in New South Wales, an enthusiasm for the gallows was fanned by fears that the island's swelling convict population could not be controlled. The Tasmanian Attorney-General remarked in 1832 that his house and life were unsafe in a colony surrounded by 'men whom it appears spend their time planning schemes of escape and plunder, and who evade the watchfulness of the most vigilant guards'.[53] Under such circumstances he thought 'an effective check' was needed to control crime in a society 'surrounded as we are by the most abandoned characters'.[54] The Tasmanian scaffold began to see only the worst offenders climb its stairs after 1837; two-thirds of criminals following that calendar year were executed for homicide-related offences only.[55]

In the case of Victoria, prior to the establishment of its Supreme Court in 1852, a resident judge of the New South Wales Supreme Court could hear capital cases in the Port Phillip District from 1841.[56] Trevor Porter has tallied 187 executions between the years 1840 and

---

[50] Mark Finnane and Chris Leppard, 'The Hanging Years: Research Brief 30', *The Prosecution Project* 2018, https://prosecutionproject.griffith.edu.au/the-hanging-years/, viewed 5 October 2019.

[51] Finnane and Leppard, 2018.

[52] Davis, 1974, p. 13.

[53] David Plater and Jenny Crofts, 'Bushrangers, the Exercise of Mercy and the "Last Penalty of the Law" in New South Wales and Tasmania 1824–1856', *University of Tasmania Law Review*, vol. 32, no. 2, 2013, p. 309.

[54] Plater and Crofts, 2013, p. 309.

[55] Finnane and Leppard, 2018.

[56] 'Our History', *Supreme Court of Victoria* 2019, https://www.supremecourt.vic.gov.au/about-the-court/our-history, viewed 15 December 2019.

1967 in Victoria with 165 of them taking place in the colonial period.[57] Meanwhile, Kathy Laster and Roger Douglas place the final execution count in Victoria slightly less at 185 people.[58] As the gold rushes caused the population of the colony to grow sevenfold, the number of executions naturally increased. Victoria was home to some of the most notorious criminals ever executed in the Australian colonies. Ned Kelly's career as a bushranger, ending at the Melbourne Gaol in 1880, is already a well-known tale. Less recall the murderer Frederick Bailey Deeming, once labelled by Melbourne papers as the 'criminal of the century' for his murder of six people on two separate occasions—once in England, the other while resident in Australia.[59] Deeming disposed of his victims (four of whom were his own children) by cementing them under the fireplaces where he lived before travelling on. Francis Knorr, the so-called 'Brunswick Baby Farmer' was another criminal executed amid much fanfare for the murder of multiple infants under her paid care.[60] Her wrongdoing was discovered when a new tenant in Knorr's old property was preparing a garden bed, only to find a baby buried with a cord around its neck.[61] If one cares to eye the profile of either one of Kelly, Deeming or Knorr they can still do so at the Old Melbourne Gaol where all three were executed. More than just a macabre memento, popular phrenologists had a foothold in Melbourne by the mid-nineteenth century. Their public lectures and published accounts erroneously pointed to the cranial features of hanged criminals as casual factors in the commission of their crime.

---

[57] Trevor J. Porter, *Executions in the Colony and State of Victoria 1842–1967*, Adelaide: The Wednesday Press, 1999.

[58] Laster and Douglas, 1991, p. 146.

[59] Barry Jones, 'Deeming, Frederick Bailey (1853–1892)', *Australian Dictionary of Biography* 1981, http://adb.anu.edu.au/biography/deeming-frederick-bailey-5940, viewed 12 December 2019.

[60] 'Baby farming' was the much-maligned Victorian practice of caring for (usually illegitimate) infants for a lump payment and sometimes, though less frequently, for a periodical fee. As one summary of the practice of lump payments for infant care ominously noted: 'It was to the pecuniary advantage of the baby-farmer to hasten the death of the child'. Many protection bills across the British world in the late nineteenth century came about, in part, because of a panic over the practice, see Hugh Chisholm (ed.), *The Encyclopaedia Britannica*, eleventh edition, New York: The Encyclopaedia Britannica Corporation, 1910, p. 97.

[61] Porter, 1999, pp. 70–71.

Early Queensland history is marked by the Moreton Bay penal settlement located on the mouth of the Brisbane River that operated between 1824 and 1842. Twelve convicts were executed for capital crimes committed while serving out their sentence at the penal outpost. However, given the settlement was administered by New South Wales, offenders needed to travel south to Sydney to be prosecuted in the early days. Ten of the condemned Moreton Bay convicts were actually hanged at Sydney Gaol in George Street following their trial while only two were returned to the Brisbane River for execution.[62] As the settlement grew in size and more free settlers arrived, serious crimes started to be heard in Queensland itself by a circuit assize and then by a resident judge—both operating under the authority of the New South Wales Supreme Court. The Queensland Supreme Court, empowered to handle capital cases from the outset, was established in 1861 in the years following separation from New South Wales.[63] As to exactly how many people were executed in Queensland, a variety of estimates currently exist. Following separation in 1859, Hugh Mac Master counts 82 executions in Queensland; 63 of those taking place before Federation in 1901.[64] Ross Barber covered the same period but came to a figure of 81 hangings instead.[65] John McGuire used a variety of primary documents to place the number of executions at 90 in the years after 1850.[66] Finally, local writer, Christopher Dawson, goes the furthest back in time, stating that 94 people were executed in Queensland from 1830.[67] As was typical for later settling colonies, those who were actually executed in Queensland were usually guilty of homicide-related crimes rather than those concerning property. To adapt Ross Barber's numbers and categorisations for those executed in

[62]Christopher Dawson, *Dirty Dozen: Hanging and the Moreton Bay Convicts*, Brisbane: Inside History, 2007, p. 54.

[63]'Queensland Courts', *The Prosecution Project* 2019, https://prosecutionproject.griffith.edu.au/other-resources/queensland-courts/, viewed 12 December 2019.

[64]Hugh Mac Master, *Mostly Murder*, North Rockhampton: Hugh Mac Master, 1999, pp. 147–171.

[65]Barber, 1967, pp. 193–197.

[66]John McGuire, 'Punishment and Colonial Society: A History of Penal Change in Queensland, 1859–1930s', unpublished PhD thesis, The University of Queensland, 2002, p. 266.

[67]Christopher Dawson, *No Ordinary Run of Men: The Queensland Executioners*, Brisbane: Inside History, 2010, p. 3.

the colony after 1859, 80.2% were hanged for murder (including accessory to murder), 17.3% for rape and 2.5% for robbery under arms with wounding.[68] A key point of difference for Queensland was the number of Pacific Islanders in that jurisdiction—most of whom were engaged in the cotton and sugar cane industries. Their presence in the colony was reflected in the execution statistics where, after 1865, nearly a dozen Melanesians went to the gallows for either murder or rape.[69]

Western Australia's overworked Courts of Quarter Sessions was officially empowered to try capital offences from 1832 so long as it was heard before three justices. The Supreme Court was established in 1861 and sat in Perth but, after the 1880s, circuit sittings became more common in faraway rural centres.[70] A fine-grained study of eleven capital cases (mostly from the colonial period) by Simon Adams shows that many of those who were hanged in Western Australia were from diverse backgrounds—Afghan, Chinese, Malay, Indian, Greek and French among them.[71] His analysis serves as a reminder of the diversity of colonial society as well as the capacity for episodes of crime and punishment to excite settler anxieties around race, gender, convictism and even political threats like Fenianism. Brian Purdue has already provided a brief overview of each individual case and concludes that 154 people were executed in Western Australian history, 120 of those in the colonial period.[72] One of the most interesting executions in Western Australia was the death of an Indigenous Australian named Midgegooroo in May 1833 for a fatal attack on a European settler. Purdue excludes it from his count of legitimate executions because his death was not authorised by the then operational Court of Quarter Sessions with the familiarities of a trial judge, prosecution, defence and regular court procedure. It was,

---

[68] Barber, 1967, p. 198.

[69] Mark Finnane and Jonathon Richards, 'Aboriginal Violence and State Responses: Histories, Policies and Legacies in Queensland, 1860–1940', *Australian and New Zealand Journal of Criminology*, vol. 43, 2010, p. 252.

[70] 'Western Australian Courts', *The Prosecution Project* 2019, https://prosecutionproject.griffith.edu.au/other-resources/western-australian-courts/, viewed 12 December 2019.

[71] Simon Adams, *The Unforgiving Rope: Murder and Hanging on Australia's Western Frontier*, Perth: UWA Publishing, 2009.

[72] Brian Purdue, *Legal Executions in Western Australia*, Perth: Foundation Press, 1993. This number is repeated in, Adams, 2009, pp. xii–xiii.

however, ordered pursuant to a brief hearing in front of the Executive Council and Frederick Irwin, then the colony's chief military officer, who acted for Governor Stirling in his absence. Following the hearing Midgegooroo was blindfolded, tied to the gaol door and shot dead by firing squad. When justifying his decision to a disapproving Colonial Office in London, Irwin wrote that his course of action was necessary given recent killings of local settlers. It was founded on his personal knowledge of the 'character and disposition of the aborigines, after nearly four years intercourse'.[73]

South Australia was the jurisdiction where the least executions were carried out. Between 1838 and 1964 it witnessed 68 judicial hangings with 46 of them taking place in the colonial period.[74] Established just days following the Proclamation of the colony, capital cases were made the concern of the South Australian Supreme Court. For many capital offences committed in rural districts, all of the parties (including the witnesses) had to travel to Adelaide for the hearing—though some circuit sittings of the Supreme Court were initiated after the 1860s (starting in the colony's southeast).[75] The earliest executions in the colony were almost entirely made up of either Indigenous offenders or one-time convicts. The spectacle of an execution was harnessed to pacify resistance to European colonisation, particularly on the Eyre Peninsula where Indigenous men were hanged at the very site of their crime (see Chapter 7). As for the execution of European offenders, seven of the first eight executed in the colony were former or escaped convicts who had committed a crime since arriving from across the border—a strange fact considering the colony's 'convict-free' foundation myth. The rhetoric surrounding these hangings reaffirmed anxious free settlers

[73]Adams, 2009, pp. 13–17, quote on p. 16.

[74]This number is revised up from an earlier figure, see Steven Anderson, 'Punishment as Pacification: The Role of Indigenous Executions on the South Australian Frontier, 1836–1862', *Aboriginal History*, vol. 39, 2015, p. 6.

[75]'South Australian Courts', *The Prosecution Project* 2019, https://prosecutionproject.griffith.edu.au/other-resources/south-australian-courts/, viewed 2 December 2019. A South Australian hanging that stands apart from the others was following the *Maria* Massacre where two Indigenous men were summarily tried and executed on the sands of the Coorong under the watchful eye of Major Thomas O'Halloran, see Anderson, 2015, pp. 7–9.

that the promise of a 'convict-free' society would be made good.[76] The administration was clearly concerned about an influx of 'illegitimate' settlers, like those with conditional pardons, travelling to South Australia in the early years. '[T]he strongest possible prejudice against a convict population has always existed here', wrote the Governor to the Colonial Secretary in 1845, they are 'a class of persons who are disliked and are regarded as a separate and distinct class, placed in an inferior social state to the rest of the population'.[77] Other than when an Indigenous offender was involved, the majority of South Australian executions took place in and around the Adelaide Gaol with a rare hanging taking place at a regional site such as Mount Gambier.

Not included in the above numbers for South Australia are the judicial executions that occurred in the area now belonging to the Northern Territory, which it administered from 1863 to 1911. Darwin (originally founded as Palmerston) hosted criminal trials from 1884 under the authority of the South Australian Supreme Court, though circuit court sittings were held there as early as 1875.[78] From 1891 the number of jurors on capital trials conducted in the Territory was expanded from six to twelve. Moreover, the previously narrow grounds for appeal to the Supreme Court in Adelaide were generously expanded to incorporate issues relating to both evidence and law.[79] The South Australian Attorney-General was frank when registering his concern for how serious crimes were being tried in the Northern Territory: 'As a general rule the Supreme Court there was conducted by gentlemen who, although fair Magistrates in ordinary petty cases, had little or no legal training, and still less experience in criminal law'.[80] From what is known of criminal trials held in the Northern Territory between 1884 and 1913 via a judge's report, seven were executed for murder—five were Indigenous

---

[76]Steven Anderson and Paul Sendziuk, 'Hang the Convicts: Capital Punishment and the Reaffirmation of South Australia's Foundation Principles', *Journal of Australian Colonial History*, vol. 16, 2014, pp. 83–111.

[77]Governor Grey to Lord Stanley, 6 September 1845, as quoted in, Anderson and Sendziuk, 2014, pp. 94–95.

[78]'South Australian Courts', *The Prosecution Project* 2019, https://prosecutionproject.griffith.edu.au/other-resources/south-australian-courts/, viewed 9 December 2019.

[79]South Australia, no. 532 of 1891, *An Act to Amend 'The Northern Territory Justice Act, 1875'.*

[80]*South Australian Parliamentary Debates*, House of Assembly, 18 November 1891, p. 2066.

Australians, and two were Chinese.[81] These numbers can be supplemented by newspaper accounts of at least two executions occurring prior to 1884.[82] After 1913 only another two criminals were hanged in the Northern Territory but that was in the early 1950s.[83]

By putting the numbers together from each jurisdiction it is possible to get a well-founded estimation of those executed in Australia for the first time. From British settlement in 1788 to the last execution in 1967 approximately two thousand people were executed in Australian history as the result of a judicial sentence. The vast majority of those executions (over 90%) took place before Federation in 1901. Outside of the possibility of any inaccuracies or oversights in different scholars' estimates, some minor issues still need to be resolved between the existing execution counts before a more precise number can be arrived at.[84] Nevertheless, this broad figure of Australian executions does allow for some comparison with Britain's other major settler colonies. Take New Zealand for instance, it only executed 85 people in its history—all but one was a convicted murderer.[85] Although the use of capital punishment in Canada can be traced to the earliest years of European settlement, concise numbers emerge only after Confederation in 1867—thereafter

---

[81] Heather Douglas and Mark Finnane, *Indigenous Crime and Settler Law: White Sovereignty After Empire*, Basingstoke: Palgrave Macmillan, 2012, p. 76.

[82] The newspaper reported that the execution of Charles Flannagan in 1893 was the Northern Territory's first, see *The Advertiser,* 17 July 1893, p. 5. For the execution of Wandy Wandy hanged soon afterwards, see *South Australian Register*, 9 August 1893, p. 6.

[83] For confirmation of the last executions in the Northern Territory (held in 1952), see 'Jerry Koci and John Novotny', *National Archives of Australia* 2019, http://guides.naa.gov.au/records-about-northern-territory/part2/chapter16/16.11.aspx, viewed 20 November 2019.

[84] This estimation relies on the numbers cited in published secondary accounts available for each jurisdiction at the time of writing. There are three key issues that need to be resolved between these different accounts before a concrete number, as opposed to a well-founded approximation like the one provided here, can be given. First, the minor discrepancies between existing scholars' estimates for the same jurisdiction need to be resolved. This is particularly an issue for Queensland and Victoria where different numbers are provided by researchers for the same time period. Second, the possibility of double counting the same execution needs to be eradicated. The New South Wales Capital Convictions Database overlaps with executions already counted by scholars in Tasmania, Victoria and Queensland prior to their separation—understandable in many ways given they were, technically, sentenced to death under the authority of the New South Wales judiciary at the time. Third, more research needs to be directed at a small number of very early colonial cases in New South Wales where it is unclear whether or not the execution actually took place.

[85] Sherwood Young, *Guilty on the Gallows*, Wellington: Grantham House, 1998, pp. 281–282.

706 people were hanged in the country.[86] South Africa is a region which, at least for nineteenth-century scholars of British settler societies, is sometimes compared to the Australian colonies. However, numbers for the nineteenth century are patchy at best while apartheid rule in the twentieth century makes an overall comparison of execution numbers difficult.[87] Meanwhile, England and Wales hanged more people between the years 1805 and 1840 than Australia did for all of its history.[88] Australia could, however, occasionally outpace England in a single year according to Tim Castle—for example, 50 people were hanged in New South Wales in 1830 compared to 46 in England and Wales combined.[89]

Despite the obvious differences in population numbers, demographics, and the frequency of crime across these international jurisdictions, these figures demonstrate that the gallows were never far from view in Britain's colonial offshoots. For each criminal executed in the Australian colonies, those in positions of power (whether it be lawmakers, judges or prosecutors) saw the example of death as a necessary punishment for those that broke the rules of both law and decency in these young settlements. But, to get the complete understanding of Australia's hanging years, it is important to also reinforce the point that the crimes people were actually executed for changed over the colonial period. As documented in the early history of Tasmania and New South Wales, a variety of crimes (including many property offences) were frequently the cause of a criminal's demise. Yet, after many of the English reforms to their capital statutes had been passed on by the late 1830s, murder was most often the crime associated with those hanged. It seems

[86]Carolyn Strange, 'Capital Punishment', in G. Hallowell (ed.), *The Oxford Companion to Canadian History*, Oxford: Oxford University Press, 2004.

[87]For instance, at least 137 people were executed in 1985, even more people were hanged two years later as the political climate intensified, Patrick Laurence, 'Twenty-One Hanged in Seventy-Two Hours', *Mail and Guardian* 11 December 1987, https://mg.co.za/article/1987-12-11-00-twenty-one-hanged-in-seventy-two-hours, viewed 15 November 2019.

[88]2175 people were hanged in England and Wales between 1805 and 1840, see V.A.C. Gatrell, *The Hanging Tree: Execution and the English People 1770–1868*, Oxford: Oxford University Press, 1994, p. 617, numbers adapted from Table 2.

[89]Tim Castle, 'Watching Them Hang: Capital Punishment and Public Support in Colonial New South Wales, 1826–1836', *History Australia*, vol. 5, no. 2, p. 43.2.

that the list of capital offences on the statute books always appeared to be longer than the list of crimes people were executed for in the colonies. Only after knowing more about the prerogative of mercy can a complete picture emerge as to how capital punishment operated in the colonial period.

The Prerogative of Mercy

New South Wales' First Charter of Justice, a document that authorized the establishment of its criminal courts, determined that every death sentence needed the approval of the Governor himself.[90] Thus, from the earliest days of Australian settlement, it was clear that the Governor (acting as a representative of the British Crown in the territory) was to be the focal point for granting mercy in individual capital cases—whether it was a full pardon being sought or a commutation of a death sentence to a lesser punishment. After 1825, colonial Governors were assisted by an Executive Council, initially made up by various government officials appointed by the Crown, including the Chief Justice of the colony.[91] By the latter part of the nineteenth century though, each Executive Council was comprised solely of elected government ministers and presided over by the Governor (i.e. the 'Governor-in-Council' was a commonly used term).[92] Although the Governor was not compelled to accept the opinion of his Executive Council, it was unusual for him to deviate from their advice—especially once the colony attained responsible government. Unless the case intersected with imperial interests or outside jurisdictions, the advice of local ministers was to be heavily weighted.[93] If executive review determined that a remission of the sentence was warranted it was deemed to be an instrument of

[90]'New South Wales Charter of Justice, Letters Patent, 2 April 1787', State Records of New South Wales, SRNSW:X24.

[91]Castles, 1982, pp. 131–132.

[92]Harold Thornton, 'Executive Councils and Their Place in Australian Westminster Systems', *Legislative Studies* vol. 10, no. 1, 1995, pp. 65–80.

[93]Alpheus Todd, *Parliamentary Government in the British Colonies* [1880], second edition, Clark: The Lawbook Exchange, 2006, p. 439.

clemency alone. Altering the sentence did not, by letter of the law, reverse the verdict like a modern court of appeal might.[94] Rarely was a criminal ever given an unconditional pardon and released. More commonly the punishment of death was commuted to a period of penal servitude—transportation or forms of corporal punishment were also known substitutes for death in earlier times.[95]

Despite the decision to execute or commute being determined by the Executive, there were two main ways that the trial judge could influence the outcome. In the first instance, a written report was always communicated to the Executive Council prior to its deliberations and, oftentimes, the trial judge or chief justice would attend the meeting in person. They were (among other things) at liberty to review key pieces of evidence, the strength of the prosecution's case, the criminal history of the condemned and if they had been extended mercy before. The judge then offered his own recommendation as to whether the criminal's life ought to be spared or not. Illustration 2.1 gives a visual window into these deliberations where a criminal's life was in the balance. It depicts the Victorian Executive Council discussing the case of the notorious murderer Frederick Bailey Deeming. Present in the Executive Chamber is the Governor and his Ministers discussing the case with Justice Henry Hodges who presided over Deeming's trial. On this occasion, Deeming was not extended mercy and was executed in accordance with the sentence of the court in May 1892.

Another means the judge could influence the Executive Council was made available following the passage of the 1823 *Judgement of Death Act* in England.[96] In any case short of murder and treason, it created the distinction between 'death recorded' and 'death pronounced'. As one nineteenth-century dictionary of English phrases noted:

---

[94]Todd, 2006, p. 347.

[95]Even South Australia, the proudly 'convict-free' colony, had no qualms transporting its reprieved capital offenders to Australian penal colonies in the first decades of settlement, see Paul Sendziuk, 'No Convicts Here: Reconsidering South Australia's Foundation Myth', in R. Foster and P. Sendziuk (eds), *Turning Points: Chapters in South Australian History*, Adelaide: Wakefield Press, 2012, pp. 33–47.

[96]United Kingdom, Chapter 48 of 1823, *An Act for Enabling Courts to Abstain from Pronouncing Sentence of Death in Certain Capital Felonies*.

Illustration 2.1 The Executive Council in Victoria discussing the case of Frederick Bailey Deeming in 1892 (*Source* J. Macfarlane, 'The Executive Council Considering a Death Sentence, 1892', print of a wood engraving, Melbourne: David Syme and Co., held by State Library Victoria)

> *Death recorded* means that the sentence of death is *recorded* or written by the recorder against the criminal, but not verbally pronounced by the judge. This is done when capital punishment is likely to be remitted. It is the verbal sentence of the judge that is the only sufficient warrant of an execution.[97]

Foreshadowing the remission of a sentence at the very moment it was being delivered may seem odd to modern eyes. However, the sentence of 'death recorded' gave the trial judge the flexibility to rule in line with England's penal code (then replete with over two-hundred capital crimes) while simultaneously signalling from the outset that the prisoner before

[97]Ebenezer Cobham Brewer, *Dictionary of Phrase and Fable: Giving the Derivation, Source, or Origin of Common Phrases, Allusions, and Words That Have a Tale to Tell* [1870], Cambridge: Cambridge University Press, 2014, p. 740 [italics original].

him was a suitable candidate for clemency. Though the Executive was still free to act as they wished in every case, it was very rare that an execution should follow from a sentence of 'death recorded'.[98] The Australian colonies were known to utilise this now antiquated judicial mechanism when sentencing criminals in the nineteenth century. New South Wales, for example, repealed the English 1823 Act locally in 1883 during a partial consolidation of its criminal law.[99] Other scholars, particularly those working with Tasmanian and Victorian court records, have also noticed its use there.[100]

In addition to the judge, the jury also had some levers at their disposal to influence the Executive Council. In the first instance it was in their remit to attach a recommendation of mercy to a guilty verdict in a capital case. In instances where the Executive Council appeared like they might ignore their recommendations for clemency, it was not unheard of for jurors to organise a petition to reiterate their position. This was what happened in the South Australian case of Charles Streitman in 1877 who was, against the wishes of the jury that found him guilty, hanged for fatally stabbing a man.[101] The other means by which jurors might influence the outcome of a trial was through variations of what Blackstone labelled 'pious perjury'. He noted in his *Commentaries* that it was a habit of many English juries to deliberately undervalue stolen goods to allow the offender to escape the capital charge and be tried for a lesser offence. Later Blackstone elaborated on how English jurors 'through compassion' would often 'forget their oaths' and set the guilty man free.[102] Hobart's *Mercury* recognised it as a problem in the 1870s: 'The difficulty of getting the typical twelve to convict on the capital charge, though the evidence be as clear as day, has become proverbial'.[103] Moreover, Australian opponents of capital punishment had long complained that the very severity of the death penalty deterred juries from convicting

[98] Laster and Douglas, 1991, p. 148.

[99] New South Wales, no. 17 of 1883, *An Act to Consolidate and Amend in Certain Respects the Criminal Law*, first schedule.

[100] For Tasmania, see Finnane and Leppard, 2018; for Victoria, see Laster and Douglas, 1991, pp. 150–151.

[101] Alfred Joseph Taylor, *Additional Notes on Capital Punishment*, Hobart Town: Printed at the 'Mercury' Steam Press Office, 1878, p. 3.

[102] Blackstone, 2016, p. 12.

[103] *The Mercury* as quoted in, Taylor, 1878, p. 3.

offenders (see Chapter 8). Regardless, the jury's opinion on the case mattered a great deal. As the Minister for Justice in New South Wales said in 1896, if a jury happened to recommend mercy in a specific case, it was 'one of the strongest elements which weighed with the Executive in coming to a decision'.[104]

Members of the public were also free to voice their opinion on death sentences passed by the colonial courts. The Executive Council was not impermeable to such influence, especially given that it was comprised of elected politicians for large portions of the nineteenth century. Petitions were the most common mechanism through which the general public could formally express their thoughts. For instance, successive capitally convicted Norfolk Island mutineers in the mid-nineteenth century were the subject of petitions for mercy, both large and small, from very diverse sectors of society: religious leaders, social reformers, penal officers, the prisoners themselves, legal counsel, as well as everyday members of the public.[105] It was not unknown for a deputation to accompany the delivery of the physical petition; often organisers were afforded an audience with the Governor to explain their rationale.[106] Newspapers were also leaders of public opinion in many cases. For example, Van Diemen Land's Daniel Priest, nicknamed 'The Friendly Bushranger' in some quarters, had the local newspapers to thank for his revised punishment in 1845. In sentencing the Chief Justice told Priest that his crime of robbery under arms was a 'shocking outrage not to be tolerated in any civilised country' and that he would not recommend mercy.[107] The judge's sentencing remarks were combated by both the *Launceston Examiner* and the *Cornwall Chronicle* which reminded readers of Priest's cooperative conduct while in custody and the lack of violence accompanying the crime he was indicted for. In the end the Tasmanian Executive

---

[104] *New South Wales Parliamentary Hansard*, Legislative Assembly, 7 July 1896, p. 1357.

[105] David Plater and Sue Milne, '"The Quality of Mercy Is Not Strained": The Norfolk Island Mutineers and the Exercise of the Death Penalty in Colonial Australia 1824–1860', *Australian and New Zealand Law and History Society e-Journal*, 2012, pp. 15, 36–37.

[106] *Sydney Morning Herald*, 19 April 1884, p. 8; *Evening News*, 10 September 1888, p. 5; *Daily Telegraph*, 4 January 1889, p. 6.

[107] Plater and Crofts, 2013, pp. 324–329, quote on p. 325.

Council went against the wishes of the judge, reducing his sentence of death to life imprisonment.

Although the judge, jury and general public had the means by which they could express their thoughts on the case, the final decision was purely the responsibility of the Executive. And, to return to the intricacies of their deliberations, it was a duty they took very seriously—even for the most repugnant criminals.[108] Yet, after responsible government was granted some ambiguity emerged as to the correct decision-making process. One colonial governor was sanctioned for leaving blank (but signed) pardon slips to be used in his absence; another later complained that local ministers did not assist him enough when coming to a decision.[109] Successive dispatches between the British Colonial Secretary and the Australian colonies in the 1860s and 1870s confirmed that the decision-making burden was to be shared. Ultimately, ministers were accountable to Parliament for their advice on the case while the Governor was responsible to his British superiors for the decision taken.[110] Executive review always took place in private, away from the public eye; by convention (but not always in practice) the reasons for a decision needed only to be minuted on occasions when the Governor deviated from the Executive Council's advice.[111] For some, the ability of the Executive to override a decision made by an impartial judiciary—often with information available to them that was not permissible in a court of law—was beyond the pale. As New South Wales MP, Thomas Ewing, described it in 1900: 'Capital punishment is the only portion of the law that is not administered, if I can use the term, in accordance with the law'.[112]

[108] David Plater and Sue Milne wrote that mercy was not a 'random lottery' while John Hirst wrote that 'great care was taken in the choice of those to be saved', see Plater and Milne, 2012, pp. 39 and 43.

[109] Todd, 2006, pp. 351–353.

[110] Todd, 2006, pp. 350–359.

[111] Todd, 2006, p. 347.

[112] Thomas Ewing as quoted in, Carolyn Strange, 'Discretionary Justice: Political Culture and the Death Penalty in New South Wales and Ontario, 1890–1920', in C. Strange (ed.), *Qualities of Mercy: Justice, Punishment, and Discretion*, Vancouver: UBC Press, 1996, p. 158.

Strange as it may sound, the moment a prisoner was sentenced to death in an Australian courtroom the odds strongly favoured an outcome where they did not end up at the gallows with a rope around their neck. In the context of Tasmania from 1806 to 1946 Mark Finnane and Chris Leppard have concluded that, of the 1469 death sentences handed down, only 545 executions were actually carried out.[113] According to Brian Purdue's numbers in Western Australia, from 1840 to 1964 a total of 596 people were sentenced to death of which 154 were hanged.[114] In Victoria, Kathy Laster and Roger Douglas found that between 1842 and 1967 a total of 606 people were sentenced to death but only 185 executed.[115] In South Australia, at least for the colonial period (1836–1900), 108 death sentences were handed down of which 46 were carried out.[116] As for New South Wales, between 1788 and 1954 around two-thirds of the 3171 capital offenders were extended some form of clemency according to Macnab, Castle and Kaladelfos' database. A key turning point came in 1819 for those sentenced to death in that colony. Before then executions outnumbered commutations in New South Wales but afterwards (barring a brief aberration around the year 1850) the opposite held true.[117] In Queensland, the figures from Mark Finnane and Jonathan Richards show that, between the years 1865 and 1922, a total of 186 people were sentenced to death of which 65 were executed.[118] Shakespeare's oft-repeated quote from *The Merchant of Venice* that 'mercy seasons justice' might be inappropriate in the context of Australian capital cases; mercy was the main dish served up by the patchwork of Executive Councils.

---

[113]Finnane and Leppard, 2018.

[114]Purdue, 1993, pp. 61 and 79.

[115]Laster and Douglas, 1991, p. 146.

[116]These numbers are compiled from the following sources: 'Execution, Whippings and Commuted Death Sentence Register', State Records of South Australia, GRS 2625/1; David J. Towler and Trevor J. Porter, *The Hempen Collar: Executions in South Australia, 1838–1964: A Collection of Eyewitness Accounts*, Adelaide: The Wednesday Press, 1990; Alan Pope, *One Law for All? Aboriginal People and the Criminal Law in Early South Australia*, Canberra: Aboriginal Studies Press, 2011, p. 103.

[117]Macnab, Castle, and Kaladelfos, 2013.

[118]Finnane and Richards, 2010, p. 252.

Raw commutation and execution numbers are valuable but they can sometimes obscure the whole story. For example, on face value South Australia had a comparatively low commutation rate but that was only because they had just two capital crimes on the statute books after 1876. Contrast that with other jurisdictions that were much slower to reduce their capital code like Victoria which still had nine capital crimes in 1900.[119] Criminals there might be sentenced to death for a less serious crime (say, robbery with wounding) where an actual execution was never going to be the likely outcome (and thereby swelling long-term commutation rates). Furthermore, if one delves deeper in search of a singular causal factor to account for the extension of mercy, then the variables are so numerous that they are difficult to properly weigh. Take, for example, the following considerations as a starting point: the type of crime (i.e. violent, property-based, sexual); the circumstances around its commission (i.e. impulsive, calculated, aggravated, accidental); location (i.e. urban or country districts); historical periods (i.e. 1790s, 1850s, 1890s); the disposition of key actors (i.e. judges, jurors, executive councillors); and precedent (i.e. how like offenders were treated in the jurisdiction). This is a dizzying array of factors which all played one part or another in the final decision to grant or withhold mercy. The granular details of each separate case also ignores the broader cultural and historical contingencies prevalent in each jurisdiction. For example, Carolyn Strange argued that the 'snap of the lash and the clang of convict chains' still 'rang in the ears' of the mercy inclined New South Wales' Executive Council as late as the 1890s.[120] Here, I will briefly discuss the tendencies of the various Executive Councils as it related to criminals of a particular gender, ethnicity and age to show how these overarching characteristics of the criminal (as opposed to the nature of the crime's commission) could influence outcomes.

To start with gender, female offenders were one group in colonial society who were far less likely to be executed. In the colonial period Victoria executed four females. In Western Australia there were two,

[119] Lennan and Williams, 2012, pp. 667–668.

[120] Strange, 1996, p. 133.

while South Australia and Queensland had only one each.[121] Investigations into New South Wales and Tasmania also demonstrate a comparatively small number of females hanged there too.[122] To be sure, colonial women were not as commonly indicted for capital crimes to begin with but, once convicted, they were, to quote Kathy Laster in the Victorian context, 'treated more favourably than men'.[123] Likewise, Plater and Milne have recognised the 'general reluctance' to carry out the death penalty on women in the colonies.[124] At least one Adelaide newspaper picked up on this trend at the time, commenting in 1860 that female capital offenders 'now almost invariably escape the extreme penalty of the law'.[125] More than in other categories of criminals, the way in which an individual female was stereotyped in the public mind (as either 'virtuous' or 'vicious') mattered a great deal to the outcome of the executive review.[126] Political factors could also play a role as in 1890s Melbourne when a panic around infanticide caused a sudden upshot in executions for the crime in that city—despite the offence previously attracting sentences less severe than death.[127] A more obscure reason for granting mercy to females (known in England as the 'benefit of the belly') was when pregnancy intersected with the law's wishes. For instance, the first female executed in Australia, Ann Davis in 1789, attempted to avoid the gallows by asserting she was 'quick with child' but was executed anyway after a physical examination found no evidence to

[121]For Victoria, see Kathy Laster and Kerry Alexander, 'Chivalry or Death: Women on the Gallows in Victoria, 1856–1975', *Criminology Australia*, vol. 4, no. 2, 1992, p. 7. For Western Australia, see Purdue, 1993, pp. 5 and 21. For South Australia, see David Plater, Joanne Duncan, and Sue Milne, '"Innocent Victim of Circumstance" or "a Very Devil Incarnate"? The Trial and Execution of Elizabeth Woolcock in South Australia in 1873', *Flinders Law Journal*, vol. 15, 2013, pp. 315–380. For Queensland, see Mac Master, 1999, pp. 136–140.

[122]Plater and Milne, 2014.

[123]Kathy Laster, 'Arbitrary Chivalry: Women and Capital Punishment in Victoria, 1842–1967', in D. Philips and S. Davies (eds), *A Nation of Rogues? Crime, Law and Punishment in Colonial Australia*, Melbourne: Melbourne University Press, 1994, p. 167.

[124]Plater and Milne, 2014, p. 100.

[125]*Adelaide Weekly Chronicle*, 14 January 1860.

[126]Plater and Milne, 2014, p. 136.

[127]Laster, 1994, pp. 171–176.

support her claim.[128] Though the reasoning for each female commutation was complex, notions of chivalry (albeit arbitrarily deployed) has been invoked by Laster to try and explain why so many females were extended mercy.[129] Certainly in arenas other than the gallows, the culturally informed desire for men to both 'save' and 'protect' females was commonplace.

Where statistical information is available, it demonstrates that race played a curious role in the application of mercy in the Australian colonies. For all of Western Australia's history, the commutation rates for capital offenders (i.e. those sentenced to death but not executed), when separated by racial grouping, were as follows according to Purdue: Indigenous Australians (82.9%); Europeans (64.1%) and Asian (47.7%).[130] For Queensland, the work of Douglas and Finnane show how commutation rates between 1865 and 1922 were arranged in a similar order: Indigenous Australians (79.6%); Melanesians (72.5%); European (57.3%); Chinese (40%) and other (28.6%).[131] Surprisingly, these statistical breakdowns indicate that the most likely recipients of mercy in these jurisdictions were Indigenous Australians. Certainly, in these later settling colonies there was a high frequency of Indigenous hangings but they were often concentrated in the formative years of settlement.[132] As the colonies matured, notions of 'tribal custom' were often raised in *inter se* cases (i.e. where the offender and victim were both Indigenous Australians) which often led to a commuted death sentence. In fact, there appears to be a general reluctance by colonial courts to interfere with crimes perpetrated between Indigenous individuals or groups.[133] As an aside, it has long been suspected that European settlers who committed capital crimes upon Indigenous Australians were

[128]David Collins, *An Account of the English Colony in New South Wales, from Its First Settlement in January 1788, to August 1801: With Remarks on the Dispositions, Customs, Manners & c. of the Native Inhabitants of That Country*, second edition, London: T. Cadell and W. Davies, 1798, p. 86.

[129]Laster, 1994.

[130]Adapted from, Purdue, 1993, pp. 61 and 79.

[131]Adapted from, Finnane and Richards, 2010, p. 252.

[132]For instance, every Indigenous offender executed in the history of South Australia was hanged in the first 26 years of European settlement, see Anderson, 2015, p. 6.

[133]Douglas and Finnane, 2012, see especially pp. 78–86.

unlikely to end up at the gallows. For instance, only one European was executed in South Australian history for murdering an Indigenous person.[134] There is however, in South Australia as elsewhere, extensive evidence of European killings of Indigenous Australians on the frontier.[135] Another key finding from Queensland and Western Australia is that criminals of Asian descent (especially Chinese offenders) were less likely than other groups to be extended mercy. One wonders just how pivotal the anti-Asian sentiment that existed in the Australian colonies, from the gold rush and beyond, had on deliberations in their individual cases.

More needs to be understood about the relationship between youth and mercy in the Australian colonies than is currently the case. Collections of city-youths were the subject of widespread concern in the colonial period—from the various 'pushes' of Sydney and Melbourne to the 'cabbage-tree mobs' of the earlier convict era.[136] Yet punishing the young, particularly in capital cases, would always run into thorny questions of criminal responsibility given their age. Tasmania's *Juvenile Offenders Act* of 1875 signalled to the judiciary that some discretion for capital offenders under the age of nineteen was warranted. Instead of handing down a sentence of death recorded, the law permitted Tasmanian judges to gaol them and, during their incarceration, mandate that they instead be 'once, twice, or thrice privately whipped'.[137] There is certainly evidence of young people (at least for modern standards) meeting an end at the gallows later in the nineteenth century than one might think. The infamous Mount Rennie gang-rape case in Sydney committed by

---

[134]Anderson and Sendziuk, 2014, pp. 100–103. See also Sendziuk, 2012, pp. 33–47.

[135]Lyndall Ryan, 'Colonial Frontier Massacres, Australia: 1780–1930', *The University of Newcastle Website*, https://c21ch.newcastle.edu.au/colonialmassacres/map.php, viewed 18 October 2019.

[136]Alastair Greig, *The Australian Way of Life: A Sociological Introduction*, Melbourne: Palgrave Macmillan, 2013, p. 408.

[137]Tasmania, no. 6 of 1875, *An Act for the More Effectual Punishment of Juvenile Offenders*, s2. Similar legislation relating to juvenile offenders was passed in most Australian jurisdictions in the second half of the nineteenth century but none appeared to follow Tasmania's lead in suggesting alternatives for capitally convicted juveniles, See, for example, South Australia, no. 35 of 1872, *Juvenile Offenders Act*; Victoria, no. 951 of 1887, *The Juvenile Offenders Act*.

members of the 'Waterloo Push' during the 1880s involved the execution of multiple perpetrators under the age of twenty.[138] As late as 1892 Francis Horrocks, guilty of murder, was the youngest man to be hanged in Queensland at age seventeen.[139] However, as early as 1872 the perpetrator's age appeared to weigh on the minds of Queensland juries in favour of mercy.[140] According to Ross Barber's numbers, only 7.4% of those executed after 1859 in Queensland were known to be under the age of 22 at the time of death.[141] For colonies that placed so much hope on its youth and future, their interactions with the criminal law were problematic and confronting.

In an abstract sense the prerogative of mercy, as wielded by the Executive in capital cases, was a check and balance upon the majority of the legislature that determined the capital code and the members of the judiciary who adjudicated upon it. In practice, however, it was seen by many as a benevolent 'act of grace' by an administration not wishing the criminal to experience the severity of the law. Yet, by the late nineteenth century the impulse to codify and rationalise criminal law in Australia was strongly felt.[142] As such, the residual pocket of discretionary decision-making power held by the Executive Council was difficult to countenance for a growing number of colonists. As Carolyn Strange points out, the Executive tried to justify a 'secret, highly discretionary process' as one that was instead 'an opportunity for a considered second thought, free from the passions and prejudices of the courtroom, and receptive to arguments and evidence ruled out by the law'.[143] More recently, legal-minded scholars like David Plater and Sue Milne have noticed that, given the limited appeal options available to Australia's colonial criminals, the Executive Council functioned imperfectly as the

---

138 K. Gleeson, 'From Centenary to the Olympics, Gang Rape in Sydney', *Current Issues in Criminal Justice*, vol. 16, no. 3, 2004, p. 189.

139 H.C. Tait, 'Convictism to Codification: The Prerogative of Mercy in Colonial Queensland', *Australian Bar Review*, vol. 38, no. 3, 2014, p. 321.

140 *Queensland Times, Ipswich Herald and general Advertiser*, 7 November 1872, p. 4.

141 This percentage is adapted from the numbers presented in, Barber, 1967, p. 198.

142 Tait, 2014, pp. 319–331.

143 Strange, 1996, p. 160.

nearest thing there was to a Court of Criminal Appeal.[144] The reasons for intervention, or non-intervention, by the Governor, and later the Governor-in-Council were varied and case-by-case. The raw numbers demonstrate that mercy was the likely outcome in capital cases, though overarching characteristics of the criminal, such as gender, race and age, had the potential to load the dice in favour of a particular outcome.

* * *

If one takes the long view of Australia's hanging years, it is a story not of the ascendance of capital punishment but its reverse. Yet, the parameters of capital punishment in the colonies were always being amended to accord with the shifting contingencies of settlement. After spiking in the 1820s and 1830s during the convict period, execution numbers declined in proportion to a growing population. Moreover, in the first third of the colonial period, all sorts of crimes (including many property offences) would regularly see a person hanged. In the last two-thirds of the colonial period, however, murder was the main crime likely to be associated with a hanged criminal. As for the application of mercy in the colonies, the most striking fact was just how frequently it was handed out. Culturally informed opinions about race, gender and youth all had different impacts on the likelihood or otherwise of capital sentences being carried out. The number of capital crimes on the statute books in the Australian colonies was also on a downward trajectory. As the nineteenth century progressed, colonial lawmakers increasingly restricted the death penalty to only the most severe crimes—though not always at the same pace. Sexual crimes, aggravated forms of burglary, attempted murder and many defence or security-related crimes lingered in Australia as capital offences for longer than in England. Almost always the unique circumstances of settlement were invoked as grounds for their retention—whether it be the gender imbalance, the isolation of the frontier, or the existence of the convict system. Despite the excesses of capital punishment being tempered in the nineteenth century, Australia's hanging years consisted of generations of

---

[144]Plater and Milne, 2012, p. 41.

colonial lawmakers, judges and administrators who supported the use of death punishments in at least some circumstances. The criminals, crimes and courtrooms may have changed but their sentiment remained the same—for lawbreakers of the deepest dye, only death could deter.

3

The Ideal and Reality of Execution Procedure

The practice of executions in colonial Australia aimed to communicate a simple message to both the criminal and the onlooker—crime has consequences. Underlined by the symbolism of death, this punitive message was an easy one to decipher then as it is now. More convoluted and hidden, however, was how this lesson of the Australian gallows was constantly being derailed by failures in execution procedure. For example, when Joseph Mutter was decapitated in Brisbane by an unusually hard and thin rope, unwisely left exposed to the effects of overnight frost, the press were flabbergasted. '[H]orrible', 'disgraceful', 'disgusting', 'sickening' and 'atrociously revolting' are a select list of adjectives extracted from just one short paragraph that appeared in *The Brisbane Courier* describing the event.[1] Instead of concentrating on the gravity of the murder Mutter had committed and the warning hangings sent to potential wrongdoers, the Queensland press were busily mounting a case for an official inquiry into the matter. This chapter gives a broad but informative sweep of the changing practice of executions

[1] *The Brisbane Courier*, 10 June 1879, p. 2.

S. Anderson, *A History of Capital Punishment in the Australian Colonies, 1788 to 1900*, Palgrave Histories of Policing, Punishment and Justice,
https://doi.org/10.1007/978-3-030-53767-8_3

in the Australian colonies from 1788 to 1900. It uses a memorandum sent out by the Colonial Office in London in 1880 as a template to discuss each component—from sentencing through to taking the limp body down from the gallows. The decapitation of Mutter may be an extraordinary example but the fact remains that even in minor cases of mismanagement a botched hanging took away from the intended lesson of punishment. The frequent bungling of colonial executions caused unnecessary pain, suffering and disfigurement upon the body of the criminal that reflected badly on the justice of the sentence as a whole. Beneath cries of 'barbarism' and 'savagery', the lesson of deterrence was lost when an execution was not performed correctly.

A Memorandum on Execution Procedure Arrives from London

In late 1880 a curious circular, not for general publication, arrived in the Australian colonies from London. It was courtesy of John Wodehouse 1st Earl of Kimberley, the then Secretary of State for the Colonies.[2] On the cover letter to the Circular was written the following:

> The attention both of my predecessor and myself has been called to cases where, through mismanagement or an adherence to barbarous usages, the execution of criminals has been attended with revolting circumstances, the recurrence of which it is necessary, in the interest both of humanity and decency, to prevent by every possible means.[3]

[2]All Australian colonies received a copy of these documents, as was the usual procedure with 'circulars' sent out by the Colonial Office. In this chapter the Queensland set are cited, see 'Circulars on Capital Punishment, 27 June 1880 to 28 December 1880', Queensland State Archives (hereafter QSA), Series ID 12690. For the individual items within this series, see 'Circular from the Secretary of State for the Colonies, Regarding a Memorandum on the Practice of Executing Criminals, 27 June 1880', QSA, Series ID 12690, Item ID 1839167; 'Memorandum Upon the Execution of Prisoners by Hanging with a Long Drop, June 1880', QSA, Series ID 12690, Item ID 1139511; 'Circular from the Secretary of State for the Colonies, with Attached Plan and Section of the Gallows at Newgate Gaol, 28 December 1880', QSA, Series ID 12690, Item ID 1839168.

[3]'Circular from the Secretary of State for the Colonies, Regarding a Memorandum on the Practice of Executing Criminals, 27 June 1880', QSA, Series ID 12690, Item ID 1839167.

Enclosed was a 'Memorandum' on the subject of proper execution method using the long drop, a document that was developed in close consultation with the Public Executioner in England.[4] It aimed to standardise execution procedures and thereby prevent the constant bungling of hangings that seemed, from London at least, to be the scourge of most colonial jurisdictions. From the time of sentencing to the preparation of the dead body for medical inspection, the Memorandum was comprehensive in its attempt to regulate execution procedure in the colonies. Diagrams of up-to-date equipment and techniques were also included for the benefit of practitioners. Only a few months later a very large, colour-printed, technical drawing of the gallows at London's Newgate Gaol was sent out as an accompaniment to the Memorandum.[5] By the 1890s a standardised 'Table of Drops' began appearing in colonial jurisdictions that used a specifically developed formula to calculate the appropriate drop length for each individual criminal.[6] These documents suggest that the kind of guesswork and amateurism that characterised Australian execution procedure for the majority of the colonial period was increasingly replaced by more professional and standardised methods by the time of Federation in 1901.

As this chapter concerns the procedure of hangings in colonial Australia, the 1880 Memorandum (full title: 'Memorandum upon the Execution of Prisoners by Hanging with a long Drop') is used below in an uncommon way. In italics the original document is quoted in full, but in a piecemeal fashion, broken up so that there is a focus on each individual point in turn (for a copy of this Memorandum see Illustrations 3.1 and 3.2). Juxtaposed to this ideal execution procedure, as conceived by the Colonial Office in 1880, is the historical reality of executions in the Australian colonies up until that point. Only by contrasting the ideal

[4]'Memorandum Upon the Execution of Prisoners by Hanging with a Long Drop, June 1880', QSA, Series ID 12690, Item ID 1139511.

[5]'Circular from the Secretary of State for the Colonies, with Attached Plan and Section of the Gallows at Newgate Gaol, 28 December 1880', QSA, Series ID 12690, Item ID 1839168.

[6]The 'Table of Drops' is reprinted in the following secondary sources, Kevin Morgan, *The Particulars of Executions 1894–1967: The Hidden Truth About Capital Punishment at the Old Melbourne Gaol and Pentridge Prison*, Melbourne: The Old Melbourne Gaol, 2004, pp. 12–13; Ross Ward, *The Office of the Sheriff: A Millennium of Tradition*, Sydney: Department of Courts Administration, 1992, p. 57.

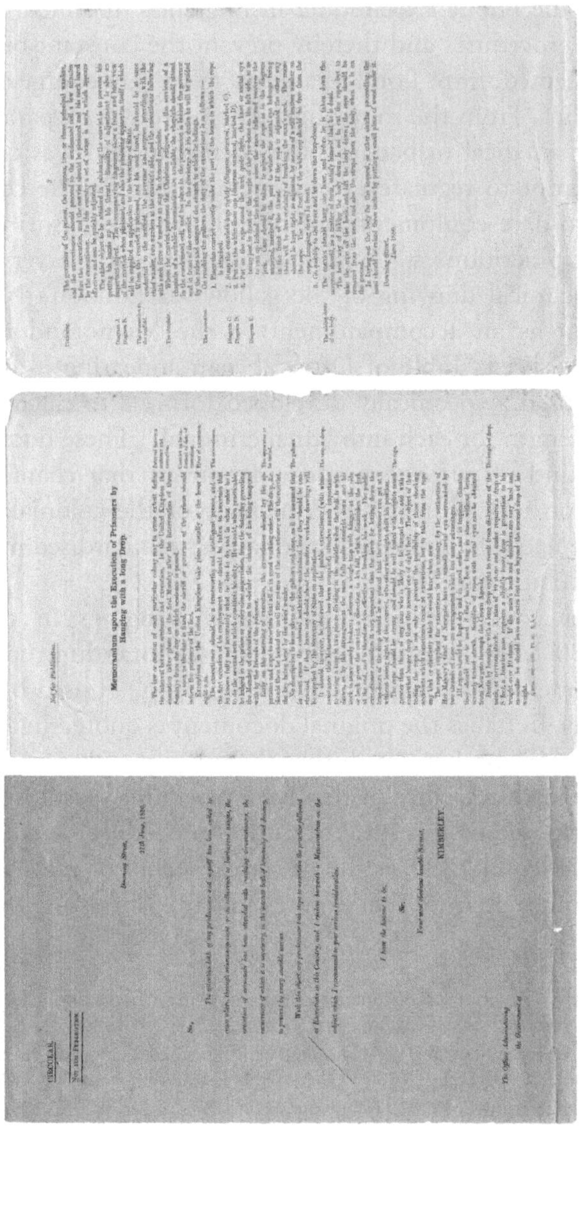

Illustration 3.1 The 1880 Memorandum on Execution Procedure (cover letter included) sent to the Australian colonies from the Secretary of State for the Colonies in London, June 1880 (*Source* 'Memorandum Upon the Execution of Prisoners by Hanging with a Long Drop, June 1880', Queensland State Archives, Series ID 12690, Item ID 1139511)

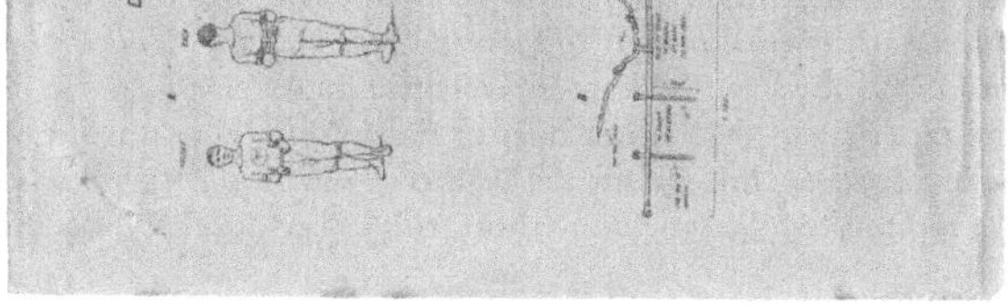

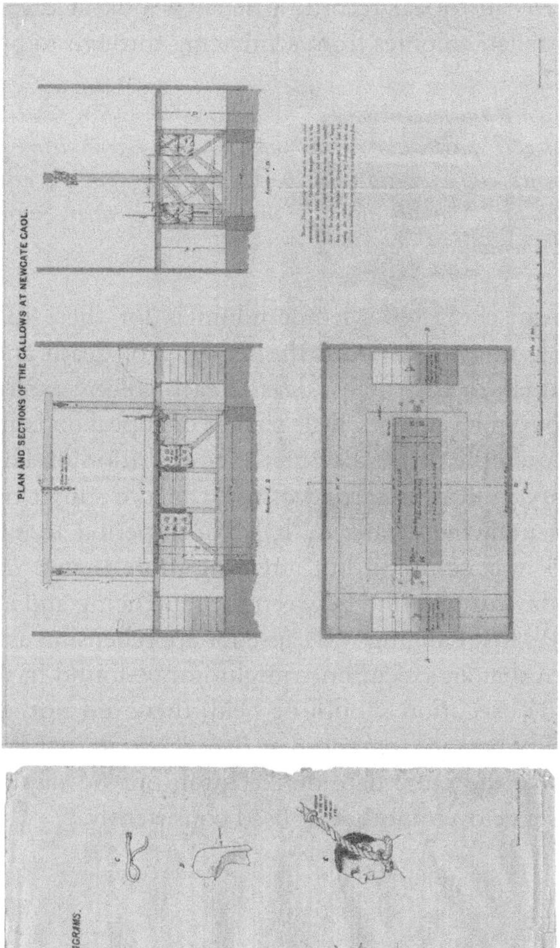

Illustration 3.2 The drawings sent by the Colonial Office in England to the Australian colonies in June and December 1880 regarding new execution equipment and the design of the Newgate gallows in London. (*Source* 'Memorandum Upon the Execution of Prisoners by Hanging with a Long Drop, June 1880', Queensland State Archives, Series ID 12690, Item ID 1139511; 'Circular from the Secretary of State for the Colonies, with Attached Plan and Section of the Gallows at Newgate Gaol, 28 December 1880', Queensland State Archives, Series ID 12690, Item ID 1839168)

with the reality of executions will the bungling nature of colonial hangings be fully grasped. Moreover, it is a useful opportunity to provide, for the first time in the historical record, a detailed look at execution procedure in the Australian colonies from sentencing through to burial.

> *[Interval between sentence and execution.]*
> *The law or custom of each particular colony may to some extent define the interval between sentence and execution. In the United Kingdom the execution takes place on the first Monday after the intervention of three Sundays from the day on which sentence is passed.*

The first point made in the 1880 Memorandum is for there to be a regular and predictable interval between the sentence of death and the execution of the criminal. In the earliest days of each colony executions seemed to be carried out in haste, with little chance of appeal on behalf of the condemned. For example, Australia's first-ever execution of Thomas Barrett on 27 February 1788 was carried out just before sunset on the very same day of his sentencing.[7] Later in the colonial period an interval of a little over a week was common but anything more than a month appears rare. The six-day turn around between the sentencing and execution at South Australia's first hanging was cause for apprehension as there was legitimate concern that an executioner might not be found in time.[8] As for the day that the execution should be held, there did not appear to be a fixed rule. Guilty persons sentenced at the same criminal sessions were very likely to have the same date of execution but no day of the week was given preference over another or used consistently.

---

[7]Watkin Tench, *A Narrative of the Expedition to Botany Bay, with an Account of New South Wales, Its Productions, Inhabitants, & c. to Which Is Subjoined, a List of the Civil and Military Establishments at Port Jackson* [1789], Sydney: Sydney University Library, 1998, p. 36. Barrett's execution was hastened by the fact that in the earliest days of the colony there was no means to appeal a criminal sentence. For more on this point, see 'Officer', *An Authentic and Interesting [sic] Narrative of the Late Expedition to Botany Bay* [short title], London: W. Bailey, 1789, pp. 20–22.

[8]For a thorough account of Michael Magee's execution, see T. Horton James, *Six Months in South Australia* [1838], Adelaide: Public Library of South Australia, 1962, pp. 54–61.

[Convict to be informed of date of execution.]
As soon as the date is fixed, the sheriff or governor of the prison should inform the prisoner of the fact.

Informing the condemned of the execution date gave them the opportunity to come to terms with their impending fate and prepare accordingly. An example of this intimate exchange is relayed in the personal diary of John Buckley Castieau who was at one time the Governor at Beechworth and Melbourne Gaols. After the arrival of a letter from the Chief Secretary's Office that fixed the date and time for the execution of James Cusack, one of the prisoners under his supervision during his time at Melbourne Gaol, Castieau immediately went to the prisoner's cell to convey the news.[9] Tying back to the question of the interval between sentencing and execution, Cusack provides a useful case study. Sentenced to death on 16 August 1870, he was informed of his execution date by Castieau on 22 August and hanged on 30 August—an interval of exactly two weeks between sentencing and execution.[10]

[Hour of execution.]
Executions in the United Kingdom take place usually at the hour of eight a.m.

Besides exemplary cases like that of Thomas Barrett (described above) who was executed near sunset, Australian executions were always conducted early in the morning. 8 a.m. was the most common time but anywhere from 7 a.m. till 11 a.m. has been mentioned as the hour of execution. For instance, Cusack's execution occurred at 10 a.m., identical to the time set for the two other men executed at Melbourne Gaol that year.[11] Early morning executions were preferred as it minimised the chance of a rowdy, carnival-like atmosphere developing among the

---

[9]John Buckley Castieau, *The Difficulties of My Position: The Diaries of Prison Governor John Buckley Castieau, 1855–1884*, M. Finnane (ed.), Canberra: National Library of Australia, 2004, p. 87.

[10]For details of Cusack's sentencing, notification of execution date by Castieau and hanging at Melbourne Gaol see, *The Argus*, 17 August 1870, p. 6; Castieau, 2004, pp. 87–89.

[11]For details of the execution of the two other men at Melbourne Gaol in 1870, see *The Argus*, 5 August 1870, p. 6; *The Age*, 14 November 1870, p. 2.

crowd. The general public were welcome to watch the execution so long as they were in the habit of rising early and not oversleeping.

> *[The executioner.]*
> *The executioner should be a trustworthy and intelligent person, and on the first occasion of his employment care should be taken to ascertain that he knows fully and accurately what he has to do, and in what order he is to do the several acts which constituted his duty. He should, when practicable, be lodged in the prison or under close supervision, from the Saturday preceding the Monday of execution, so as to obviate the chance of his being tampered with by the friends of the prisoner.*

The fact that the Memorandum had to state explicitly that the hangman ought to be a dependable individual and competent at the task at hand says something about their previous quality. Extended studies of specific executioners in Australia reveals, among other things, their poor character, rampant alcoholism and bungled handiwork.[12] For the majority of the colonial period hangmen were chosen from among the prisoners themselves. Sometimes they performed the undesirable task in exchange for a reduction of their sentence or a relatively large pecuniary reward.[13]

The position of executioner in colonial Australia was an ignoble one, laden with superstition and social stigma. It was a fact that led many executioners to don disguises at the colonial gallows. Hangmen with fake beards, goggles, masks, costume dress and faces smeared with various emulsions were seen on the colonial scaffold.[14] When Henry Flude's

[12] Ray Beckett and Richard Beckett, *Hangman: The Life and Times of Alexander Green, Public Executioner to the Colony of New South Wales*, Melbourne: Thomas Nelson Australia, 1980; Christopher Dawson, *No Ordinary Run of Men: The Queensland Executioners*, Brisbane: Inside History, 2010a; Steve Harris, *Solomon's Noose: The True Story of Her Majesty's Hangman of Hobart*, Melbourne: Melbourne Books, 2015.

[13] For example James Freeman, the man who hanged Thomas Barrett, had also been sentenced to death that very same day. However, Freeman was reprieved by Governor Arthur Phillip on the proviso that he act as the colony's hangman for the remaining period of his sentence. See Dawson, 2010a, p. 7; Ward, 1992, p. 33. As of 1819 the salary of the executioner in Hobart Town was £25 per annum, only £5 less than that of the turnkey at the Gaol. See 'Return of All Civil Officers and Persons Receiving Salaries from the Police Fund of Van Diemen's Land', in *Historical Records of Australia*, series 3, vol. 3, Sydney: The Library Committee of the Commonwealth Parliament, 1921, p. 538.

[14] Dawson, 2010a, p. 50.

identity as the hangman of Queensland was revealed he left Brisbane and his successful grocery store behind such was the shame attached to the job.[15] Long-term executioners like Alexander Green in New South Wales and Soloman Blay in Tasmania cared less about protecting their identity, as their vocation and status was already well known in the colony. Other executioners even tried to distance themselves from the act of killing itself. Robert Howard, or 'Nosey Bob' as he was known, was the public executioner of New South Wales but delegated to an assistant the task of putting the rope around the neck of the victim and activating the drop.[16] 'It's not a fact that I ever hung a man – never, sir, never' he told *The Bulletin* in 1880.[17]

A willingness to do the job was the only prerequisite of the colonial hangman; aptitude for the task was a secondary concern. For instance, the convict who had agreed to play hangman for the first-ever execution in 1788 was so reluctant to perform his duty that he complied only once the Provost Marshal and others had threatened to shoot him.[18] The non-existence of formal training left any shortcomings in technique uncorrected until either intuition or experience told them to adjust their methods. Knowledge of proper execution method was, for the most part, hard-won through trial and error. By 1876 the Sheriff of New South Wales, Charles Cowper, was tired of the lack of professionalism among executioners. In writing a letter to the Department of Justice he demanded an increase in their salary and an end to employing criminals for the job. He was, to quote from the letter, 'daily beset' by the nuisance of previous executioners under his service.[19] Their addiction to drink, lack of respectable attire and need for a personal handler when attending a regional execution was particularly irritating to the Sheriff.

---

[15] Dawson, 2010a, p. 41.

[16] 'Robert "Nosey Bob" Howard (1832–1906)', *Waverley Council* 2009, http://www.waverley.nsw.gov.au/__data/assets/pdf_file/0020/8732/Hangman_Waverleys_First.pdf, viewed 11 November 2014.

[17] *The Bulletin*, 31 January 1880, p. 5.

[18] Arthur Bowes Smyth, *The Journal of Arthur Bowes Smyth: Surgeon, Lady Penrhyn, 1787–1789*, in P.G. Fidlon and R.J. Ryan (eds), Sydney: Australian Documents Library, 1979.

[19] The letter written by Sheriff Charles Cowper to the Under Secretary of the Department of Justice, dated 1 June 1876, is reprinted in Ward, 1992, pp. 46–55.

Sheriff Cowper would have been pleased to hear that in colonies like Queensland the professionalisation of the executioner was not far off. Withholding the name and address of the hangman from the public record combined with the new secrecy of private executions led to a better class of person being appointed to the post of hangman in that colony. In 1886 twenty-six people applied for a publicly advertised vacancy to become the new executioner of Queensland. The successful applicant had no criminal record and even sported a reference from the former Mayor of Brisbane. In 1900 when the same position became available, over one hundred people applied for the job, demonstrating just how much things had changed over the intervening century.[20]

> *[The apparatus to be tested.]*
> *Early on the morning of execution, the executioner should try the apparatus and rope to ascertain that all is in good working order. The drop, &c. should then be locked up until the return of the executioner with the convict, the key being kept by the chief warder.*

Testing the apparatus prior to the actual hanging was a rare event, or at least it does not show up strongly in the historical record. That said, Edmund Finn in *The Chronicles of Early Melbourne* (1888) tells one story of how the executioner of three condemned criminals in 1842 did indeed put in some prior practice. Earlier in the year the same hangman had horribly blundered an execution in such a way where 'the two poor wretches got jambed [*sic.*], and twisted and writhed convulsively in a manner that horrified even the most hardened'.[21] Being Victoria's first-ever execution the untested and hastily constructed scaffold, 'only a degree removed from the proverbial "bucket"', was mostly to blame.[22] Finn testifies that the executioner 'was so universally censured' by his first effort that he was 'fearful of losing the "appointment"'.[23] So as to

[20] Dawson, 2010a, pp. 42 and 45.

[21] The execution was of two Indigenous Australians named 'Bob' and 'Jack' on 20 January 1842. See Edmund Finn (pseudonym 'Garryowen'), *The Chronicles of Early Melbourne 1835 to 1852: Historical, Anecdotal and Personal* [1888], centennial edition, Melbourne: Heritage Publications, 1976, pp. 394–396, quote on p. 396.

[22] Finn, 1976, p. 396.

[23] Finn, 1976, p. 398.

avoid the same mistakes and in the hope of 'making his post a permanency' the hangman 'procured the straw effigy of a human figure, and upon this model was in the habit of taking frequent private rehearsals'.[24] Practice, as the saying goes, makes perfect. The three men died 'without a struggle' when the drop was activated for the second time in Victoria's history.[25]

> *[The gallows.]*
> *No description is here given of the gallows and drop, as it is assumed that in most cases the colonial authorities understand how they should be constructed. If they have any doubt about the matter, working drawings will be supplied by the Secretary of State on application.*

At the earliest executions in each colony, particularly the very first, the gallows were primitive constructions. The five executions that occurred in 1788 in Sydney appeared to have been conducted on a tree with the help of a ladder that was quickly pulled away.[26] At South Australia's first execution in 1838 the culprit was hanged using an overhanging tree branch and a cart that was slowly removed from under him by a horse. Performed and prepared by an amateur hangman of no experience it was, unsurprisingly, horribly botched.[27] The first execution in Moreton Bay was at the convict barracks but the second in 1841 occurred atop a windmill in the heart of the settlement that had been refitted for the occasion.[28] These early executions were very likely to be bungled since there was little technical expertise on hand to direct the build and, more

---

[24] Finn, 1976, p. 398.

[25] Finn, 1976, p. 398.

[26] For primary accounts of the five convicts executed in 1788, see John Cobley, *Sydney Cove 1788*, London: Camelot Press Ltd., 1962, pp. 87–88, 134, 169, and 259–260.

[27] For first-hand written accounts of how the execution was set up, see James, 1962, pp. 59–60; John Fogg Taylor, 'Letter from John Fogg Taylor of Tundemunga, Near Adelaide, 1840, to "John" in Wigan, Lancashire, England, Dated September 1840', State Library of South Australia, D 7310, p. 21.

[28] Christopher Dawson, *The Hanging at the Brisbane Windmill*, Brisbane: Inside History, 2009.

to the point, an all too hasty turnaround time between sentence and execution.

After these initial hangings each colony soon developed the appropriate infrastructure to deal with the execution of criminals. In Queensland, a trusty set of portable gallows—ten feet long, six feet wide and ten feet high—could hang up to three criminals at a time and were in use for many years at the Petrie Terrace Gaol.[29] These were later replaced by a cellblock gallows at Boggo Road Gaol. A similar set of portable gallows was erected out the front of Adelaide Gaol and then within the gaol yard after the introduction of private executions. A permanent drop was constructed in the 'A' wing of the Adelaide Gaol in the 1890s before a 'hanging tower' was constructed in the 1950s.[30] The same portable gallows that were used at the George Street Gaol in Sydney for many years were transferred to the yard at Darlinghurst Gaol after it opened in the early 1840s. During the year 1844 a new permanent drop was commissioned at Darlinghurst whereby the prisoner mounted the scaffold from a ladder inside the prison walls but emerged above the drop outside its walls. In full view of the crowd, the criminal fell into the space below the entranceway on the given signal.[31]

When public executions were abolished (see Chapter 7), many hasty alterations were made to these long-standing structures across the colonies. In November 1855 the colony of Victoria had its first private execution, a triple hanging at Melbourne Gaol, where such an alteration was made. 'The machine of death remains in the place it formerly occupied', wrote *The Argus*, 'but having been roofed in, the condemned are enclosed from public view'[32]. At the first private execution in Queensland in 1857 a thick black cloth was wrapped around the top half of the scaffold to prevent people from seeing the platform from over the low

[29] Christopher Dawson, *A Pit of Shame: The Executed Prisoners of Boggo Road*, second edition, Brisbane: Inside History, 2010b, p. 12.

[30] David J. Towler and Trevor J. Porter, *The Hempen Collar: Executions in South Australia, 1838–1964: A Collection of Eyewitness Accounts*, Adelaide: The Wednesday Press, 1990, pp. 148–149.

[31] Arthur L. Wintle, 'The Abolition of Public Executions in New South Wales', unpublished BA (Hons) thesis, La Trobe University, 1973, p. 23.

[32] James Condon, John Dixon and Alfred Henry Jackson were the names of the men executed. See *The Argus*, 23 November 1855, p. 5.

lying walls.[33] At Western Australia's first private execution in Perth Gaol in 1871, the gallows remained in the same location inside the gaol yard but it was simply erected at a lesser height so that it could no longer be seen over the walls.[34] A similar tact was taken inside the prison yard of the Murray Street Gaol in Hobart. The long wooden legs of the scaffold were all but removed while a large hole was dug to the depth of seven feet and the trap placed above it.[35] The once proud gallows, soaring over the prison walls, now became invisible to the world outside the prison through a variety of hasty alterations made in accordance with the spirit of the Private Execution Acts.

> *[The trap or drop.]*
> *It should, however, be observed that the public executioner (with whose assistance this Memorandum has been compiled) attaches much importance to having a trap in two pieces dividing in the middle when the bolt is withdrawn, as by this arrangement the man falls quite straight down and his neck is more surely broken; whereas a single trap with hinges at the side or back gives the convict a direction in his fall, which diminishes the jerk at the end, and is therefore less effective in breaking his neck. The public executioner considers it very important that the lever for letting down the trap-doors of the drop should be so placed that the executioner can get at it without losing sight of the convict, who otherwise might shift his position.*

The specific design aspects of the construction of the trap door are best explained by reprinting the technical drawing of the Newgate Gallows sent to the Australian colonies in December 1880 (see Illustration 3.2). This document was not included in the original Memorandum from the Colonial Office dated June 1880. As noted by the Secretary of State for the Colonies, copies were arranged and dispatched only after 'numerous applications' were received from the colonies regarding the 'Working drawings of a Gallows and Drop'.[36] The technical drawing clearly details

---

33 The man executed was named William Teagle. See Dawson, 2010a, p. 26.

34 *The Inquirer and Commercial News*, 19 April 1871.

35 Richard Davis, *The Tasmanian Gallows: A Study of Capital Punishment*, Hobart: Cat and Fiddle Press, 1974, p. 59.

36 'Circular from the Secretary of State for the Colonies, with Attached Plan and Section of the Gallows at Newgate Gaol, 28 December 1880', QSA, Series ID 12690, Item ID 1839168.

the trap being made from two pieces that part in the middle as suggested by the Memorandum. When the stop pin was removed the floor very quickly gave way. A sudden drop and a clean death should result, providing the drop length was calculated properly and the knot fixed in the appropriate position.

Given there was no central directive on the question of gallows construction until after this document was sent out in 1880 the design of the apparatus varied in the Australian colonies. Still, descriptions of drops designed later in the nineteenth century give the impression of a much more efficient and reliable apparatus that was far superior to earlier incarnations. In 1896 one Melbourne writer wrote of 'springs, bolts, and [a] pulley' when describing the gallows at Melbourne Gaol.[37] Even an 'India-rubber tube' was strategically placed below the drop with the aim of 'deadening any noisy slam'.[38] The Boggo Road gallows in Brisbane constructed in the early 1880s was similarly complex and had a pulley system that could gently lower the criminal's body to the ground after the execution was complete.[39] Some of these late colonial constructions reference aspects of the Newgate drop in their design but to state with confidence that they could trace their lineage directly to this drawing sent out in 1880 is difficult to determine.

> *[The rope.]*
> *The rope should be strong, and should be well tested with weights much greater than those of any man who is likely to be hanged on it, and with a somewhat longer drop than the normal one of eight feet. The object of thus testing the rope is not only to prevent the possibility of those shocking accidents which sometimes occur at executions, but to take from the rope any kink or elasticity which it would have when new.*
> *The ropes supplied for executions in this country by the authorities of Her Majesty's Gaol of Newgate have a smooth metal eye surrounded by two strands of rope – an arrangement which has many advantages.*

[37] Waldemar Bannow, *The Colony of Victoria, Socially and Materially*, Melbourne: McCarron, Bird & Co., 1896, p. 43.

[38] Bannow, 1896, p. 43.

[39] Dawson, 2010b, p. 12.

All ropes should be kept dry and in good order, and in tropical climates they should not be used if they have been long in store without being severely tested afresh. Supplies of ropes with metal eyes can be obtained from Newgate through the Crown Agents.

Some executioners took pride in the rope and knot they were capable of producing. In New South Wales, Robert Elliot reportedly spent many hours 'manipulating the rope with grease to make it soft and pliable' before every execution.[40] Grease, or a similar lubricant, was always applied to the rope to make the knot slide over itself more easily. If appropriate care was not taken with the rope it could stretch or even snap in two at the crucial moment. For example, when a government party travelled to the Coorong from Adelaide in 1840 to hang the perpetrators of the 'Maria Massacre' the rope was not hung with weights prior to the summary execution. The result was that it stretched well beyond its resting length. The sand had to be cleared away from under the feet of the two condemned men before a second attempt on their lives could be made.[41]

Unwanted stretching was one thing but a clean snap of the rope could be just as harrowing and certainly more painful. It even engendered the possibility of the condemned being extended mercy because of the trauma involved. In 1803 Joseph Samuels mounted the Sydney gallows three times over. On the first attempt the rope broke in a 'singular manner', on the second attempt 'the cord unrove at the fastening' and on the third attempt the 'cord again snapped in twain'.[42] Each time Samuels slammed to the ground from the height of the platform. When the rope failed a third time the Provost Marshal rode to the Governor and

---

[40] Dawson, 2010a, p. 27.

[41] A watercolour painted by E.C. Frome at the scene of the hanging in 1840 clearly demonstrates the hole dug below the feet of the two men to accommodate the stretched rope. The work is reprinted in Robert Foster, Rick Hosking and Amanda Nettelbeck, *Fatal Collisions: The South Australian Frontier and the Violence of Memory*, Adelaide: Wakefield Press, 2001, p. 14. For a written primary account of the two attempts to execute these men, see Alexander Tolmer, *Reminiscences of an Adventurous and Chequered Career at Home and at the Antipodes, Volume 1* [1882], facsimile edition, London: Gilbert and Rivington Ltd., 1972, p. 189.

[42] G. Paterson, *The History of New South Wales from Its First Discovery to the Present Time* [short title], Newcastle-upon-Tyne: Mackenzie and Dent, 1811, p. 385.

'feelingly represented these extraordinary circumstances' to him.[43] The Governor, in response, granted Samuels a reprieve from the penalty of death. On another occasion in 1826 William Curtin received a commutation of his death sentence after a problem with the rope caused him to fall to the ground from a 'considerable height' and receive heavy injuries.[44] Mercy was not always forthcoming, however, as William Johnson found out in 1828. He too fell to the earth after the rope snapped so the Sheriff took leave from the execution scene to inquire into the possibility of Johnson being granted mercy. It was a 'trying moment', according to the *Australian*, where the criminal sat on his coffin for almost an hour 'painfully vibrating between hope of mercy, and doubt, and fear'.[45] Unfortunately for Johnson, the Sheriff returned and announced that 'the law shall take its course'.[46]

The traditional 'hangman's knot' was tied with varying degrees of success in the colonies. One journalist who witnessed the hanging of the perpetrators of the Mount Rennie rape case at Darlinghurst Gaol in 1887 stated how the knot that pressed against the neck of the condemned men approached the 'size of an ordinary quart bottle, if not larger'.[47] Not only did the rope reek of freshly applied tar that 'permeated the whole building', it was also 'stout' enough to tie a 'steamer up to a wharf'.[48] The correspondent called these arrangements 'barbarous in the extreme' because he thought it caused prolonged strangulation rather than the immediate dislocation of the neck. A poorly tied knot was also a point of concern. At one of the executions presided over by Alexander Green in 1853 a faulty knot he had tied around the neck of one criminal caused him to fall to the ground from a reported height of twenty feet. Paralysed but still living the criminal was, limp-limbed, carried up to the drop once more to be hanged a second time.[49]

---

[43]Paterson, 1811, p. 385.

[44]'Executive Council Minute no. 6, 17 February 1826', in *Historical Records of Australia*, series 1, vol. 12, Sydney: The Library Committee of the Commonwealth Parliament, 1919, p. 245.

[45]*Australian*, 25 March 1828.

[46]*Australian*, 25 March 1828.

[47]*The Riverine Grazier*, 11 January 1887, p. 4.

[48]*The Riverine Grazier*, 11 January 1887, p. 4.

[49]*Bathurst Free Press*, 16 April 1853.

The rope used for hangings was an object of fascination to many colonists. Robert Elliot, the aforementioned hangman who took great pride in preparing his rope for executions, appeared before a Magistrate for drunkenness in 1857. It was revealed in court that he became unsociably drunk after being given free 'nobblers' by publicans around Sydney for exhibiting to excited patrons the two lengths of rope he had used at a recent double execution.[50] After the death of Solomon Blay, the long-term Tasmanian executioner, one newspaper claimed that two-hundred pieces of rope were found among his personal effects. Housed in a box they were said to be labelled and ticketed with the details of each of his executions.[51] Sometimes the rope was profitably sold off as a relic of the hanging. The rope used to hang a man named Thomas Griffin in Queensland was later cut up and sold at one shilling each. 'The genuineness of this rope was doubted', wrote one settler in his published recollections, 'but the buyers were satisfied'.[52] The existence of such stories and an unwanted fascination with the rope led, in Queensland at least, for it to be burnt by prison authorities immediately following executions conducted after the 1860s.[53]

> *[The length of drop.]*
> *Death by hanging with a long drop ought to result from dislocation of the neck, or nervous shock. A man of 10 stone and under requires a drop of 8 feet, a heavier man requires a slightly lesser drop in proportion to his weight over 10 stone. If the man's neck and shoulders are very hard and muscular he should have an extra foot or so beyond the normal drop of his weight.*

The correct drop length, calculated with reference to the weight of the prisoner, would result in a quick dislocation of the neck and an immediate death. A decade after this Memorandum appeared giving general estimates of appropriate drop length a much more precise 'Table of Drops' began appearing in the colonies, sent out as a 'confidential

---

[50] *Empire*, 16 May 1857.

[51] Harris, 2015, p. 314.

[52] W.R.O. Hill, *Forty-Five Years' Experiences in North Queensland, 1861 to 1905, with a Few Incidents in England, 1844 to 1861*, Brisbane: H. Pole & Col., Printers 1907, p. 180.

[53] Dawson, 2010a, p. 6.

circular'.[54] The table itself is dated April 1892 and has two columns 'weight of the prisoner in his clothes' and 'length of drop'.[55] The hangman and sheriff could easily refer to these corresponding columns on the day of execution. In rare circumstances, where an abnormally heavy or light prisoner was in their care, they could even calculate the drop length themselves since the specific formula underpinning these standard drop lengths was also included.

According to the Table of Drops anywhere from four to eight feet was acceptable but anything beyond these parameters could be disastrous. Set the drop too short and extended strangulation would result, too long and decapitation was a very real risk. John Hatton, Queensland's longest serving executioner who plied his trade from 1862 to 1885, was in the habit of setting the drop length far too long. When Patrick Collins was hanged in 1872, Hatton set an enormous drop length of 12 feet. A 'fearful gash' was thereby made to Collins' neck that nearly took off his head; 'blood spurted forth violently, deluging the clothes he wore, and pouring down over his trousers on to the ground underneath his feet'.[56] Solomon Blay in Tasmania was at the opposite end of the spectrum hanging every criminal regardless of weight with a drop of 1.5 metres, or just under five feet.[57] Light-framed criminals would therefore be choked over many minutes rather than a clean break of the neck being made. The insufficient drop length that Blay persisted with in Tasmania was even raised repeatedly by one MP at the 1884 Select Committee into Gaol Discipline.[58] Though dislocation of the neck was the intention, it was no sure thing in the colonial era. Such informative guides as the Table of Drops and the 1880 Memorandum provided welcome instruction to tenured hangmen who did not appear to be quick learners.

---

[54] Morgan, 2004, pp. 12–13.

[55] Morgan, 2004, pp. 12–13.

[56] *The Maitland Mercury*, 11 June 1872, p. 4.

[57] George Brown, David Button, Elizabeth Mercer, Peter Mercer, and Brian Rieusset, *The Penitentiary Chapel Historic Site*, Tasmania: National Trust of Australia, 2007, p. 42.

[58] Tasmania, 'Gaol Discipline: Report from the Select Committee, with Minutes of Proceedings and Evidence', *Tasmanian Parliamentary Papers*, no. 177 of 1884, pp. 8 and 11.

> *[Pinioning.]*
> *The governor of the prison, the surgeon, two or three principal warders, and the executioner should proceed to the condemned cell a few minutes before the execution, and the convict should be pinioned and his neck bared by the executioner. In this country a set of straps is used, which appears effective and can be quickly adjusted.*
> *The chief object to be attained in pinioning the convict is to prevent his getting his hands up to his throat. Rapidity of adjustment is also an important object. The accompanying diagrams show a front and back view of the convict when pinioned, and also the pinioning apparatus itself; which will be supplied on application to the Secretary of State.*

Executioners who were either forgetful or untrained in the necessities of pinioning paid a price for their negligence. At the hanging of Charles Streitman at Adelaide Gaol for example, the executioner forgot to strap the prisoner's legs together beforehand. Owing to the drop length being a mere three feet, Streitman managed to raise his legs to the platform above but they were soon kicked back into the drop. 'His chest heaved and fell at long intervals in the attempt to breathe', wrote one observer, 'It was not until twenty-two or twenty-three dragging minutes had passed that all signs of life had ceased'.[59] At Darlinghurst Gaol in 1863 Henry Manns' untied arms, 'repeatedly rose and fell, and finally, with one of his hands, the unfortunate man gripped the rope as if to tear the pressure from his head, a loud guttural noise … proceeding from his throat and lungs, while blood gushed from his nostrils, and stained the cap with which his face was covered'.[60] The whole scene lasted over 10 minutes according to the reporter. Pinioning the limbs of the criminal ought to be one of the easiest things to control on the day of execution. The imprecision of drop lengths, uncertainties over the type of rope and placement of the knot, were much harder to get right. Still, many executioners either completely forgot to do so, or remembered but failed to do it properly.

[59] *South Australian Register*, 9 August 1877.

[60] *The Sydney Morning Herald*, 27 March 1863.

[The procession to the scaffold.]
When the convict is pinioned, and his neck bared, he should be at once conducted to the scaffold, the governor and surgeon preceding with the chief warder, two warders at the convict's side, and the executioner following with such force of warders as may be deemed requisite.

In the earliest days of each colony, when the place of confinement and the execution site could be spread out across town, there was something of a procession for the public to witness. In early Port Phillip there were three separate processions of the 'death cart' (as one writer called it) in 1842—at the execution of 'Bob' and 'Jack' in January, Daniel Jepps, Charles Ellis and Martin Fogarty in June, and finally, of 'Roger' in September.[61] A watercolour, painted by W. F. E. Liardet, depicts the start of the very first procession that took place in the settlement.[62] A bullock team pulls the cart conveying the two Indigenous criminals away from waiting officials, there are military guards in tow while a crowd is visible walking adjacent to the cart. The procession travelled down Collins Street, William Street, Lonsdale Street and Swanston Street to the site chosen for the execution.[63] On the second occasion the route taken to Swanston Street was only very slightly altered but, this time, the cart had been loaded with three coffins which the condemned bushrangers were required to sit atop.[64] On both occasions crowds lined portions of the streets to see it pass by. Less is known about particulars of the procession of an Indigenous male nicknamed 'Roger' in September, though one writer from the time notes that one did indeed take place.[65]

In Adelaide and Launceston a similar horse and cart procession is recorded at one time or another but only very early on in the history of each settlement.[66] In none of the colonies did it come close to the

[61] For information about the three separate processions of the criminal to the site of execution, see Finn, 1976, pp. 394–395, 397, and 399, quote on p. 394.

[62] W.F.E. Liardet, 'The First Execution', watercolor, pencil, pen and ink, 8.7 × 16.4 cm, 1875, State Library of Victoria, H28250/14.

[63] Finn, 1976, p. 395.

[64] Finn, 1976, p. 397.

[65] Finn, 1976, p. 399.

[66] In Adelaide this occurred at the execution of Michael Magee in 1838 according to the account of T. Horton James. In Launceston a man named Jefferies in 1826 was carted to the gallows

scale, formality or carnival atmosphere that was detectable at London's 'Tyburn Processional'. In fact, processions ceased immediately following the main gaol being built in each colony. For instance, Port Phillip's processions stopped after the Melbourne Gaol opened in 1845. Thereafter the 'procession' to the scaffold consisted of nothing more than collecting the criminal from his/her cell to wherever the gallows had been erected within the gaol precinct.

> *[The chaplain.]*
> *Where the convict professes the Christian religion, and the services of a chaplain of a suitable denomination are available, the chaplain should attend in the condemned cell, and his place in the procession is behind the governor and in front of the convict. In the discharge of his duties he will be guided by the rules and usages of the church to which he belongs.*

Religion was an important part of the execution ritual, clergymen time and again helped guide the condemned criminal both at the execution itself and in the days leading up to it (see Chapter 4). The overwhelming majority of criminals received some variety of Christian comfort in their final moments. For many subsections of colonial society the importance of religion was heightened as it functioned as a key marker of their identity in an adopted home. For example, Irish Catholics came to the Australian colonies in large numbers, either as convicts or free settlers, and were particularly diligent in expressing their faith on the scaffold. There are repeated references across the colonies to Catholics, sometimes but not always, being dressed in pure white with a large black cross emblazoned across their chest, back or cap.[67] Rosaries and crucifixes were also a common sight on the scaffold among many Catholics sentenced to death. Although most criminals mounted the scaffold empty-handed, objects like flowers or the Bible did sometimes appear across the denominational divide.

---

among a hostile crowd. See James, 1962, pp. 54–61; Geoffrey Chapman Ingleton, *True Patriots All, or News from Early Australia*, Sydney: Angus and Robertson, 1952, p. 107.

[67]William Ullathorne, *The Autobiography of Archbishop Ullathorne with Selections from His Letters*, London: Burns & Oates Ltd., 1891, p. 103.

The narrow definition of Christian attention suggested in the Memorandum was sometimes exchanged for spiritual advisors of religious minorities. At the execution of Edward Davies, a bushranger of Jewish heritage, he was assisted by a reader at the Sydney Synagogue throughout proceedings and later buried in the Jewish portion of the Devonshire Street Cemetery.[68] At the execution of an Afghan Muslim named Goulam Mahomet in Western Australia his spiritual advisor passed the Quran over his chest, traced the words of a holy prayer on his forehead and told him to recite that same prayer as the drop fell. After his execution he was buried with 'Mohammedan rites', as it was labelled by the newspaper, outside the walls of Fremantle Prison by twenty of his fellow countrymen.[69] Some sheriffs also respected the wishes of Indigenous criminals in death. Wera Meldera was executed at Adelaide Gaol in 1845 and wanted no white man to touch him in death or at the burial—a request that was 'strictly complied with' according to the *South Australian Register*. After his hanging a collection of local Aborigines 'received him in their arms, placed him in the coffin, and buried him in the gaol yard by the side of the other murderers'.[70] Only very rarely was spiritual advice refused entirely as in the case of Arthur Buck, an atheist executed at Melbourne Gaol in 1895. He 'respectfully received' the prison chaplain but was most unusual in his request for the 'usual prayers and devotional exercises' not to be carried out in his final moments.[71]

> *[The execution.]*
> *On reaching the gallows the duty of the executioner is as follows: –*
>
> 1. *Place the convict exactly under the part of the beam to which the rope is attached.*
> 2. *Strap the convict's legs tightly (diagram annexed, marked C).*
> 3. *Put on the white linen cap (diagram annexed, marked D).*

[68] G.F.J. Bergman, 'Davis, Edward (1816–1841)', *Australian Dictionary of Biography* 1966, http://adb.anu.edu.au/biography/davis-edward-1964, viewed 15 March 2015.

[69] Albert Frederick Calvert, *My Fourth Tour in Western Australia*, London: W. Heinemann, 1897, p. 157.

[70] *South Australian Register*, 29 March 1845.

[71] *The Argus*, 2 July 1895, p. 7.

4. *Put on the rope round the neck quite tight, the knot of metal eye being just in front of the angle of the jaw-bone on the left side, so as to run up behind the left ear when the man falls and receives the jerk. Care should be taken to adjust the rope as in the diagram annexed, marked E, the part to which the metal eye belongs being [sic.] in the front of the throat. If the rope is adjusted the other way there will be less certainty of breaking the man's neck. The noose should be kept tight, as adjusted, by means of a stiff leather washer on the rope. The long front of the white cap should be free from the rope, hanging down in front.*
5. *Go quickly to the lever and let down the trap-doors.*

Once the preparation was made and the knot accurately adjusted under the neck, the procedure was rather straightforward. Rather than talk through these points one by one it is much easier to see how they pair with the illustrations included in the 1880 Memorandum (see Illustration 3.2). The equipment and technique drawn in these diagrams were seen by the executioner in England as being most appropriate for the job at hand. Buckled leather straps replaced plain lengths of rope for ease of adjustment and quick use. A newly fashioned hood replaced the rather nondescript calico bag that was usually placed over the heads of dying criminals. It kept the back and sides of the neck clear for the precise positioning of the rope while the plunging flap extending down near the chest of the culprit made it an even more remote possibility that the contortions of the face would be visible to the onlookers. To be sure that this execution equipment was used in the proper fashion additional diagrams were included. Clarification on how to fix the leather pinioning straps onto the upper body of the criminal was also demonstrated for the benefit of practical application. The new method employed by the English hangman of a metal washer instead of the 'hangman's knot' is drawn very clearly. So too is the positioning of the washer in relation to the criminal's neck.

An illustrated account published in *The Bulletin* of an execution conducted in the months prior to the circulation of the 1880 Memorandum (and therefore in the absence of these new techniques) depicts the hanging of Andrew George Scott (known as 'Captain Moonlite') and Thomas Rogan at Darlinghurst Gaol on 20 January 1880. The 'hangman's knot' was still in use as are the rather nondescript calico bags placed over the criminal's faces, their hands appear to be pinioned but the legs left free. 'Nosey Bob', the executioner of New South Wales, confidently stands cross-armed to the left of a reliable platform that was purpose-built for such an occasion. Even without explicit guidance from England like that contained in the 1880 Memorandum, by the final decades of the nineteenth century the basics of hangings were being performed well when a competent executioner was on hand. Visually, at least, the Australian gallows were similar to elsewhere and the suggestions of the Memorandum appear to be sometimes small, obvious or incidental. However, critical mistakes were frequently made in regards to technique. As documented above, even very minor oversights could produce a variety of very painful outcomes for the criminal involved. Fortunately for Scott and Rogan, 'Nosey Bob' performed his task admirably on this occasion with skill and judgment derived from years of first-hand experience. As far as Australian colonial executions are concerned, both men died as well as could be hoped.

> *[The taking down of the body.]*
> *The convict should hang one hour, and before he is taken down the surgeon should, as a matter of form, satisfy himself that he is dead.*
> *The best way of taking the body down is not to cut the rope, but to take the rope off the hook, and lift the body down; the rope should be removed from the neck, and also the straps from the body, when it is on the ground.*
> *In laying out the body for the inquest, or other similar proceeding, the head should be raised three inches by putting a small piece of wood under it.*

These instructions on how to deal with the criminal's body in death are the final procedural guidelines included in the 1880 Memorandum. Historically criminals were always left hanging for at least one hour following their execution to ensure that, without any doubt, death had run its course. In the era of private executions sometimes this length of time was shortened. Either because the surgeon could quickly confirm the death or since the execution was so horribly botched that it was quite clear that the criminal was deceased. For example, at an execution in Brisbane in 1901, the criminal was only left hanging for a mere 10 minutes after death—a motionless body, expired pulse and a blood-soaked cap caused by the fall was more than enough confirmation for those present.[72] The Private Execution Acts passed during the 1850s did not specify a period of time for the body to be left hanging and it was, therefore, a proviso that was open to interpretation.

The display of the body for any more than an hour would only occur in the rare decision that it should be 'hung in chains'. This practice was certainly not the norm at colonial executions and it was only prevalent in the very early annals of New South Wales and Tasmanian history. On such occasions, the dead criminal's body could be left hanging for months, standing as a lasting warning for visitors to the district. Frances Morgan, for instance, was hung in chains on a small island in the middle of Sydney Harbour. According to one early chronicler, the 'clothes shaking in the wind, and the creaking of his irons' reminded local Indigenous Australians of the supernatural and therefore presented a 'much greater terror to the natives, than to the white people, many of whom were more inclined to make jest of it'.[73] 'Hunter's Island' was the place to gibbet dead criminals in Hobart until the year 1816 when the Lieutenant-Governor of Van Diemen's Land, Thomas Davey, ordered these 'Objects of Disgust' to be moved elsewhere.[74] Following the example of the British Parliament in 1834, the practice of hanging in chains was abolished by New South Wales and Van Diemen's Land in 1837.[75]

Dissection was another indignity that could be imposed upon the early Australian criminal before burial. When John Fenlow was executed in early Sydney his body was, pursuant to his sentence, turned over to a surgeon for dissection. David Collins, the first Judge Advocate of the infant colony, described what happened when Fenlow's post-dissection body was able to be inspected by the general public: '[T]hey had no

[72] Dawson, 2010b, p. 58.

[73] Paterson, 1811, p. 254.

[74] A 'Point of Land near Queensborough' was, according to the words of Lieutenant-Governor Davey's order, to be the new site of executions. See *The Hobart Town Gazette and Southern Reporter*, 8 June 1816, p. 1.

[75] For the original British Act, see United Kingdom, Chapter 26 of 1834, *An Act to Abolish the Practice of Hanging the Bodies of Criminals in Chains*. For confirmation of the adoption of the British Act by New South Wales and Van Diemen's Land, see New South Wales, no. 2 of 1837, *Imperial Acts Adoption Act*; Tasmania, no. 1 of 1837, *An Act for Extending to This Colony Sundry Statutes Passed for the Amendment of the Criminal Law.*

sooner signified that a body was ready for inspection, than the hospital was filled with people, men, women, and children, to the number of several hundreds'.[76] Collins says these spectators consisted of the 'lower class' and lamented how none 'appeared moved with pity for his fate, or in the least degree admonished by the sad spectacle before their eyes'.[77] Dissection was commonly recorded at very early executions, though the degree of publicity given to Fenlow's executed body in 1796 stands out as a rare occurrence.[78] Dissection was finally abolished in the two oldest Australian colonies of New South Wales and Van Diemen's Land in 1837 by the same legislative instrument that outlawed hanging in chains.

The taking down of the body was only occasionally documented by witnesses to the execution as it was viewed as ephemeral to the central drama of the event. At the private execution of Thomas Williams and Charles Montgomery one unnamed journalist writing in *The Bird O' Freedom* did, however, give an extended personal account of what it was like to stay behind and witness this part of the scene. It was stated that the executioner's assistant held the body while 'Nosey Bob', the hangman, cut through the noose using a sharp knife, lowering the bodies gently into a prepositioned basket. What was most 'repulsive' to the journalist was when he spotted the executioner, 'coolly wiping the grease of the rope from his hands with a towel' before moving onto the second body.[79] Once dissection was outlawed, the inspection of the body following death by medical practitioners was a much more passive exercise. The bodies of Williams and Montgomery were carried away individually in the large basket to the gaol morgue. The doctor then assessed each body for the exact cause of death and noted it down—suffocation for Williams and the dislocation of the neck in

---

[76] David Collins, *An Account of the English Colony in New South Wales, from Its First Settlement in January 1788, to August 1801: With Remarks on the Dispositions, Customs, Manners & c. of the Native Inhabitants of That Country*, second edition, London: T. Cadell and W. Davies, 1804, p. 330 [above, and hereafter, the arcane use of the 'f' has been replaced with 's' where appropriate for passages quoted from Collins' work].

[77] Collins, 1804, p. 330.

[78] For example, Henry Muggleton was executed in 1830 at Sydney Gaol and was then sent off for dissection but no note was made of the public being admitted to the hospital afterwards. See *Sydney Gazette*, 1 June 1830.

[79] *The Bird O' Freedom*, 2 June 1894, p. 5.

the case of Montgomery.[80] Victoria has an unusually thorough record of these medical examinations of executed criminals, at least from 1894 onwards.[81]

These instructions on what to do with the criminal's body after the execution was the last detail in a long list of procedural elements outlined in the 1880 Memorandum. In addition to the Memorandum itself, the technical drawings of the gallows at Newgate Prison and the Table of Drops was the extent of the documents sent out by the Colonial Office regarding execution procedure to the Australian colonies. All of these efforts were made to ensure that a previously haphazard practice might become standardised and error-free in the future. Yet it was not the last contact the Colonial Office in London had with the Australian colonies pursuant to this correspondence. Recipients were encouraged to procure helpful equipment from the Colonial Office—'ropes with metal eyes' and the 'pinioning apparatus' are mentioned as examples.

Instantaneous and Painless? Execution Procedure After 1880

The hangman at Adelaide Gaol in the 1880s and 1890s was one person who was keen to try out the new techniques outlined in the Colonial Office's documents. At the execution of William Burns in 1883 the journalist remarked how:

> The old hangman's knot in use on former occasions, gave place in this instance to the style of noose adopted by [William] Marwood, the English hangman. The knot is replaced by a thimble neatly spliced at one end of the rope, and the other end being passed through this thimble forms the noose … This has proved to be a far better arrangement than the old one.[82]

[80] *The Bird O' Freedom*, 2 June 1894, p. 5.

[81] Morgan, 2004.

[82] *South Australian Register*, 19 January 1883.

Moreover, a decade later in 1894, the newspaper remarked on how the hangman was now using a rope fixed by a 'copper eyelet' paired with a 'closely fitting leather washer' to prevent it from slipping.[83] Both remarks suggest a technique that aligned closely that was suggested by the Colonial Office over a decade earlier.

Despite help from the Colonial Office to make colonial hangmen less error-prone, it is still unclear whether it was entirely painless and instantaneous exercise from the perspective of the condemned criminal. Take the execution of Joshua Beard in 1897 at Adelaide Gaol. It made use of these improved methods and it was said to have gone smoothly by the journalist present—or at least nothing was noted to the contrary.[84] However, Dr. W. Ramsay Smith testifies that Beard's heartbeat did not expire until precisely 14 minutes and 45 seconds after the drop had been activated. As the medical officer on duty he stood alongside the criminal the moment the drop fell, immediately checking him for physiological signs of death. Beard's declining heart rate was noted as 160 beats per minute at two minutes after the hanging, 120 at three minutes and 60 at 11 minutes. After 11 minutes his heartbeat became irregular before finally stopping at the stated 14-minute mark. Upon publishing his findings in a small pamphlet Ramsay argued that this fact challenged the idea that the heart ceases to act after death.[85] Later commentary on his publication from the local press offered this as conclusive proof to its readers that hanging was not 'instantaneous, as is imagined popularly, but is really strangulation'.[86]

The belief that hanging may not be the best way to execute society's criminals was not a new one and the 1890s saw a plethora of new suggestions for the Australian colonies to consider. Indeed, each new method promised to be more painless and less confronting than that of hanging. 'HUMANITY', in a Letter to the Editor of *The Brisbane Courier*, suggested that drowning the criminal in an iron tank would avoid any disfiguration of the body, be both 'certain' and 'painless',

---

[83] *South Australian Register*, 25 August 1894.

[84] *South Australian Register*, 12 June 1897.

[85] W. Ramsay Smith, *Stoppage of the Heart in Death from Violence*, Adelaide: William M. Warren Publisher, 1902.

[86] *Adelaide Times*, 15 November 1906.

while also being 'devoid of all risks from bungling or miscalculation' that currently existed with death by hanging.[87] In a letter sent to the same newspaper the previous year, 'D.H.F.' suggested 'asphyxiation with carbonic acid gas' in an airtight shaft would be 'rapid, painless, and unaccompanied by disgusting concomitants'.[88] The peculiarly American form of death by electrocution that was emerging late in the nineteenth century was rejected by the *South Australian Register* for there was an even greater risk of error.[89] *The Sydney Morning Herald*, also commenting on developments in America, thought that not enough was known about electricity to guard against its misuse at executions.[90] The guillotine, a very effective killing machine, was far too French to be given a fair hearing in the Australian colonies.

Colonial authorities stuck firmly to the punitive methods bestowed on them by England and a legal heritage that privileged hanging over other forms of execution. The response of Australian authorities was therefore not to adopt a new method of execution altogether but to bury the practice of hanging further away from public view. For instance, by the early 1890s, newspaper reports of executions at Melbourne Gaol begin to reference the existence of a 'curtain' below the drop.[91] The warder, stationed on the platform itself, would release the curtain the very same moment the trap door was activated. It completely hid the full-body contortions undertaken by the criminal in death. A full-length curtain hiding the body was something of an upgrade on the calico hood that had—for as long as executions were conducted in Australia—prevented the contortion of the eyes and mouth from being seen by the onlooker. Across the border in South Australia a similar arrangement with a black cloth was in place for the execution of William Burns inside Adelaide Gaol.[92] Even into the 1960s the use of obscuring tarpaulins were being

[87] *The Brisbane Courier*, 18 July 1893, p. 7.

[88] *The Brisbane Courier*, 27 April 1892, p. 7.

[89] *South Australian Register*, 26 October 1891, p. 4.

[90] *The Sydney Morning Herald*, 21 December 1895, p. 4.

[91] For example, at three separate executions at Melbourne Gaol in 1891—that of John Phelan, Fatta Chand and William Colston—the use of a curtain below the drop is mentioned in newspaper reports. See *Mercury and Weekly Courier* 19 March 1891, p. 3; *Mount Alexander Mail*, 25 August 1891, p. 3; *The Maffra Spectator*, 30 April 1891, p. 3.

[92] *South Australian Register*, 19 January 1883.

referenced in journalist's accounts of executions.[93] Once the curtain was installed the rope leading into the newly hidden space below the drop was the only way for journalists to make a judgement on the extent of the criminal's suffering. Whether it twitched violently or swayed slowly back and forth spoke too much of what was going on behind the curtain. The curtain prevented anyone but medical men and experienced gaol officials from viewing the bodily spasms typical at executions but alarming to journalists and their readers.

* * *

Australian executions were practised in order to communicate to both the criminal and onlooker the consequences of crime. However, if this was indeed a didactic exercise, mistakes were frequently made in its implementation. Faulty equipment and a lack of technical guidance until late in the nineteenth century made it an even chance whether a solemn display of state justice would morph into a gory spectacle. By circulating the 1880 Memorandum, the Colonial Office in London was attempting to rectify long-standing procedural mistakes it had witnessed taking place at the Australian gallows from afar. For colonists striving to be seen as more refined and in step with the age, the unnecessary suffering inflicted upon the body of a criminal through frequent procedural mistakes was difficult to stomach. This was certainly the case even in circumstances far less dramatic than Joseph Mutter's decapitation in Queensland that opened this chapter. To repeat the words of the Colonial Secretary who signed off on the 1880 Memorandum, it was hoped that 'humanity and decency' might be restored to the gallows by following the document's instructions. In order to restore the communicative potential of capital punishment, professionalism and expertise needed to replace the amateurism that had characterised execution practice for the majority of the colonial period. It seems that by the time Australia entered the twentieth century, an execution performed 'correctly' was one that was entirely painless for the criminal to undergo.

---

[93] Mike Richards, *The Hanged Man: The Life and Death of Ronald Ryan*, Melbourne: Scribe, 2002, pp. 369–396, quote on p. 388.

4

The Criminal at the Gallows

The history of the Australian gallows is littered with examples of condemned criminals who gave unhelpful dying speeches, committed acts of violence on the scaffold, or were perceived to behave inappropriately given the gravity of the event. In Adelaide, Hugh Fagan appeared to one local newspaper as a 'mere animal' because he 'smoked his pipe with the coolest indifference', approached the gallows with disturbing haste and swore at the executioner for appearing nervous with the rope.[1] In Hobart, Samuel Williams struggled with the hangman and repeatedly got his pinioned hands free to remove the hood placed over his face.[2] In Victoria there were many unhelpful protestations of innocence at the last moment; in fact about one-fifth of those hanged denied that they were actually guilty of the crime.[3] In Sydney one 'young desperado' in 1830 reportedly tackled the executioner off the scaffold platform to the

[1] *Adelaide Observer*, 17 April 1878.

[2] Steve Harris, *Solomon's Noose: The True Story of Her Majesty's Hangman of Hobart*, Melbourne: Melbourne Books, 2015, pp. 114–115.

[3] Kathy Laster, 'Famous Last Words: Criminals on the Scaffold, Victoria, Australia, 1842–1967', *International Journal of the Sociology of Law*, vol. 22, 1994, p. 10.

S. Anderson, *A History of Capital Punishment in the Australian Colonies, 1788 to 1900*,
Palgrave Histories of Policing, Punishment and Justice,
https://doi.org/10.1007/978-3-030-53767-8_4

ground below in a fit of rage.[4] Speaking generally, the *Brisbane Courier* did well to capture the variety of criminal behaviour displayed at the colonial gallows:

> Some [are] penitent, praying and peacefully receiving those priestly consolations which smooth down the pain of death, or its dreadful anticipations; some, alas! Hardened, full of bravado, refusing all the offerings of spiritual advisers, and desirous of going to their last account with ostentatious indifference; others, full of strange fears, deeply wrought in spirit, suffering mental agonies worse than a thousand deaths.[5]

This chapter concerns the behaviour of colonial criminals in their dying moments. It starts with the premise that the criminal's behaviour, words and demeanour went some way in shaping how their punishment was 'read' by the onlooker. Those running the execution desired a penitent criminal above all else, one who gave the outward appearance of agreement with the justice of their sentence. Yet, many factors worked against this outcome on the day of execution. Crucially, there was the widespread cultural expectation in the Australian colonies that the criminal 'die game'—that is, with a degree of premeditated pluckiness and bravado. This cultural belief, appropriated from England, encouraged many criminals to misbehave in their final moments and show little remorse for their crimes. Fully aware of the criminal's propensity to misbehave, those charged with running the execution employed various mechanisms to guide the criminal away from 'gameness' and towards penitence. By limiting forms of resistance it was hoped that the lesson of the Australian gallows would remain shaped by the hands of the state, rather than that of the criminal.

---

[4]J.H. Heaton, *Australian Dictionary of Dates and Men of the Time: Containing the History of Australasia from 1542 to May 1879*, Sydney: George Robertson, 1879, p. 90.

[5]*Brisbane Courier*, 3 July 1883.

The Art of 'Dying Game'

In consultation with Francis Grose's well-known *1811 Dictionary of the Vulgar Tongue* a working definition of 'dying game' can be ascertained. Published in London and initially having a wide circulation within the lower orders of society, under the entry for 'game' is written the following: 'To die game; to suffer at the gallows without shewing any signs of fear or repentance'.[6] Various editions of John Camden Hotten's equally well-circulated English publication, *A Dictionary of Modern Slang, Cant, and Vulgar Words* (1859), offers a similar definition. The usage examples for 'game' in the 1859 edition were: 'are you GAME? Have you courage enough?'[7] While the 1874 edition included a new entry for 'gameness' that was said to denote, 'pluck, endurance, courage generally'.[8] The practice of 'dying game' was inherited from English folk culture but flourished in its southern colonial outpost during the nineteenth century.[9] This cultural expectation was present in all Australian colonies and affected every criminal in the executioner's care. The pressure placed on the dying to behave in an unhelpful way also heightened the crowd's sense of excitement on the day of execution. A 'game' criminal was perceived by many writers to threaten the lesson of capital punishment and make a hero out of the criminal.

The degree to which the crowd anticipated and expected the condemned to 'die game' should not be underestimated or considered peripheral to the larger narrative of the occasion. The manner in which the criminal took his or her death was central to the execution as

---

[6]Francis Grose, *1811 Dictionary of the Vulgar Tongue. A Dictionary of Buckish Slang, University Wit, and Pickpocket Eloquence* [1811], Adelaide: Bibliophile Books, 1981.

[7]John Camden Hotton, *A Dictionary of Modern Slang, Cant, and Vulgar Words*, London: Antiquarian Bookseller, Piccadilly, 1859, p. 43.

[8]John Camden Hotton, *The Slang Dictionary, Etymological, Historical and Anecdotal: A New Edition, Revised and Corrected, with Many Additions*, London: Chatto and Windus Publishers, 1874, p. 172.

[9]For more on 'dying game' in the English context, see Andrea McKenzie, *Tyburn's Martyrs: Execution in England, 1675–1775*, London: Hambledon Continuum, 2007, pp. 191–224; Andrea McKenzie, 'Martyrs in Low Life? Dying "Game" in Augustan England', *Journal of British Studies*, vol. 42, no. 2, 2003, pp. 167–205; Michael Ignatieff, *A Just Measure of Pain: The Penitentiary in the Industrial Revolution, 1750–1850*, New York: Pantheon Books, 1978, pp. 21–24.

public attraction. 'Such an event', wrote the *Bathurst Free Press* in 1853, 'becomes a holiday occasion to the depraved, and whether the shedder of human blood has died or is likely to "die game", is a subject of brutal speculation'. To prove its point the newspaper then recounted one story where a 'Vandemonian pugilist' walked for fifty miles to attend a local execution to see if the criminal named Whilmore—whom the traveller labelled a 'plucked un'[10]—would 'show the white feather' or not. The newspaper then lamented that such 'beastly phraseology' was all too common among spectators at the foot of the gallows.[11] At an execution the year before, Sydney's *Empire* wrote how the 'cursing and the hustling, and the language circulating among the crowd' was fully devoted to 'the speculation as to whether he will die "game" or like a "brick"'.[12] Clearly, to see whether the criminal would 'die game' was a great unknown that drew many spectators towards the foot of the public scaffold for all the wrong reasons.

Perth's *The Inquirer and Commercial News*, among many other colonial publications, tells how the attitude of the crowd could quickly shift from agreement with the justness of the punishment to all-out admiration for the courage of the criminal if performed correctly. It was a common gestalt switch that damaged the intended ends of the punishment irrevocably:

> The mind of the lower classes, and they are the majority, it has been found, is only too apt to sympathise with the so-called victim of the law, and particularly if a man shows physical pluck and dies what is styled game. This sympathy changes to a certain admiration, which makes a lasting and dangerous impression on the minds of those whose animal propensities outweigh their mental ones.[13]

---

[10]'Plucked un' was a common phrase for a 'stout or brave fellow' who 'dares face anything' according to John Camden Hotton's dictionary. See Hotton, 1874, p. 256.

[11]*Bathurst Free Press*, 9 July 1853, p. 2.

[12]*Empire*, 27 September 1852, p. 3.

[13]*The Inquirer and Commercial News*, 8 April 1874, p. 2.

The Argus in Melbourne concurred in thinking that the 'sight of a hardened ruffian closing his career by "dying game" upon the scaffold, is not a spectacle calculated to have a warning effect upon people of the same stamp in the crowd'.[14] *The Courier* of Hobart shared a similar dislike of 'gameness' viewing it as destructive to the mind-set of the criminal and dangerous in the way public perceptions were so easily altered:

> He is supported, in the contemplation of a violent death, by the same feeling which animated the warriors of old in the day of battle. He knows that in his last moments he will be hailed as the hero of the scene, and that if he dies 'game,' he will depart amidst the plaudits of a thousand spectators.[15]

Fervent opponents of capital punishment pounced on the fact that 'gameness' was rife at the Australian gallows. Alfred J. Taylor, for example, wrote an abolitionist pamphlet in 1877 that touched on the scourge of 'dying game' in a tone that echoed the concern of many colonial newspapers. It was used as strong evidence for Taylor's belief that the death penalty was not a deterrent:

> It cannot be denied that to the criminal mass murderer who dies what is called 'game' is as much a hero as the man who dies with the flag of victory waving over his head is to his fellow soldiers, or the martyr who burns at the stake for his religion is to his disciples.[16]

Earlier Taylor states that: 'There should exist in all cases the general impression that the infliction of a certain penalty is just'.[17] Otherwise, he argued, a series of negative consequences would result: '[S]ympathy for the criminal often amounts to forgetfulness of his crime, public feeling revolts against the sentence under which he suffers, and the blood-dyed villain gets to believe that he is regarded as a martyr rather than as a

---

[14] *The Argus*, 25 April, 1853.

[15] *The Courier*, 3 August 1855, p. 2.

[16] Alfred Joseph Taylor, *Capital Punishment: Reasons Why the Death Penalty Should Be Abolished; with Suggestions for an Efficient Substitute*, Hobart Town: Davies Bros. Printers 'Mercury' Steam Press Office, 1877, p. 20.

[17] Taylor, 1877, p. 5.

justly punished offender'.[18] The art of 'dying game' was clearly a threat to the very meaning of a punishment that required a penitent criminal to successfully communicate the grave consequences of committing a crime. A criminal's last words, their demeanour and appearance, were all closely examined by the crowd who decided what to make of the death.

Though the concept of 'gameness' had far-reaching consequences, it appears to be applied only in the case of male executions. Female criminals escaped the cultural expectation that they too must 'die game', or, in any other manner that could be expressed in a comparatively coherent manner. Certainly, special care was taken by journalists to document the emotional state, appearance and family ties of female criminals on the scaffold. Moreover, the comparatively rare hanging of a female criminal was read into predictable nineteenth-century narratives of fallen womanhood and broken morals. Yet, an anticipation or knowledge of these worn narratives did not seem to alter the behaviour of women in their final moments in anywhere near the same way. By contrast, courage and bravado in the face of death can easily be tied to expressions of colonial masculinity. Even executioners defined the gallows as a manly space and strongly disliked having to hang female criminals, lest it impinge on their own sense of masculinity.[19]

To demonstrate the advantages of a penitent criminal over a 'game' one from the perspective of the authorities it is worth considering the example of Daniel Jepps (sometimes spelt Gepps), Charles Ellis and Martin Fogarty—three bushrangers hanged in Melbourne for attempted murder in June 1842. Their execution, and the demeanour of Jepps in particular, stands out as an ideal display of penitence on the Australian scaffold. It is recounted in detail by Edmund Finn in his *Chronicles of Early Melbourne* (1888). At the foot of the gallows near modern-day Swanston Street 'not less than seven thousand persons' were present

---

[18]Taylor, 1877, p. 5.

[19]The most spectacular example of this came in 1894 when Melbourne's *The Argus* reported that, in the days leading up to the execution of Frances Knorr, 'Jones the Hangman' had committed suicide over a fear that 'the persecutions of his neighbours … would be still more hostile if he hanged a woman'. See *The Argus*, 8 January 1894, p. 5 quoted in Kathy Laster and Kerry Alexander, 'Chivalry or Death: Women on the Gallows in Victoria, 1856–1975', *Criminology Australia*, vol. 4, no. 2, 1992, p. 7.

according to Finn.[20] Upon arriving at the scaffold, Jepps and Ellis immediately began to kneel in prayer while Fogarty engaged in a private devotion with his own spiritual advisor. After Jepps had finished praying he delivered his gallows' speech to the crowd below while being supported by the arm of a clergyman. It was a penitent and dignified address but one that also served as a deterrent to potential bushrangers, a key issue that worried the government of the day:

> Fellow Christians! You see before you three young men in the prime of life and strength about to suffer on the scaffold for the crime of bushranging. I trust you will all take warning by our untimely fate, and avoid those crimes which have brought us to this end. Good people, I most humbly beg your prayers to the Almighty on our behalf. I die in the faith of our salvation through the blood of our Divine Redeemer.[21]

One historian described Jepps' attempts to 'persuade the spectators at his execution of the correctness of his punishment' as the desired outcome for a state that got 'lucky' on this occasion.[22] Jepps' eloquence may be attributed to the fact that he was originally a native of Boston with 'highly respectable connexions' who received a 'liberal education' before commencing a career on whaling vessels in the South Sea.[23] Finn goes on to describe how gentlemanly the three convicted bushrangers acted among themselves as the hangman made the final adjustments:

> When the three wretches were standing together under the gallows, they shook hands one with the other, and Fogarty, looking at Jepps, exclaimed 'Farewell! We shall soon meet in eternity.' The executioner then shook hands twice with each of them, adjusted the ropes, and drew the caps down over their faces; and whilst operating upon Jepps, the latter said to him, 'May God bless you and your poor soul.'[24]

---

[20]Edmund Finn (pseudonym 'Garryowen'), *The Chronicles of Early Melbourne 1835 to 1852: Historical, Anecdotal and Personal* [1888], centennial edition, Melbourne: Heritage Publications, 1976.

[21]Finn, 1976, p. 397.

[22]Laster, 1994, p. 10.

[23]Finn, 1976, p. 398.

[24]Finn, 1976, p. 398.

Jepps, Ellis and Fogarty were models for a disposition most desirable to those running the execution. They were easy to manage and did not physically or verbally resist their fate. Contrition was evident in Jepps' speech to the crowd and their dignified behaviour was appropriate to the solemnity of the event. The three men behaved in agreement with the fundamental tenets of their punishment as the just, commendable and right action to take under the circumstances. For these reasons, the authorities were intent on producing a penitent criminal on the scaffold if at all possible. Understanding exactly how those running the execution on the day itself worked towards this outcome is where this discussion now turns.

Penitent Minds: The Role of Religious Advisors

The role the church performed at the gallows was a key factor in helping guide the criminal towards a penitent death that was conducive to the aims of the sheriff. Any diligent clergyman sought a criminal brimful of forgiveness and remorse, prepared for the coming judgment of God. It was a disposition very distant from that of the 'game' and mischievous criminal defiant to the very end. In the heightened symbolic world of executions, the church took on a large portion of responsibility for initiating its ritualistic elements. The outward signs of penitence on the part of the criminal were invaluable in buttressing the overall 'look' of the punishment as just and commendable. Religion has always been closely linked to the execution ceremony and historians of Europe and North America have already explored this connection in detail.[25] The church is

[25]In scholarly book-length historical studies of German, French, Dutch, and American executions the prominent role of the church on the day of execution been widely examined, see Paul Friedland, *Seeing Justice Done: The Age of Spectacular Punishment in France*, Oxford: Oxford University Press, 2012, pp. 101–107; Richard J. Evans, *Rituals of Retribution: Capital Punishment in Germany, 1600–1987*, Oxford: Oxford University Press, 1996, pp. 77–86; Louis P. Masur, *Rites of Execution: Capital Punishment and the Transformation of American Culture, 1776–1865*, Oxford: Oxford University Press, 1989, pp. 33–39; Pieter Spierenburg, *The Spectacle of Suffering: Executions and the Evolution of Repression; From a Preindustrial Metropolis to the European Experience*, Cambridge: Cambridge University Press, 1984, pp. 59–66. More specific

frequently depicted in these studies as deliberately acting on behalf of the state by lending divine legitimacy to the sentence of the law.[26] It was a neat collision of interests that applies to the Australian situation as well.

The idea that the diligence of the clergy fitted conveniently with the needs of the state is exemplified twice in the autobiography of William Ullathorne, a devout Catholic who was at one time the Vicar General of Sydney.[27] On the first occasion Ullathorne travelled with an Anglican priest to comfort two convicts (one Catholic, the other Anglican) who had recently beaten an overseer to death. By recalling a conversation he had with the Anglican priest prior to the hanging, Ullathorne reveals a great deal about his own methods of preparing the criminal for death:

> The Anglican clergyman again wished to see me. He asked what I should do on the way and on the scaffold? I told him that my poor man was well instructed, that on the way I should repeat a litany which he would answer, and I should occasionally address words to him suited to his state. 'Very good, Sir; and what will you do on the scaffold?' 'The man,' I replied, 'is well taught to offer his life to God for his sins, which he will do with me in the words I have taught him. And when the executioner is quite ready for the drop he will give me a sign, and I shall descend the ladder and pray for his soul.'[28]

studies appear in various academic journals, see J.A. Sharpe, '"Last Dying Speeches": Religion, Ideology and the Public Execution in Seventeenth-Century England', *Past and Present*, no. 107, 1985, pp. 144–167; Daniel A. Cohen, 'In Defense of the Gallows: Justifications of Capital Punishment in New England Execution Sermons, 1674–1825', *American Quarterly*, vol. 40, no. 2, 1988, pp. 147–164.

[26]In Australia, Sturma forwarded the case for the church was deliberately acting in ways that bolstered the New South Wales colonial administration, see Michael Sturma, 'Public Executions and the Ritual of Death, 1838', *Push from the Bush*, no. 15, 1983, pp. 4–6. For other passing mentions to the role of the church at Australian colonial executions, see Hamish Maxwell-Stewart, *Closing Hell's Gates: The Death of a Convict Station*, Sydney: Allen & Unwin, 2008, p. 215; Laster, 1994, p. 8. Tim Castle also noted that religion was one of three major themes in newspaper reports of hangings during Sydney in the nineteenth century, the others being 'authority' and 'humanity', see Tim Castle, 'Constructing Death: Newspaper Reports of Executions in Colonial New South Wales, 1826–1837', *Journal of Australian Colonial History*, vol. 9, 2007, pp. 51–68.

[27]T.L. Suttor, 'Ullathorne, William Bernard (1806–1889)', *Australian Dictionary of Biography* 1967, http://adb.anu.edu.au/biography/ullathorne-william-bernard-2750, viewed 6 May 2015.

[28]William Ullathorne, *The Autobiography of Archbishop Ullathorne with Selections from His Letters*, London: Burns & Oates Ltd., 1891, p. 92.

Upon arriving at the gallows the convict under Ullathorne's care wanted to make a final speech and meet with some friendly faces gathered below. However, this did not align with Ullathorne's plan and he successfully persuaded him out of the interaction:

> The young man was bent on speaking to his comrades below, but I would not let him: for such speeches at the dying moment are commonly exhibitions of vanity. He obeyed me, I pressed his hand, and he was cast off.[29]

On another occasion Ullathorne travelled to Norfolk Island to comfort thirteen convicts who were executed for the 'mutiny' of 1834.[30] According to his autobiography, Ullathorne gave them spiritual guidance and comfort at every available hour in the week leading up to the hangings. On the night prior to their execution the mutineers were granted a rare 'indulgence' to fuel their religious fervour: 'My Men asked as a special favour … to be allowed some tobacco, as with that they could watch and pray all night'.[31] On the day of execution, the condemned convicts displayed their obedience to Ullathorne's instructions in a passage that is worth quoting at length:

> When the irons were struck off and the death warrant read, they knelt down to receive it as the will of God; and next, by a spontaneous act, they humbly kissed the feet of him who brought them peace. After the executioner had pinioned their arms they thanked the jailers for all their kindness, and ascended the ladders with light steps, being almost excitedly cheerful. I had a method of preparing men for their last moments, by associating all that I wished them to think and feel with the prayer, 'Into Thy hands I commend my spirit; Lord Jesus, receive my soul.' I advised them when on the scaffold to think of nothing else and to say nothing else

---

[29]Ullathorne, 1891, p. 93.

[30]For more information on the 'mutiny' of 1834, see Manning Clark, *A History of Australia*, vol. 2, Melbourne: Melbourne University Press, 1968, p. 215; Frank Clune, *The Norfolk Island Story*, Sydney: Angus & Robertson, 1967, p. 145; William Molesworth, *Report from the Select Committee of the House of Commons on Transportation: Together with a Letter from the Archbishop of Dublin on the Same Subject and Notes*, London: Henry Hooper, 1838, pp. xv–xvi.

[31]Ullathorne, 1891, p. 103.

> … As soon as they were on the scaffold, to my surprise, they all repeated the prayer I had taught them, aloud in a kind of chorus together, until the ropes stopped their voices forever. This made a great impression on all present, and was much talked of afterwards.[32]

Travelling across both colony and denomination, Reverend William Bedford was another who was no stranger to properly preparing the guilty for an impending death. Before migrating to Van Diemen's Land in 1823, Bedford was made an Ordinary at London's Newgate Prison that turned out to be an ideal preparation for the sombre task he took on in his new home. After a decade in the colony Bedford was already a veteran of the gallows, comforting many fellow Anglicans awaiting their fate. Speaking at an early meeting of the Hobart Temperance Society in 1832 he told them that he had already attended to the dying needs of condemned criminals at 'no less than 3 and 400 executions'.[33] In the next breath he stated that '19/20ths' of those criminals who were hanged owed their fate to alcohol and the effects of drunkenness.[34]

Bedford made a habit of speaking to the crowd on behalf of the criminal in his or her last moments. These addresses were often structured with a general confession of the crime bookended by statements of remorse and requests for divine forgiveness.[35] To say that these final remarks were further coloured with gushes of moral feeling comes as little surprise given his statements made to the Temperance Society. For example, at the execution of Thomas Jerries in 1826 Bedford, in his speech, took care to highlight the elements of the parable that were contained in his path to the gallows:

[32]Ullathorne, 1891, p. 103.

[33]*The Hobart Town Courier*, 28 April 1832, p. 4. This fact is repeated in John West, *The History of Tasmania* [1852], A.G.L. Shaw (ed.), Sydney: Angus and Robertson, 1971, p. 663, fn. 247.

[34]*The Hobart Town Courier*, 28 April 1832, p. 4.

[35]For examples of Bedford making speeches at the gallows on behalf of the criminals under his care, see *Hobart Town Gazette and Van Diemen's Land Advertiser*, 25 February 1825, p. 2; *Colonial Times and Tasmanian Advertiser*, 2 September 1825, p. 4; *Hobart Town Gazette*, 25 August 1827, p. 6.

> The unhappy man, Jeffries, now before you, on the verge of eternity, desires me to state, that he attributes all the crimes which he has committed, and which have brought him to his present awful state, to the abhorrent vice of drunkenness. He acknowledges the whole of the crimes with which he has been charged, and he implores of you all to take warning by him, and to avoid the commission of the sin of drunkenness, which infallibly leads on to all other crimes.[36]

Years later in 1845, a criminal named Gardiner requested that Bedford state to the crowd gathered that: 'Sabbath-breaking and disobedience to parents had been the first steps of an evil course of life which was thus about to be terminated by a premature and shameful death'.[37] Bedford's orations framed how the crime and execution ought to be perceived by those gathered at the foot of the scaffold and overlaid the whole ceremony with a deep spiritual significance. As for the criminals in Bedford's care, this practice removed a major opportunity for displays of 'game' indifference and manly bravado in the face of death.

Bedford, like Ullathorne, ensured that the criminal was prepared for his or her fate well before the actual day of execution. When two particularly obstinate criminals presented themselves to Bedford in 1832 he organised for prison officers to take turns reading scripture to the men during the hours when he, or another religious advisor, were absent.[38] Bedford prepared another man named Charles Routley in a similar manner. Routley was given a 'sense of the awful situation in which he was placed' by the repeated exertions and prayers of the experienced Bedford in the week leading up to his hanging.[39] It was something of a triumph according to *The Hobart Town Courier* because, before Bedford's intervention, the criminal was 'one of the most horrid and most bloodthirsty monsters that have yet disgraced the annals of humanity'.[40] On the scaffold Routley confessed to all his crimes, prayed for the King and

[36] *Colonial Times and Tasmanian Advertiser*, 5 May 1826, p. 3.

[37] *The Courier*, 26 June 1845, p. 2.

[38] *The Hobart Town Courier*, 8 June 1832, p. 4.

[39] *The Hobart Town Courier*, 18 September 1830, p. 3.

[40] *The Hobart Town Courier*, 18 September 1830, p. 3.

Governor of the colony by name and, in his own words, offered the crowd a first-hand account of the slippery slope he took to the gallows:

> He implored all those who heard him to set its due price on the gospel, and not undervalue its glad tidings as he had done, and he besought them, if they would avoid his awful end, immediately to forsake all wicked and dissipated courses of life, for he said the beginnings of crime though at first small, and often committed without discovery, gradually led to offences more and more deep, until at last robberies and murders like his would be committed.[41]

Being chief comforter to Anglican criminals during the reign of Lieutenant-Governor George Arthur (1824–1836) meant that Bedford was a dependable hand on the scaffold during a period of Tasmanian history in which the frequency of hangings was unparalleled (see Chapter 2). Bedford's 'sincerity and devotion' to the numerous prisoners under the sentence of death even drew personal praise from Governor Arthur himself.[42]

William Ullathorne and William Bedford were models for conscientious and well-meaning men of religion whose want for the criminal to die penitent was foremost in their efforts. As already noted by Australian historians, this desire was something that dovetailed handily with the needs of those who ran the execution.[43] However, it should be pointed out that clergymen did not work on behalf of the state in some grand conspiratorial manner. Men of faith like Ullathorne and Bedford placed existential demands on the condemned before death out of a sincere concern for the spiritual welfare of those in their care. Clergymen of any denomination would have wanted a penitent criminal, remorseful as they countenanced eternal life and steeled for the coming judgment of God. It was merely a matter of mutual convenience that, with the help

---

[41] *The Hobart Town Courier*, 18 September 1830, p. 3.

[42] 'Bedford, William (1781–1852)', *Australian Dictionary of Biography* 1966, http://adb.anu.edu.au/biography/bedford-william-1760, viewed on 28 October 2013.

[43] Laster, 1994, p. 8; Maxwell-Stewart, 2008, p. 215; Sturma, 1983, pp. 4–6.

of spiritual advisors, the sheriff was more likely to have a contrite and dignified criminal on the scaffold.

Penitent Bodies: The Sheriff and Executioner

A criminal with a soul properly prepared to meet the afterlife often delivered the executioner a body of little resistance. However, this was never a fait accompli since the clergy were not always successful in their attempts at getting the criminal to repent. An example of this was at the execution of John Jenkins in colonial Sydney. He was under the care of the experienced Father John McEncroe on the scaffold, a man who had attended some seventy-five executions in three years.[44] Yet Jenkins used his dying speech to falsely confess to the crimes of his prison associates and encourage everyone watching to take to the bush and commit more murders.[45] In these situations it often fell to the sheriff and executioner to take charge of the situation. The executioner could apply physical coercion directly to the body of the criminal whereas the sheriff, as representative of the law, ran the ceremony to his pleasure and could use other means to reduce the likelihood of criminal misbehaviour.

To assess the role of the sheriff on days of execution a good place to start is with the hanging of John Troy and Thomas Smith, two highway robbers who mounted the scaffold in Sydney after being found guilty under the Bushranger Act.[46] Smith was coolheaded in putting the case to the crowd that his companion, due at the gallows only a few days later, was to hang for a crime that he had in fact committed. Troy then came forward to state that Smith was innocent, placing full responsibility for the crime in question upon his own shoulders. One correspondent present at the hanging records how these claims were subtly dealt with by the Sheriff:

---

[44]Patricia K. Phillips, 'John McEncroe', unpublished M.A. thesis, The University of Sydney, 1965, p. 29; *The Sydney Herald*, 13 November 1834, p. 2.

[45]For more on Jenkins, see Russel Ward, *The Australian Legend*, Melbourne: Oxford University Press, 1958, pp. 138–139.

[46]For a record of Troy and Smith's trial, see *Australian*, 10 August 1832, p. 3.

> The Sheriff here interrupted him, observing that 'he had done very right in allowing the justice of his own sentence, but begged he would not arraign the justice of another's. He did not like to interrupt him at such an awful moment, but it was his painful duty.' On hearing this, Smith again spoke, 'surely Mr. Sheriff, you do not begrudge us these few moments to speak our minds.' The Clergymen … recommended that their last words should be in prayer.[47]

Another example of a Sheriff, or in this case the Under-Sheriff, intervening to the advantage of proper decorum was at the 1848 execution of William Fyfe, a Moreton Bay convict who was tried and hanged in Sydney. Found guilty of murder, Fyfe was convinced of his innocence and carefully penned a speech to recite on the gallows that reflected this sentiment. However, Fyfe was never able to read his hand-written speech as it was 'surreptitiously' taken off him by the Under-Sheriff while the criminal was still in his cell.[48] A less than pleased Reverend William Richie told a newspaper the following day that the condemned man in his care 'knew nothing of the loss [of his speech] till he put his hand into his bosom to feel for the document, which assuredly was there when about to leave his cell'.[49] Ritchie agreed that Under-Sheriff Prout had the right to strip the prisoner of such material before leaving for the gallows but to do it without informing him was unreasonable. 'If this be not theft', wrote the Reverend, 'I know not how to designate the deed'.[50] On the scaffold, the Under-Sheriff read the death warrant aloud to the waiting crowd but when Fyfe repeatedly declared his innocence the cap was hastily pulled over his eyes by the executioner and the bolt was drawn.[51] *The Sydney Morning Herald* did not care for the wish of the authorities to suppress Fyfe's plea of innocence and published his pre-prepared speech alongside the details of his hanging. The troublesome document that was taken off the body of Fyfe concluded with the line:

47 *The Sydney Gazette and New South Wales Advertiser*, 21 August 1832, p. 3.

48 *The Sydney Morning Herald*, 6 July 1848, p. 3.

49 *The Sydney Morning Herald*, 6 July 1848, p. 3.

50 *The Sydney Morning Herald*, 6 July 1848, p. 3.

51 *Sydney Chronicle*, 8 July 1848, pp. 2–3; *Bell's Life and Sporting Reviewer*, 8 July 1848, p. 3.

'I shall appear at the bar of Almighty God as innocent as the child in its mother's womb'.[52]

If the Sheriff, or his representative, was unable to prevent the criminal from misbehaving, it was left to the executioner who, as a last resort, would muscle the condemned into place. Executioners were not averse to the physicality required for the job, with the official post of hangman so undesirable that vacancies were mostly filled from within the criminal class.[53] Alexander Green, one of Australia's most well-known colonial executioners, was himself transported to New South Wales in 1824 for shoplifting. He soon became chief 'scourger' at the gaol before assuming the position of the colony's official executioner in 1828.[54] His post as chief hangman of New South Wales lasted from 1828 to 1855 during which time he was said to have executed 490 criminals.[55] A biographical work on Green recounts numerous episodes of him carrying through with his duty in the face of violent resistance on the part of the criminal. Examples range from being pushed off the scaffold himself by a wild felon to restraining another from jumping off the scaffold and committing suicide.[56] It demonstrates how Green was there to make sure the law's wishes were fulfilled, no matter the level of verbal or physical hostility emanating from the criminal.

[52] *The Sydney Morning Herald*, 5 July 1848, p. 3.

[53] Testament to his convict background, when Green accompanied Ullathorne to Norfolk Island in 1834 he recognised an old friend while in the process of pinioning his arms: '[Green] suddenly recognised him, and exclaimed: "Why, Jack, is that you?" "Why Bill", was the answer, "is that you?" He then shook his old friend by the hand, and said: "Well, my dear fellow, it can't be helped"', see Ullathorne, 1891, pp. 104–105.

[54] Ray Beckett and Richard Beckett, *Hangman: The Life and Times of Alexander Green, Public Executioner to the Colony of New South Wales*, Melbourne: Thomas Nelson Australia, 1980, pp. 6, 31, and 67.

[55] Beckett and Beckett, 1980, pp. 67 and 185.

[56] Beckett and Beckett, 1980, pp. 97 and 144–146.

Penitent Spaces: The Role of Private Executions

It is important to realise that the time-tested ritual of the execution ceremony, passed down from England to Australia in a colonial exchange, was, in and of itself, configured to induce complicity from the criminal. Regardless of what the criminal actually thought about the justice of their sentence, so long as they passively complied with the ritualistic elements of the execution ceremony it conveyed the look of outward agreement with the punishment being meted out. An important, though often overlooked, aspect of the event was the backdrop upon which the final act of the criminal was played out. Once the appropriate penal infrastructure was established in the colony, executions were carried out in front of the main gaol, and then inside of it. The practical advantages for the authorities to do this are obvious (i.e. proximity to execution equipment, relevant officials, and the criminal) but the dramaturgical benefits were also clear. It bolstered the notion of this being a state-sanctioned act, and built upon the symbolic weight of the prison as a site of punishment and correction.

The introduction of private hangings in Australia during the 1850s (see Chapter 6) did nothing to touch the fundamental interaction between the criminal and his minders. However, this new execution space was more likely to induce penitence for one major reason—it removed the criminal's interaction with the general public. To demonstrate how pernicious this interaction could be consider the example of a criminal in Adelaide who, at his public execution in 1840, had some old friends stationed below the drop. According to the eyewitness account of Joseph Fogg Taylor, the criminal smoked on the scaffold, made faces at the clergyman, kicked the hangman's shins and dared him to remove his disguise. These behaviours were, according to Taylor, 'greatly applauded by his comrades'.[57] Moreover, these very same men, wrote Taylor, were satisfied with the occasion only because their friend 'was game & died

[57]The criminal described in the letter went unnamed, see John Fogg Taylor, 'Letter from John Fogg Taylor of Tundemunga, near Adelaide, 1840, to "John" in Wigan, Lancashire, England, dated September 1840', State Library of South Australia, D 7310, pp. 20–21.

like a "pebble"'.[58] Public executions were not spaces that were likely to elicit penitence from the criminal since they exposed them to the expectations of the rowdy onlooker. If it was not familiar faces below to play up to, jeering and abuse might lead to similarly unhelpful responses. Moreover, execution crowds in Australia could range from several hundred to several thousand and it was hard to tell in advance how someone might react to such an occasion.

Contrast that account with the private execution of Andrew George Scott at Darlinghurst Gaol in 1880. Scott was not subject to the gaze of the general public but was executed in front of a select crowd of government and gaol officials. In his cell the famous bushranger had expressed a desire to make a speech to those gathered in the gaol yard. His testimony would be a final chance to shape the narrative of his life and crimes before the hangman activated the drop. Yet, when Scott mounted the scaffold, he hesitated and called upon the chaplain for advice. The chaplain told Scott that there was 'no one except magistrates and officials present' to witness his final testimony.[59] Upon hearing this Scott changed his mind and 'did not insist upon making any address' to those gathered in the gaol yard.[60]

There are, of course, individual temperaments to consider in these two examples but it is hard to deny that replacing a large and boisterous crowd with the detached faces of officialdom removed a key incentive to criminal misbehaviour before death. By making officials the only witnesses present, the criminal was thereafter shielded from the immediacy of the public gaze and their expectations of a 'game' death. As a result of private executions Perth's *The Inquirer and Commercial News* even suggested that the practice of 'dying game' was almost extinct in the Australian colonies. Writing in 1874 the newspaper remarked how, 'the gameness or cowardice of the depredator is veiled from the eyes of the public'.[61] Thus, displays of 'gameness' had 'gradually disappeared' from

[58] Taylor, 1840, pp. 20–21.

[59] *The Brisbane Courier*, 21 January 1880, p. 3.

[60] *The Brisbane Courier*, 21 January 1880, p. 3.

[61] *The Inquirer and Commercial News*, 8 April 1874, p. 2.

the scaffold in consequence of private executions.[62] The private execution space worked to the advantage of those running the execution by removing this key incentive to misbehaviour and made it more likely for outward displays of penitence to be observed.

Ned Kelly and the Limits of State Control

At the gallows the criminal was in the peculiarly privileged position to influence the narrative of his or her very own death. The criminal's final words, actions and demeanour was an uncontrollable and unpredictable element of the spectacle that could shape its very legitimacy. It is the reason why, as explored above, those running the execution were so keen to placate the criminal and ensure that he or she played the penitent. With this in mind it is instructive to look at the case of Ned Kelly, Australia's most famous executed criminal, to assess the limits of state power and control over the 'message' that the execution spectacle could convey—even one that went exactly according to plan.

Ned Kelly was raised in Victoria's High Country but was in and out of prison after he first got into trouble with the law at age fourteen for assaulting a Chinese man. A subsequent altercation with a policeman at the Kelly family home led Ned and his brother to take to the bush. Between 1878 and 1880 the 'Kelly Gang' were fully fledged bushrangers, robbing banks and homesteads (among other exploits). Earlier on they killed three policemen at Stringybark Creek who had been sent to arrest them. At their final showdown with police in the town of Glenrowan two years later, three of the Kelly Gang were killed. Ned Kelly—clad in his now-iconic homemade metal armour during the confrontation—was arrested soon afterwards and sentenced to hang.[63] Newspaper reports from the time indicate that Kelly died a 'clean' death on the scaffold and that he complied with the requests of his religious advisors as well as the sheriff and executioner. Moreover, his was a private execution. No one

---

[62] *The Inquirer and Commercial News*, 8 April 1874, p. 2.

[63] Bill Gammage, 'Kelly, Edward Ned (1855–80)', in G.J. Davison, J. Hirst, and S. Macintyre (eds), *The Oxford Companion to Australian History*, revised edition, Melbourne: Oxford University Press, 2001.

but officials and journalists were present at the hanging with members of the public completely excluded from the scene. As far as Ned Kelly's death was concerned, it was an execution to the letter, the best the state could hope for by the standards of the day.

It goes without saying that the execution of Ned Kelly had a long-lasting impact on the cultural memory of Australia. It started with Kelly's final words being reported in the colonial press. These last words—'Such is Life'—have since floated out of the cellblock window and into the public vernacular.[64] Moreover, Kelly's execution gave rise to a peculiarly Australian turn of phrase—'As game as Ned Kelly'—which connoted 'the ultimate in bravery'.[65] As an example of usage, Father John Brosnan was the Catholic comforter to Ronald Ryan in 1967 (the last criminal to be executed in Australia) and used it to describe his final moments. Brosnan commented on the 'courage' of Ryan; how his 'step did not falter' as he mounted the gallows and looked the executioner squarely in the eye.[66] At the conclusion of Brosnan's eyewitness account he wrote that: 'Murderer or not, the condemned man died well, "like a Kelly", as they say'.[67] The symbol of Ned Kelly has since entered the Australian popular psyche, not as an index to punishment or triumphant state power, but as a celebration of 'Australianness' itself. When stage performers at the Sydney Olympic

---

[64]'Such is life' were the words recorded by a 'Melbourne Correspondent' who wrote a report of the execution that found circulation in many of Victoria's regional newspapers such as the *Geelong Advertiser* and *The Ballarat Star*. By contrast, *The Argus* and *The Sydney Morning Herald*'s correspondents make no mention of this phrase, instead recounting variations of his alleged last words—'Ah well, I suppose it has come to this' and 'Ah, well! It's come to this at last'. A gaol warden who was present at the execution and in close proximity to Kelly the moment the drop was activated disputes that he ever uttered the words 'Such is life'. See *Geelong Advertiser*, 12 November 1880, p. 3; *The Argus*, 12 November 1880, p. 6; *The Ballarat Star*, 12 November 1880, p. 2; *The Sydney Morning Herald*, 12 November 1880, p. 5.

[65]John V. Barry, 'Kelly, Edward (Ned) (1855–1880)', *The Australian Dictionary of Biography* 1974, http://adb.anu.edu.au/biography/kelly-edward-ned-3933, viewed 12 November 2013. For a more substantial discussion of this phrase, see Amanda Laugesen, 'As Game as Ned Kelly', *Ozwords: A Blog from the Australian National Dictionary Centre* 2012, http://ozwords.org/?p=3014, viewed 12 November 2013. Graham Seal even titled his study of Ned Kelly in popular culture with this phrase in mind, Graham Seal, *Tell 'em I Died Game: The Legend of Ned Kelly*, second edition, Melbourne: Hyland House, 2002.

[66]Tom Prior and John Brosman, *A Knockabout Priest: The Story of Father John Brosnan*, Melbourne: Hargreen Publishing Company, 1985, p. 1.

[67]Prior and Brosman, 1985, p. 1.

Opening Ceremony in 2000 were playfully dressed in Kelly-like tin armour one historian suggested that, 'it is probably fair to say that Ned Kelly meant nothing more for many young people than something uniquely Australian, like water tanks, windmills, kookaburras and kangaroos: things that evoked the bush'.[68]

For those who know the story well, the reasons for Ned Kelly's execution living on in the Australian consciousness are obvious enough. He was an Irish Catholic who felt short-changed by the Anglo-Protestant orthodoxy of the day and positioned himself in opposition to the local police and wealthy landowners. Many Victorians, especially those of the High Country, identified with such sentiments and it caused them to take a lesser view of the very real crimes the Kelly Gang committed. In fact, at the time of his execution, some 60,000 signatures were collected protesting Kelly's execution, almost a fifth of the population of Melbourne.[69] Eric Hobsbawm's work on 'social bandits' and 'primitive rebels' is not out of place when talking about Ned Kelly in this light.[70] A violent and criminal subversion of dominant economic, power and social structures of colonial society was fodder for contemporary and later mythmakers who saw in Kelly a symbol of popular resistance.

What is interesting about the execution of Ned Kelly is that he behaved in total complicity with the executioner, clergy and sheriff yet Australian culture managed to find a way to subvert the official narrative of his punishment. Even when an execution went entirely according to plan, killers could become heroes and thugs the object of collective sympathy. Kelly is an obvious example of this phenomenon but it proves that the public still had it within their grasp to side with the criminal in counterproductive ways for the state. Clearly, the official lesson of the gallows—that crime had consequences—could always be amended, rejected or reinforced by those looking on. Despite the best efforts of

---

[68] Bob Reece, 'Tell 'Em I died Game: The Legend of Ned Kelly—Book Review', *Journal of Australian Studies*, no. 82, 2004, pp. 159–160.

[69] Peter Norden, 'Ned Kelly: Hero or Hell Raiser?', *Australian Geographic Magazine* 2014, http://www.australiangeographic.com.au/topics/history-culture/2014/06/ned-kelly-hero-or-hell-raiser/, viewed 8 February 2015.

[70] Eric Hobsbawm, *Bandits* [1969], revised edition, London: Abacus, 2001; Eric Hobsbawm, *Primitive Rebels*, Manchester: Manchester University Press, 1959.

key figures on the scaffold, there were limits on the ability of the state to control the message that a hanging communicated. The words and actions of the criminal on the scaffold could always be appropriated, or even totally disregarded, by an onlooker who was eager to interpret the merit of the punishment for themselves.

* * *

Colonial executions could go down two very different paths depending upon whether the criminal died penitent or 'game'. The first option agreed with the wishes of those who ran the execution while the latter only served to distract from its intended lesson. Religious advisors like William Ullathorne and William Bedford prepared the condemned for their impending fate in the days leading up to the execution and instructed them on how to behave when at the gallows. If the criminal did not obey religious instruction in his or her final moments, the sheriff and executioner were left to deal with any obstinacy and proceed with the penalty regardless. Private executions broke the immediacy of the criminal's interaction with the crowd and their expectations. The interior of the prison provided an appropriate backdrop in which the punishment could be carried out. Criminals were placed at the centre of the execution ceremony and their behaviour was well worth regulating for that very reason. However, as the case of Ned Kelly demonstrates, the narrative of their death was strongly influenced by individual perceptions and the way in which the broader culture reinterprets the events that took place on the scaffold. Although criminal behaviour could be manipulated in the moments leading up to their execution, there were still limits on how much the state could determine the meaning of the punishment after it had taken place.

5

The Scaffold Crowd

The Australian colonies, like England before it, saw the free and unhindered access of the general public to the death of a criminal as the central guarantor of due process. As the *South Australian Register* put it in 1854: 'The execution being in the open face of day, the whole community can testify – first, that the sentence of the law has really been carried out; and next, that no unnecessary or extra-judicial sufferings have been inflicted on the criminal'.[1] The execution crowd was the prized English principle of transparency in action, providing a check and balance on both the punished and the punisher. However, as we shall see, such noble ends of the scaffold crowd in the era of public executions were rarely acknowledged. This Chapter details the Australian 'scaffold crowd' and the changing way that people consumed an execution over the colonial period. Across the colonies the crowd at public executions was perceived to consist largely of women, children and lower class spectators. This was something deeply concerning to the middle and upper echelons of colonial society who believed that public displays of

[1] *South Australian Register*, 28 December 1854.

S. Anderson, *A History of Capital Punishment in the Australian Colonies, 1788 to 1900*,
Palgrave Histories of Policing, Punishment and Justice,
https://doi.org/10.1007/978-3-030-53767-8_5

violence only served to harden the onlooker. The attendance of these three impressionable groups at the public scaffold also conflicted with their culturally defined role in society as idealised by these same elites. Colonial anxieties were tempered once public executions finally gave way to private ones. Now the transparency of a criminal's death could be guaranteed by a select group of witnesses signing off on the fact. Or, by the journalist who cared to witness it alongside the government officials. The much-criticized masses, offering their range of emotional responses to each and every execution, were doomed to be a relic of the past.

Colonial Elites, Public Executions, and the Crowd

Elites played a key role in the exchange of ideas between the Australian colonies and elsewhere. For a start they were the most transient and mobile set of colonists who were able, over the course of a lifetime, to move between different colonies. Some even arrived in Australia with an eye to returning home to Britain after only staying for a fixed number of years. Education and a degree of wealth enabled privileged access to a communicative exchange going on between 'Home' and the colonies in the form of book and periodical purchases. For example, John Dunmore Lang, one opponent of public executions discussed below, had a private library that numbered over six hundred volumes.[2] After listing off almost every conceivable genre of book in his possession, one historian remarked: 'It seemed to comprise almost everything a nineteenth-century scholar could have wished to read'.[3] Moreover, Lang moved between the colony of New South Wales and Britain six-times before his death in Sydney in 1878.[4] The role of colonial elites

[2]Jan Kociumbas, *The Oxford History of Australia: Possessions, 1770–1860*, vol. 2, Melbourne: Oxford University Press, 1992, p. 251.

[3]George Nadel, *Australia's Colonial Culture: Ideas, Men and Institutions in Mid-Nineteenth Century Eastern Australia*, Cambridge, MA: Harvard University Press, 1957, p. 79.

[4]Nadel, 1957, p. 79.

in facilitating this exchange of ideas to Australia from elsewhere should not be underestimated when it comes to discussions around capital punishment.

The result of this relatively high level of mobility and ready access to the latest literature from England is that colonial Australians higher up the social scale were more likely to know about, and be updated on, developments in England and elsewhere regarding capital punishment.[5] Colonists knew about William Ewart's push for the total abolition of the death penalty in mid-nineteenth-century England. They were highly knowledgeable of Charles Dickens' influential letters to *The Times* about the public execution of the Mannings in London.[6] Indeed, a discomfort with the violence of executions and its perceived effect on those who watched (discussed further below) was analogous to many discussions that prominent reformers were already having in England.[7] These influences obviously had an impact in Australia since some of these worldly colonists of high social rank had time spare to write down their thoughts on executions in a published format. In the first half of the nineteenth century, these writings expressed a deep displeasure at public executions and the crowd that went to watch.

Peter Cunningham, John Dunmore Lang, and Nathaniel Kentish were three such writers who, to varying degrees of brevity, displayed concerns over the way executions were carried out. All were highly literate, white collar, well-heeled and connected Australian colonists, very far removed in their personal circumstances from the level of the perspiring labourer. All three were united in their opinion that witnessing violence

---

[5]It should be noted that the lower classes were not entirely excluded from this exchange of ideas from abroad regarding capital punishment. Colonial newspapers frequently reprinted news from 'Home' on the issue, and the spread of Mechanics' Institutes in the mid-nineteenth century did ensure that members of the working class, so long as they were literate, could freely access books and other forms of published material.

[6]According to one newspaper, 'The letter of Mr. Charles Dickens recommending the disuse of public executions has been published with approval in several of the colonial journals'. See *The Moreton Bay Courier*, 15 June 1850. For an example of where Dickens' opinions were raised in a colonial parliament, in this case the Tasmanian Parliament by the Solicitor General, see *The Courier*, 1 August 1855, pp. 2–3.

[7]Randall McGowen, 'History, Culture and the Death Penalty: The British Debates, 1840–70', *Historical Reflections*, vol. 29, no. 2, 2003, pp. 236–237; Randall McGowen, 'Civilizing Punishment: The End of the Public Execution in England', *Journal of British Studies*, vol. 33, no. 3, 1994, pp. 260–266.

demoralised the onlooker and searched for solutions to a problem framed in those terms. Together they represent some of the earliest published evidence in Australia (outside of the colonial newspapers) that sought to banish forms of execution that took place in full view of the public due to their influence on the crowd. It is a window into the cultural beliefs of a social group whose opinion carried much weight in the colonies but one that was not far removed from that of journalists and lawmakers. It also provides a welcome opportunity to investigate why the middle to upper end of colonial society tended to dislike the sight of public executions in city streets and largely stayed away from them.

Peter Cunningham was a well-travelled ship's surgeon who settled briefly in New South Wales in the 1820s after having leased farming land on the Upper Hunter River.[8] During his time in Australia he wrote a popular series of published letters containing his thoughts on the colony of New South Wales. The book went through three editions in just two years and was even translated into German. One of these letters penned in New South Wales and sent home to England expressed his disdain for public punishment in much detail.[9] Cunningham's belief was that public executions hardened the spectator and acclimatised them to violent acts. It was an effect that he could personally relate to:

> A man who has been in the habit of witnessing public punishments of any kind must feel with what different sensations he contemplated the *first* instance to the *last* … The first time I saw a man flogged, every lash made me wince as if it had fallen upon my own shoulders; but now I could see a back scarified without moving a muscle … Can it be with this view that legislators familiarize individuals to the sight of capital punishments; – to make them think lightly of the gallows, and steel their minds preparatory to the trial when their own turn may come?[10]

---

[8]L.F. Fitzhardinge, 'Cunningham, Peter Miller (1789–1864)', *Australian Dictionary of Biography* 1966, http://adb.anu.edu.au/biography/cunningham-peter-miller-1942, viewed 6 March 2015.

[9]Peter Cunningham, *Two Years in New South Wales: Comprising Sketches of the Actual State of Society in That Colony, of Its Peculiar Advantages to Emigrants, of Its Topography, Natural History, & c. &c.*, vol. 2, London: Henry Colburn, 1827, pp. 296–311.

[10]Cunningham, 1827, pp. 309–310, emphasis original.

Cunningham thought that being an eyewitness to the death penalty only served to harden the spectator rather than deter future crime. His solution was therefore to play on the imagination of the spectator rather than rely on the graphic reality of the death itself. To achieve this end the symbolic elements of the death penalty would need to be heightened:

> Every effort ought to be made to impress powerfully upon the *imagination* of the multitude the terrible nature of our punishments, without permitting them to be actual *spectators* thereof. The having [of] a black board, bearing in large letters the names, ages, and crimes of the delinquents, posted up conspicuously before the prison; a black flag with emblems of death hung out; a minute-bell tolled until the criminals [are] issued from their cells; and the clergyman to appear briefly *with them on* a stage in front of the prison, and kneeling with them to call upon the multitude to join in prayer on behalf of the unhappy culprits: – I think it might be at least worth the serious consideration of the legislature whether these solemnities, or such as these – this display of the 'pomp and circumstance' of death – this appeal, in fact, to the imagination (whose peculiar property it is to exaggerate), – may not be far better calculated to answer the purposes of warning and deterring than the actual brutal exhibition, notoriously turned by the reprobate into a disgusting joke.[11]

Cunningham's suggestion of a new mode of execution, penned while in the penal colony of New South Wales, shares much with a later account by John Dunmore Lang. Lang was a Presbyterian clergyman of many talents; a politician, educationalist, journalist, historian and anthropologist according to his entry in the *Australian Dictionary of Biography*.[12] In a larger work on the general topic of New South Wales published in 1837, Lang registered his disgust at the 'uniformly demoralizing character' of executions and the 'withering and blasting influence of the feelings they awaken'.[13] Lang's personal experience with the 'miserable

[11]Cunningham, 1827, pp. 310–311, emphasis original.

[12]D.W.A. Baker, 'Lang, John Dunmore (1799–1878)', *Australian Dictionary of Biography* 1967, http://adb.anu.edu.au/biography/lang-john-dunmore-2326, viewed 10 July 2015.

[13]John Dunmore Lang, *An Historical and Statistical Account of New South Wales, Both as a Penal Settlement and as a British Colony*, vol. 2, second edition, London: A. J. Valpy, 1837, p. 50.

perverseness of human nature' inclined him to believe that 'there are individuals who would actually be incited to crime by the prospect of such a death'.[14] Lang appealed to the colony's lawmakers to adopt a form of midnight executions that he believed to take place in Venice, whereby only officials could witness the death:

> Better surely that the system of Venice—revolting as it seems to Britons—should be revived … that the criminal should be conducted at midnight over the Bridge of Sighs, and the work of death performed by torchlight and in solemn silence, in the presence of no other witness than the jailer and the sheriff![15]

Taking the suggestions of both Cunningham and Lang together, they identify a shared problem with public executions. Namely, it hardened the innocence of the spectator, accustomed them to violence and had the possibility to incite future criminal behaviour. Moreover, their solution was, though taking on different forms, aimed at achieving the same outcome. Both Lang's support for midnight executions and Cunningham's focus on the symbolism rather than the reality of death itself sought to shield the spectator from the raw violence of the hanging.

If there was a sense of paternalism underlying an upper class dislike of public executions then it reaches its logical conclusion in an abolitionist essay written by Nathaniel Kentish in 1842. Kentish was also a member of that transient class of colonists in Australia. English born, he trained as an engineer and worked as a surveyor in New South Wales, South Australia and Van Diemen's Land while later attempting to establish an agricultural assurance scheme in Port Phillip.[16] He was, in addition, a man of literary ambition; publishing his own poetry, writing book-length commentary on current events and he was, at one point, the owner-editor of the *Sydney Times*. One of Kentish's works was titled *An Essay on Capital Punishments* (1842) where he, first and foremost, outlined

[14] Lang, 1837, p. 50.

[15] Lang, 1837, p. 50.

[16] L.J. Blake, 'Kentish, Nathaniel Lipscomb (1797–1867)', *Australian Dictionary of Biography* 1967, http://adb.anu.edu.au/biography/kentish-nathaniel-lipscomb-2302, viewed 5 January 2015.

his opposition to the punishment.[17] That said, Kentish's concerns over the effect of witnessing a violent spectacle also feature prominently throughout. Rather than merely hide the spectacle within the prison, capital punishment should be abolished completely to prevent such a corruption of innocence.

A lengthy poem was included in Kentish's *Essay* that included a key stanza focusing on the disgust he felt towards public executions. Penned in Adelaide and published in Hobart, it implies that those colonists who delighted in 'scenes of blood' had lapsed into a fallen state, despite being given all the tools by God to advance beyond mere barbarism:

> Emerging gradually from a bar'rous state,
> In which it pleased his Maker, to place Man
> With organs, faculties, and reas'ning powers,
> By exercise of which he might attain
> To all the comforts, pleasures, virtuous joys
> In store for him; it not surprising is,
> That e'en as he advanced in love of Truth –
> Of Knowledge, Virtue, and Religion too,
> His fallen nature should the seeds retain
> Of cruel habits sown 'midst scenes of blood.[18]

In the latter half of the stanza Kentish laments the large number of people attending the 'scaffold scene' calling them a stain on 'Britain's character':

> What but this *habit* and a *horrid taste*
> For tragic scenes, could cause *so foul a stain*
> *On* BRITAIN'S *character*, for valour famed,
> As that attached to every public scene
> Of woe and shame? BRITANNIA'S DAUGHTERS, *blush!*
> Blush deep for what is said – and hear, and weep!
> What's said, alas! *Is true* – to your reproach –
> Your Fathers' – Brothers' – Sons'! The Scaffold scene –

---

[17]Nathaniel Lipscomb Kentish, *Essay on Capital Punishment* [short title], Hobart Town: S.A. Tegg, 1842.

[18]Kentish, 1842, pp. 5–7, emphasis original.

> The gibbet where the trembling Culprit hangs –
> The scene of ignominy, guilt, and shame –
> Of woe commencing – (who knows *when* to end
> Or *where?*) – this is the spectacle which draws
> The largest concourse of my Country's Sons!
> I weep to own it – *of her Daughters too!!*[19]

At the conclusion of Kentish's publication he includes a proposed 'Petition to the Crown' to abolish capital punishment that also reveals his fears over the negative effect that violence has on the onlooker. This document, addressed 'To the Queen's Most Excellent Majesty', states that, '*the very exhibition* of male-factors being hanged, *has a lamentable tendency to demoralize the good, and to harden the depraved and ill-disposed*'.[20]

The thoughts of Lang, Cunningham and Kentish indicate that a person who would actively choose to watch violent spectacles offended something deep within what might be termed the 'middle class' cultural sensibility of colonial Australians. Henry Kingsley, for example, was a novelist who lived in Victoria from 1853 to 1857 and assumed the 'superiority of upper-class Englishmen' upon arrival.[21] In an outline of his life it was noted how he was briefly in the mounted Victorian police but soon quit: 'compelled by duty to attend an execution, he was so much affected that he threw up the appointment in disgust'.[22] Similarly, a 'popular pressman' named 'Bob' O'Toole, active in Melbourne during the late 1890s, was said to avoid reporting on executions at all costs:

> There are one or two things upon which he [O'Toole] prides himself, one of which is that he has always managed to escape reporting an execution. He draws the line at seeing the common hangman draw the bolt, and the *Free Lance* congratulates him upon his excellent good taste.[23]

---

[19] Kentish, 1842, pp. 5–7, emphasis original.

[20] Kentish, 1842, p. 58, emphasis original.

[21] A.A. Phillips, 'Kingsley, Henry (1830–1876)', *Australian Dictionary of Biography* 1974, http://adb.anu.edu.au/biography/kingsley-henry-396, viewed 4 April 2015.

[22] Clement Shorter, 'A Note on Henry Kingsley', in Henry Kingsley, *The Recollections of Geoffry Hamlyn*, New York: Longmans, Green & Co., 1899, pp. vii–xxiii, quote on p. xvii.

[23] *The Free Lance*, 12 September 1896, p. 3.

Even as early as 1855 executions had become, for many respectable colonists, 'A thing to shudder at, not to see', according to the *The Argus*.[24]

Even the very sight of the gallows itself was enough to disgust well-to-do colonists. After one of the 1842 executions in Port Phillip, the administration back in New South Wales had instructed Superintendent Charles La Trobe to leave the gallows permanently erected to save on the £5 cost of repeatedly assembling and dismantling the cumbersome structure. La Trobe obliged, leaving the gallows where they stood for months outside the gaol. However, the public and press were so outraged by the very sight of the idle structure that he soon ordered it to be taken down without seeking permission from Sydney.[25] While the gallows stood erect in Melbourne's streets the press viewed it as a 'standing eye-sore' and an 'outrage upon public decency'.[26] Edmund Finn was another who called the gallows an 'uncouth and repulsive looking object' when recounting this story in his own work.[27]

It is an interesting thought as to whether outwardly registering a lowly opinion of public executions had some kind of social utility. 'In the "Antipodes" as at "Home"', writes the historian Penny Russell, 'manners served to define social position in an unstable world, providing grounds for exclusion from the elites, as well as mapping the road into them'.[28] Condemning the 'barbarity' of public executions may have played some small part in defining oneself in the muddled social world of the Australian colonies in the same way that manners and bodily conduct would in many other situations. Bold displays of morbid curiosity by the scaffold crowd as well as the persistent thought that their innocence was being corrupted were very troublesome to the colonial elite.

---

[24] *The Argus*, 19 October 1855.

[25] Edmund Finn (pseudonym 'Garryowen'), *The Chronicles of Early Melbourne 1835 to 1852: Historical, Anecdotal and Personal* [1888], centennial edition, Melbourne: Heritage Publications, 1976, p. 400; H.F. Behan, *Mr. Justice J.W. Willis: With Particular Reference to His Period as First Resident Judge of Port Phillip 1841–1843*, Melbourne: Harold Frederick Behan, 1979, p. 225.

[26] Finn, 1976, p. 400.

[27] Finn, 1976, p. 400.

[28] Penny Russell, *Savage or Civilised? Manners in Colonial Australia*, Sydney: The University of New South Wales Press, 2010, p. 3.

With all this in mind, it comes as little surprise to find that the middle and upper echelons of colonial society are not mentioned as frequenters of public executions. Stay away from the public gallows, *The Argus* of Melbourne warned its readers, less you be 'ranked amongst the hopelessly-depraved classes of society'.[29] In the *South Australian Register* it was written that, 'People of refined morals or cultivated taste would feel themselves entirely out of place in the vicinity of the scaffold, which is consequently abandoned to the profligate, the thoughtless, and those whose minds are morbidly disposed'.[30] The result of this tendency for the middle classes to avoid setting foot near such 'demoralising' spectacles was very damaging to the legitimacy of public executions as a whole. It was only natural that a civil ceremony without the presence of the community's more esteemed citizens was destined to disintegrate into its very worst incarnation—a 'kind of satanic high festival' as *The Argus* labelled public executions in 1855.[31] Those lower down the social rung, meanwhile, voted with their feet and continued to engage with the spectacle of public executions until their abolition. To the last they came to watch public executions, secure in the knowledge that their attendance would be severely censured by colonial periodicals and those higher up the social ladder. Now that the dislike of the scaffold crowd has been registered among colonial elites and that they (outwardly at least) claimed not to attend, it is necessary to look deeper into the anxieties that the public execution crowd could provoke.

The Public Execution Crowd

Joseph Long Innes, police superintendent and later magistrate, is someone who provides a unique window into the composition of the crowd. He gave evidence at the 1849 Select Committee that inquired

[29] *The Argus*, 1 April 1853.

[30] *South Australian Register*, 13 December 1854.

[31] *The Argus*, 19 October 1855. For how this very same process of middle class non-attendance affected the legitimacy of capital punishment in Antebellum America, see Louis P. Masur, *Rites of Execution: Capital Punishment and the Transformation of American Culture, 1776–1865*, Oxford: Oxford University Press, 1989, pp. 95–100.

into concerns over discipline and safety at Darlinghurst Gaol in Sydney. While acting in his professional capacity Innes observed many public executions at the Gaol over a period of eight years. He was asked explicitly by the committee: 'What class of people generally attend executions?'[32] The answer given by Innes was recorded as follows: 'The labouring class, and an enormous number of women and children'.[33] Innes continued by stating how the demeanour of the public execution crowd was 'appalling' and distinguishable by their 'levity and total want of feeling'.[34] Even mothers came with their children to 'hold them up in their arms, [so] that they may have a good sight of the execution'.[35] This preliminary picture of the public execution crowd as outlined by Innes is worth investigating further. This section assesses the size of the crowd at public executions and their behaviour. It also offers a brief overview of the women, children and members of the so-called 'lower class' that were said to attend these spectacles.

A random sample of crowd estimates for the era of public executions demonstrates a large degree of variation across the colonies. The estimation of 10,000 Sydneysiders at John Knatchbull's execution in 1844 seems far and away the largest of the colonial era.[36] In Hobart 600 people attended an execution in 1827 but this number had jumped to as many as 2000 for a relatively uneventful hanging in 1853.[37] All 900 of Moreton Bay's convict population witnessed that settlement's first ever hanging in 1830.[38] South Australia's first execution was performed in front of at least 1000 people according to one witness. It was a huge proportion of Adelaide's population, which at that time was said to be

[32]New South Wales, 'Report from the Select Committee on the Darlinghurst Gaol, with Appendix and Minutes of Evidence', *Votes and Proceedings of the Legislative Council*, 1849, vol. 2.

[33]New South Wales, 1849, vol. 2.

[34]New South Wales, 1849, vol. 2.

[35]New South Wales, 1849, vol. 2.

[36]*Australian*, 15 February 1844, p. 3.

[37]For the 1827 crowd number, see Hamish Maxwell-Stewart, *Closing Hells Gates: The Death of a Convict Station*, Sydney: Allen and Unwin, 2008, p. 214. For the 1853 estimate, see *The Courier*, 14 February 1853.

[38]Two convicts were executed on this occasion. For more details, see Christopher Dawson, *Dirty Dozen: Hanging and the Moreton Bay Convicts*, Brisbane: Inside History, 2007, pp. 31–32.

around 2800.[39] That said, John M. Skipper's hastily composed practice sketches of other South Australian executions suggest a much smaller spectatorship was the norm.[40] In the absence of anything nearing an official means to record attendance at public executions these anecdotal estimates are, of course, all too susceptible to exaggeration and plain inaccuracy on the part of the observer.

Edmund Finn's record of crowd numbers in the context of Victoria is about as definitive a sample as one can get for the public execution era. Finn had a habit of making crowd estimates at the many public executions he attended in the history of early Melbourne. His estimates appear throughout *The Chronicles of Early Melbourne* (1888) and comprise the following when arranged together: 6000 spectators attended the execution of 'Bob' and 'Jack' in 1842; 7000 watched Daniel Jepps, Charles Ellis and Martin Fogarty hang in 1842; 300 for John Healy in 1847; 2000 for Augustus Dauncey in 1848, and finally, 700–800 spectators came to watch the hanging of Patrick Kennedy in 1851.[41] It goes without saying that Finn's estimates are just as anecdotal as those that appear in the newspapers. However, made by the same observer over the period of a decade, they should be given a little more weight by comparison. Taken at face value, Finn demonstrates that very large crowds would commonly appear to watch Melbourne's executions but it was not the norm. Rather than demonstrating an upward or downward trend over the longer term, crowd numbers appear to fluctuate quite dramatically depending on the profile of the person executed.

---

[39]T. Horton James, *Six Months in South Australia: With Some Account of Port Philip and Portland Bay, in Australia Felix: With Advice to Emigrants: To Which Is Added a Monthly Calendar of Gardening and Agriculture, Adapted to the Climate and Seasons* [1838], Adelaide: Public Library of South Australia, 1962, pp. 54 and 57.

[40]John M. Skipper, 'Execution of George Hughes and Henry Curran, Adelaide, 16 March 1840', Pencil on Card, 15.0 × 20.1 cm, 1840, Art Gallery of South Australia, 367D4; John M. Skipper, 'Execution of Joseph Stagg, Adelaide, 18 November 1840, Pen and Brown Ink on Paper, 10.7 × 12.8 cm, 1840, Art Gallery of South Australia, 367D5; John M. Skipper, 'Early Execution, South Australia', Pencil on Paper, 16.3 × 20.1 cm, c.1840, Art Gallery of South Australia, 367D3; John M. Skipper, 'A Sketch of South Australia's First Execution by John M. Skipper, 1838', Pencil on Paper, 13 × 18 cm, 1838, State Library of South Australia Pictorial Collection, B 7797.

[41]Finn, 1976, pp. 395, 397, 403, 405, and 406.

If the stereotype is to be believed, the public execution crowd was primarily comprised of those low in social standing. Labouring types were strongly represented as Joseph Long Innes suggests while large portions of the unemployed, perhaps even a small criminal element, were thought to lurk below the drop. One of the more sensational descriptions of the scaffold crowd was produced in Adelaide at the execution of William Wright for murder in 1853. The hanging was conducted early on a Sunday morning and the *South Australian Register* began its report by stating that there 'could hardly have been less than a thousand persons' gathered at the base of the gallows.[42] It depicted the social make up of the crowd as follows:

> [I]f there could be a more disgusting sight than the gallows itself, it was presented by the bulk of the spectators – unwashed loungers, reeking from the night's debauch, or only half recovered from its effects by a hasty hour or two of sleep; women hurrying to the spot as if pressing to join in some ordinary amusement, and some even carrying with them their shivering unweaned infants ... Every purlieu of the city's worst locality seemed to have belched forth its inmates and frequenters, and to have assembled them around the frightful structure.[43]

At an earlier execution in 1850 the very same newspaper wrote that, 'with scarcely any exception', the crowd was composed of the 'most abandon class'.[44] In Sydney it was reported that 'mechanics, labourers, vagrants, thieves, prostitutes' all swelled with a 'horrible and unnatural anxiety for the time when "the show would begin"'.[45] In Tasmania spectators to public executions were described, somewhat more politely, as being from the 'humbler classes'.[46] For a public hanging near Queen Street Gaol in Brisbane there was 'scarcely a person of respectability', to be seen, 'except [for] those required' to be present.[47] In Victoria, one letter

[42] *South Australian Register*, 14 March 1853, p. 3.
[43] *South Australian Register*, 14 March 1853, p. 3.
[44] *South Australian Register*, 6 September 1850.
[45] *Bell's Life and Sporting Reviewer*, 9 November 1850.
[46] *Colonial Times and Tasmanian Advertiser*, 6 August 1852.
[47] *Moreton Bay Free Press*, 29 August 1854.

addressed to the Editor of *The Argus* described the Melbourne crowd as 'a mixed assembly of unthinking, vicious and profane men, women, [and] children'.[48]

The mention of women at public executions was frequent in the colonial newspapers and almost always accompanied by a moralising judgement. The *Bathurst Free Press* was no exception to this rule. After demonising female spectators to a hanging in 1849, it offered a somewhat farcical suggestion to remedy their continued attendance:

> [A] very large proportion [of the crowd] consisted (as usual) of women and children. There is indeed something truly shocking in the avidity with which – in the case of ignorant and uncultivated females – these kind of spectacles are sought after. We observed more than one vehicle literally *crammed* with them, and we could not help wondering ... [what] induced a whole bevy of fair dames to undertake a journey of twenty miles in order to feast their eyes upon the dying agonies of a miserable fellow-creature! Sincerely did we wish that every female present could have been sentenced to six months incarceration, as a means of rewarding her for her gratuitous display of shameful curiosity.[49]

Another publication called for a woman so 'forgetful of her sex' as to attend executions that she deserved nothing less than 'a good whipping'.[50] The *Moreton Bay Free Press*, though it was 'blush to write it', mentioned that many women in the township had come to watch a hanging in 1854.[51] Those women who could stomach such a scene did 'no credit to her sex', according to the writer, since 'humanity is one of woman's ennobling characteristics'.[52] While Sydney's the *Australian* wondered aloud: 'Is the mind of woman, which we have hitherto admired for its gentleness, purity, and innocence, so utterly lost and debased as to delight in gazing upon the dying agonies of

[48] *The Argus*, 27 June 1848, p. 4.

[49] *Bathurst Free Press*, 27 October 1849, emphasis original.

[50] *The Atlas*, 8 July 1848.

[51] *Moreton Bay Free Press*, 29 August 1854.

[52] *Moreton Bay Free Press*, 29 August 1854.

the condemned?'[53] This disapproval of female spectators in New South Wales was on full display for an execution at Darlinghurst Gaol in 1840. A traveller to Sydney wrote about how, on this particular occasion, women were deliberately excluded from freely entering the prison yard to watch the death.[54] It is a passing example that usefully illustrates the very real concern over female attendance in the era of public executions.

The last group that Joseph Long Innes suggests attended public executions were children. In 1841 Tom Petrie was only 'nine or ten years old' when an elderly prisoner took him by the hand to view a recently hanged Indigenous man lying in his coffin:

> Stooping, he [the prisoner] pulled the white cap from the face of the dead blackfellow, exposing the features. The eyes were staring, and the open mouth had the tongue protruding from it. The horror of the ghastly sight so frightened the child that it set him crying, and he could not get over it nor forget it for long afterwards.[55]

Tom's father, Andrew Petrie, had constructed the gallows used at this particular execution in Moreton Bay so the boy's ready access to the body of the dead criminal was likely a result of this family connection and thus a rare occurrence.[56] Still, there are many more references to children viewing executions throughout the colonies. In Perth, for example, there were a 'not inconsiderable number' of children who watched the hanging of William Dodd in 1855.[57] Prior to the execution of Eliza Benwell in Tasmania there was an 'abundance' of young boys who found room on the pavement to play 'leap-frog, marbles, and other juvenile

---

[53] *Australian*, 15 February 1844.

[54] Alexander Marjoribanks, *Travels in New South Wales*, London: Smith, Elder, and Co., 1847, p. 169.

[55] This encounter was recorded much later in a memoir written by Tom Petrie's daughter, Constance Campbell Petrie. It was said to have occurred at the execution of Mullan and Ningavil at Moreton Bay in 1841. See Constance Campbell Petrie, *Tom Petrie's Reminiscences of Early Queensland*, Brisbane: Watson and Ferguson, 1904, pp. 175 and 245.

[56] For details of the Petrie family's connection with prison and gallows construction in early Queensland, see Christopher Dawson, *The Hanging at the Brisbane Windmill*, Brisbane: Inside History, 2009, p. 29.

[57] *The Inquirer and Commercial News*, 17 October 1855, p. 2.

games'.[58] At an execution at Brisbane's Queen Street Gaol in 1851 it was to the 'shame and disgrace of the town' that a large number of children could be counted among the spectators.[59]

There is a strong possibility that children were actively brought to public executions as a means to teach them the consequences of wrong-doing. In his evidence to the Select Committee, Joseph Long Innes states that children were held up by mothers to better see the gallows. It is an action that implies parental approval to view proceedings as opposed to an image of disobedient youths sneaking to the foot of the gallows without consent. Pieter Spierenburg is one scholar who briefly countenanced the idea of the gallows as a parental aid in the context of Amsterdam. According to Spierenburg, after witnessing an execution a father might say to his son: 'Take a good look; this is what will happen to you, if you stray from the right path'.[60] Public executions may have been used as a mechanism of parental instruction but, without hearing from these attendees directly and only through the lens of disapproving newspaper correspondents, it is difficult to make this claim conclusively in the Australian context.

Innes' observation that the behaviour of the lower classes, women and children at executions was 'appalling' holds true as an umbrella term for the negative construction of the crowd in the press. At one execution in Melbourne alone, Edmund Finn labelled the crowd 'white barbarians', complaining that they 'shouted and yelled and vented their gratification in explosions of uproarious merriment, as if they were participating in the greatest sport'.[61] At the same hanging the *Port Phillip Gazette* also reported that a 'most disgusting spirit' was on display, describing how spectators clambered for vantage points on nearby trees and walls, some

---

[58] *Launceston Advertiser*, 2 October 1845, p. 3.

[59] *The Moreton Bay Courier*, 29 August 1854 as quoted in Christopher Dawson, *That Gingerbread Structure: The Trials and Tribulations of the Queen Street Gaol*, Brisbane: Inside History, 2010, p. 36.

[60] Pieter Spierenburg, *The Spectacle of Suffering: Executions and the Evolution of Repression: From a Preindustrial Metropolis to the European Experience*, Cambridge: Cambridge University Press, 1984, p. 97.

[61] Finn, 1976, p. 395.

even mounting the criminal's coffins for a better view.[62] If this one execution can serve as a guide to others, negative slurs on crowd behaviour were widespread across the colonial era. In England the uncomfortably 'sporting tone' that executions took on was noted by John Pratt while Thomas W. Laqueur contextualised crowd behaviour within that nation's history of carnival days.[63] The sporting analogy is not completely out of place in the Australian colonies, especially when considering the cultural expectation of the crowd that the criminal 'die game' (see Chapter 4). However, a genuine fear of the crowd was seldom expressed in the colonies. In fact, only on one extremely rare occasion was the military guard actually called upon by the Sheriff to settle violent or interfering spectators.[64]

Although the crowd at public executions was not placed in a positive light across the Australian colonies, there are some references to spectators behaving in a way that matched the solemnity of the occasion. The colonial historian, John West, wrote how onlookers were 'affected to tears' when a group of condemned men died singing a hymn on the Hobart scaffold.[65] The travelling Scotsman, Alexander Marjoribanks, witnessed numerous hangings in both England and Australia. He suggested that the Sydney crowd was comparatively docile to those found abroad: 'The spectators behave with a remarkable degree of propriety in that country on such occasions, very different from what I have often seen in Britain'.[66] For Marjoribanks, this was best illustrated by the

[62] *The Port Phillip Gazette*, 22 January 1842.

[63] John Pratt, *Punishment and Civilization: Penal Tolerance and Intolerance in Modern Society*, London: Sage, 2002, pp. 15–34; Thomas W. Laqueur, 'Crowds, Carnival and the State in English Executions', in A.L. Beier, D. Cannadine, and J.M. Rosenheim, *The First Modern Society: Essays in English History in Honour of Lawrence Stone*, Cambridge: Cambridge University Press, 1989, pp. 305–355.

[64] In 1826 a man named Jefferies was travelling in a cart to the site of his execution in Launceston. Jeffries had, among other crimes, murdered an infant so as he travelled to the gallows: 'Several attempts were made by the people to take him out of the cart [so] that they might wreak their vengeance upon him'. As a result, 'it became necessary to send to Town for a stronger guard to prevent his immediate dispatch'. For details of this particular case, see Geoffrey Chapman Ingleton, *True Patriots All, or News from Early Australia*, Sydney: Angus and Robertson, 1952, p. 107.

[65] John West, *The History of Tasmania* [1852], A.G.L. Shaw (ed.), Sydney: Angus and Robertson, 1971, p. 421.

[66] Marjoribanks, 1847, p. 170.

way people related to the public executioner who was 'always treated with great respect'.[67] As with any stereotype there are always counter-narratives to be discovered.

It is worth probing further into the criticism directed at the public execution crowd with reference to the earlier comments made by colonial elites like Lang, Cunningham and Kentish; viz., their belief that scenes of violence were something that demoralised and hardened the spectator. Understanding this point helps to unlock the endless criticism directed at the women, children and lower classes who attended public executions. The ideal of 'improvement', for instance, was a key concept in Australia's intellectual culture from the 1830s to the 1860s.[68] The proliferation of the Mechanics' Institutes across the colonies during this time marked a desire to raise the labouring classes away from sensual pleasures to higher intellectual endeavours. Drunkenness and debauchery was a far cry from the disciplined workforce required to grow settlements from the ground up. If colonial society did indeed have an idealised cultural role for the lower classes to aspire towards, it certainly did not involve keeping company at the foot of the public scaffold.

As for the criticism that women and children attending executions received, scholars like Anne Summers and Jan Kociumbas may have part of the answer. A number of historians have identified how colonial women were placed in narrowly defined domestic, sexual and reproductive roles during the colonial period.[69] Summers' *Damned Whores*

[67]Marjoribanks, 1847, p. 132.

[68]Nadel, 1957. In identifying that the concept of improvement was prevalent in mid-nineteenth century Australia, Nadel complements the work of Asa Briggs on the Victorian period as a whole. See Asa Briggs, *The Age of Improvement, 1783–1867*, second edition, Harlow: Pearson Education Limited, 2000; Asa Briggs, *Victorian People: A Reassessment of Persons and Themes, 1851–1867*, London: Penguin Books, 1954; Asa Briggs, *Victorian Cities*, Harmondsworth: Penguin Books, 1963.

[69]See, for example, Raymond Evans and Kay Saunders, 'No Place Like Home: The Evolution of the Australian Housewife', in K. Saunders and R. Evans (eds), *Gender Relations in Australia: Domination and Negotiation*, Sydney: Harcourt Brace Jovanovich Publishers, 1992, pp. 175–167; Margaret Anderson, 'Good Strong Girls: Colonial Women and Work', in K. Saunders and R. Evans (eds), 1992, pp. 225–245; Miriam Dixson, *The Real Matilda: Women and Identity in Australia–1788 to the Present* [1976], fourth edition, Sydney: UNSW Press, 1999, pp. 138–154.

and God's Police (1975), for example, puts the birth of the 'bourgeoisie family' in Australia around the 1840s and 1850s, a period where females were told to assume 'moral guardianship of society'.[70] These types of roles designated for women, usually curated, enforced and exemplified by middle-class families, clashed with the idea of female attendance at the violent spectacle of public hangings. As for underage spectators to executions, Kociumbas' history of Australian childhood emphasises how the juvenile mind was usually conceived of as a malleable and pliable object. Schooling, play, family, discipline—all the elements of a proper upbringing—were thought to influence not just the child's individual prospects but the future health of the nation. These ideals were replicated in the raising of the children of the colonial elite, who were inculcated from birth with the virtues of good habit, respectability and appropriate gender roles.[71] The existence of children at the gallows, their corruption of innocence and crude introduction to violent death, flew in the face of all elite conceptions of proper child rearing. Children, and the mothers who brought them to watch, were thus free targets for sanction and concern in such a cultural milieu.

To return briefly to the question of the attendance of well-to-do types at public executions there is some evidence to suggest that they were, despite their outward rhetoric, spotted below the drop as well. The depiction of John Knatchbull's execution in Sydney in 1844 (see Illustration 1.1), for example, shows well-dressed men, women and children in the foreground. The horses and carriages dotted outside the gaol also betray the idea that it was a penniless rabble gathered to watch. Moreover, in Melbourne—the location where *The Argus* labelled executions a 'satanic high festival'—an eyewitness account of an execution by George Willmer exists. Willmer was an English draper who identified as one of those 'staid men, with large families, prosperous businesses, and settled habits' before leaving in search of 'golden tidings' in Victoria.[72] Upon

---

[70] Anne Summers, *Damned Whores and God's Police: Women's Lives in Australia*, second revised edition, Melbourne: Penguin Books, 1975, p. 67.

[71] Jan Kociumbas, *Australian Childhood: A History*, Sydney: Allen and Unwin, 1997, pp. 55–71.

[72] George Willmer, *The Draper in Australia*, London: W. Freeman, 1856, pp. 1–2.

arriving in Melbourne he too gathered around the drop with a travelling companion:

> This was the first sight of the kind I ever witnessed, and it was not a very agreeable introduction to the capital of Victoria. After witnessing the sad spectacle, we retired to a respectable-looking place to break our fast; but neither of us could eat much, or forget the sight just left behind us.[73]

Despite Willmer proclaiming that he was turned off his breakfast because of the scene, it still shows that men of his standing were not totally absent from public executions in Australia.

Who the Sheriff 'May Think Fit': Spectators to Private Executions

The following is the clause within the New South Wales Private Execution Act, assented to in 1854, that designates who was able to attend these new executions within the prison walls. The legislation passed in the other colonies offers very similar recommendations, albeit with slightly different wordings:

> The sheriff, under sheriff, or deputy as aforesaid, shall be present at such execution, together with the gaoler and proper officers of the gaol, including the physician or surgeon, together with all magistrates who shall think fit, and such constables, military guard, and adult spectators as the said sheriff, under sheriff, or deputy as aforesaid, may think fit.[74]

The official witnesses to private executions, noted in the legislation to be present, usually totalled no more than a dozen and provided a number of functions. The officers of the gaol were required to bring the prisoner from the cell to the scaffold and, along with any police or military present, maintain security as the private execution unfolded. The medical officer confirmed the prisoner was deceased and signed off on the fact.

---

[73] Willmer, 1856, pp. 108–109.

[74] New South Wales, no. 40 of 1853, *An Act to Regulate the Execution of Criminals*.

Magistrates, if they chose to attend, were a way for a member of the judiciary to witness that the sentence of the court was upheld. The Sheriff ran the event while the executioner and clergy rounded out those needed to perform the task. Journalists, meanwhile, communicated news of the execution to the wider public. These were the official witnesses to private executions, nothing but a distilled version of all who were legally and practically required to perform the task of hanging.

Gaining admittance to a private execution was an arbitrary decision made by the Sheriff, very much subject to his personal discretion. Sometimes it was as simple as being present outside the gaol on the day of execution in the hope of being one of the chosen few picked out. Later in the century, many sheriffs preferred to distribute 'cards of admission' in the days leading up to the execution to those who had applied.[75] William Sams in Tasmania and W. R. Boothby in South Australia are two sheriffs who provide passing examples of the different ways that one might gain admittance to a private execution. In Hobart, Sams acted as Sheriff for the hanging of John Halley and two others in 1861 and was welcomed outside the gaol by a large group of people 'most anxious to obtain admittance'.[76] 'Upon three having gained admittance', wrote *The Cornwall Chronicle*'s correspondent, 'all assembled followed the Sheriff from that lobby to the yard'.[77] For an execution at Adelaide Gaol in 1883, Sheriff Boothby had a 'large number of applications for admission to the Gaol' but granted none of them.[78] The *South Australian Register* thanked Boothby for denying the 'morbid tastes of the applicants' concluding that he conducted his duty in the true 'spirit of the Act' by attempting to prevent the criminal 'being paraded before the public' any more than was necessary.[79]

---

[75]For passing references to these 'cards of admission' granted to spectators who had applied to watch the private execution, see *Queanbeyan Age*, 24 August 1889, p. 4; *Darling Downs Gazette*, 14 November 1888, p. 3; *The Sydney Morning Herald*, 8 January 1887, p. 8; *Wallaroo Times*, 10 July 1867, p. 5.

[76]*The Cornwall Chronicle*, 25 May 1861, p. 5.

[77]*The Cornwall Chronicle*, 25 May 1861, p. 5.

[78]*South Australian Register*, 19 January 1883.

[79]*South Australian Register*, 19 January 1883.

The Sheriff often employed a good deal of discretion and calculation in deciding who should attend, especially since admittance to the scaffold scene was usually in high demand. In Queensland, two labourers of Pacific Island background were executed at the Maryborough lockup in 1877. On the day of execution some five hundred fellow Islanders showed up in the town who had been encouraged by police and local plantation owners to be privy to the event. However, of these hundreds, only 'six "representative" Polynesians' were allowed into the yard by the Under-Sheriff.[80] The sight of the six admitted into the lockup was said to have 'unmanned' one of the condemned men who burst into tears and fell silent upon seeing them.[81] On another occasion, again in Queensland, the father of a murdered daughter knocked on the gate to the Boggo Road Gaol early in the morning so that he could see her killer, James Gardiner, executed. After providing paperwork confirming his identity, the elderly man was granted permission to watch. As the execution was underway the father positioned himself directly opposite Gardiner and 'gazed long and earnestly' at the corpse after it was cut down.[82] According to *The Brisbane Courier* he left the gaol silently with a 'satisfied look on his face, and no doubt feeling in his heart that his daughter was avenged'.[83]

For high profile private executions there seems to be a sudden jump in spectator numbers, though it seems to be largely confined to New South Wales. For example, at the execution of Henry James O'Farrell, the Irishman executed for an attempt on the life of the visiting Duke of Edinburgh in 1868, the number of spectators swelled to 'upwards of a hundred persons' inside Darlinghurst Gaol.[84] This number was surpassed many years later in 1887 when the perpetrators of the Mount Rennie rape were executed at Darlinghurst Gaol. On that occasion 120 people, not including officials and policemen, were reported to be present.[85] The prison yard 'resembled a scene in a theatre' according to one newspaper:

---

[80] *Maryborough Chronicle*, 19 May 1877, p. 2.

[81] *Maryborough Chronicle*, 19 May 1877, p. 2.

[82] *The Brisbane Courier*, 16 October 1883, p. 3.

[83] *The Brisbane Courier*, 16 October 1883, p. 3.

[84] *Maryborough Chronicle, Wide Bay and Burnett Advertiser*, 28 April 1868.

[85] *The Riverine Grazier*, 11 January 1887, p. 4.

> The top gallery was set apart for the general public and visitors. The second gallery, on a level with the scaffold, was reserved for the press, members of Parliament and J's.P [*sic.*]. The floor was reserved for medical and scientific men. A strong force of police guarded each side of the scaffold. A subdued hum of voices filled the large open space, until the sheriff in stentorian tones demanded silence on pain of expulsion.[86]

The dramatic surge in numbers at very prominent private executions was in many ways to do with the upshot in interest from men of officialdom as well as journalists. At the execution of O'Farrell, for example, MPs and Justices of the Peace were strongly represented, equal to that of the 'well-known private citizens' that attended.[87] Still the large number of attendees at prominent private executions seems to be a practice limited to New South Wales. To contrast these two hangings with some of the most infamous executions to occur in colonial Victoria—say, that of Ned Kelly and, later, Frances Knorr—no private citizens were listed as being present.[88] Moreover, if counting the signatures on official witness declarations are anything to go by, the total number of spectators to private executions (including officials) rarely exceeded a dozen in the case of Tasmania.[89]

Sometimes the press accused the private spectators of being lowly and depraved just as they had the public execution crowd. At the 1861 execution of Thomas Sanders in Melbourne a 'favoured few' members of the public gained admittance but they behaved 'just like a crowd of low persons ... rushing the entrance to a theatrical pit or gallery'.[90] These members of the public displayed a 'rude eagerness' when trailing the condemned criminal to the drop in a manner that made the officials

---

[86] *The Riverine Grazier*, 11 January 1887, p. 4.

[87] *Maryborough Chronicle, Wide Bay and Burnett Advertiser*, 28 April 1868.

[88] Twenty-three spectators attended the execution of Kelly while thirteen came to watch Knorr's hanging but all were present in a professional capacity. See 'Witnesses to Kelly's Execution, 11 October 1880', Public Record Office Victoria, VPRS 4969/2/78; *The Argus*, 16 January 1894, p. 5.

[89] 'Copies of Declaration by Witnesses and Doctors of the Execution of Convicted Persons, 1 January 1856 to 31 December 1946', Tasmanian Archives, SC485/1/1.

[90] *The Mercury*, 15 June 1861.

'most unhappy'.[91] The behaviour of the private execution crowd in 1858 at the hanging of Young and Burns in Launceston was particularly scandalous. Their excitement drew comparisons to the 'refined savages who flock to bull-fights and gloat over the sanguinary scenes of the arena'.[92] The conduct of the chosen members of the public seemed to worsen in the case of botched executions, a scourge that continued unabated for much of the private execution era. The crowd hissed and jeered the hangman immediately following the execution of an Indigenous man known as 'Scabby Harry' at Goulburn Gaol in 1859.[93] The executioner, having terribly bungled the task by allowing the body to hit the ground, ran to the gaoler's quarters in fear for his personal safety but was soon recalled to suspend the criminal's corpse in the proper manner.

The controlled environment of private executions made it much easier for scientific experts to be admitted by the Sheriff for research purposes. Christopher Dawson, in the context of Queensland, unearthed the story of a Russian anthropologist named Nikolai Milkhoulo-Maclay who attended four executions in Brisbane during the year 1880.[94] The criminals were from ethnicities the anthropologist had labelled Australian, Melanesian, Malayan and Mongolian. Immediately following the execution the brain of each criminal was removed from the skull and then dissected, photographs being taken at each relevant stage. For the purposes of posterity it may be noted that Mikhoulo-Maclay found that each physical brain did not appear so different as to 'justify the concept of higher and lower races'.[95] In Victoria, on at least one occasion in 1872, local medical students were allowed into the prison to watch the post-mortem being carried out by the medical officer. In an era where cadavers were in short and unpredictable supply, the prison governor at

[91] *The Mercury*, 15 June 1861.

[92] *Melbourne Punch* reprinted in *The Colonist*, 9 November 1858, p. 3.

[93] Cries of 'scandalous' and 'shameful butchery' were just some of the phrases yelled at the executioner on this occasion. See *The Moreton Bay Courier*, 1 June 1859.

[94] For Dawson's account, see Christopher Dawson, *The Prisoners of Toowong Cemetery: Life, Death and the Old Petrie Terrace Gaol*, Brisbane: Inside History, 2006, p. 51.

[95] C.L. Sentinella quoted in Dawson, 2006, p. 51.

Melbourne Gaol wrote in his diary how both student and doctor alike 'revelled in the luxury of a fresh & healthy corpse'.[96]

Phrenology was gaining traction in the latter half of the nineteenth century and its practitioners were frequently permitted by various sheriffs to attend private executions. These men of pseudoscience were one of the main reasons for the growing prevalence of death masks being taken of executed criminals in the late colonial period.[97] Travelling phrenologists like Professor G. A. De Blumenthal claimed at lectures that, for the purposes of 'scientific research', he attended twenty-two executions in the colonies by the year 1895.[98] Taking physical measurements and casts of the head immediately following the hanging was a means to conduct an analysis of criminal character. De Blumenthal's 'phrenological chart', an analysis of the hanged criminal's head, was often published in the colonial newspapers.[99] The phrenologist's task could be a gruesome one, as in the case of Frances Knorr who was executed at Melbourne Gaol in 1894:

> The white cap was removed from the face of the dead woman, and the female warders were compelled to hold up the woman's head, with the blood streaming down all over their hands, in order that a phrenologist should take certain measurements with a tape, and the hideously contorted blood besmeared face of a decrepit little woman was exposed to the public gaze.[100]

Another prominent colonial phrenologist, Professor Archibald S. Hamilton, preferred to avoid the execution altogether and instead

96 John Buckley Castieau, *The Difficulties of My Position: The Diaries of Prison Governor John Buckley Castieau, 1855–1884*, M. Finnane (ed.), Canberra: National Library of Australia, 2004, pp. 181–182.

97 Dean Wilson, 'Explaining the "Criminal": Kelly's Death Mask', *The La Trobe Journal*, no. 69, 2002, pp. 51–58.

98 *Wagga Wagga Express*, 21 May 1895, p. 2.

99 For two examples of De Blumenthal examining the heads of deceased criminals during the year 1889, see *Bendigo Advertiser*, 19 March 1889, p. 1; *Geelong Advertiser*, 18 October 1889, p. 3.

100 *The Armidale Express and New England General Advertiser*, 19 January 1894, p. 4.

examine the culprit in the cell before death.[101] That said, Hamilton was known to seek out the death masks of criminals after their hanging as he gave his lectures surrounded by 'upwards of forty skulls, various casts, and numerous diagrams'.[102] Through the display of the heads of dead criminals phrenology tapped into the sensational possibilities of hangings, especially in the visually starved era of private executions. For instance, the death mask of Ned Kelly may have been initially commissioned for medical or scientific purposes but a wax likeness of his head appeared on public display in Bourke Street the day immediately following his execution.[103] Hamilton's personal reading of Kelly's cranium appeared in a newspaper not long after that.[104]

On the day of a private execution many members of the public still congregated outside colonial prisons just to partake in the drama of the event. Estimates of the crowd gathered outside the walls of Melbourne Gaol at the execution of Ned Kelly ranged anywhere from four to several thousand.[105] Most were 'larrikin-looking youths' and 'nearly all were of the lower orders' according to *The Mercury*.[106] The death of Frances Knorr attracted some fifteen hundred spectators outside Melbourne Gaol.[107] Many of the women gathered were said to have 'relieved their overcharged feelings with tears'—according to one report.[108] The vast majority of estimates of crowd numbers outside the walls vary and range from anywhere from a handful to several hundred. As the sun set on

[101]For details of A.S. Hamilton's career as a phrenologist, in so far as it intersected with executions, see Alexandra Roginski, *The Hanged Man and the Body Thief: Finding Lives in a Museum Mystery*, Melbourne: Monash University Press, 2015; Wilson, 2002; A.S. Hamilton, *Abstract of a Lecture on Criminal Legislation, Prison Discipline, and the Causes of Crime, and on Capital Punishments: With Delineations on the Characters of Alexander and Charles Ross*, Sydney: F. Cunningham, 1863.

[102]*Bendigo Advertiser*, 3 December 1867, pp. 2–3.

[103]Wilson, 2002, p. 51. For the original death mask, see Maximilian L. Kreitmayer, 'Ned Kelly Death Mask', Plaster, 28.0 × 21.5 × 18.5 cm, 1880, National Portrait Gallery of Australia, LOAN2000.39.

[104]*The Herald*, 18 November 1880, p. 2.

[105]National Trust of Australia, *The Old Melbourne Gaol*, Melbourne: National Trust of Australia, 1991, p. 30.

[106]*The Mercury*, 15 November 1880, p. 3.

[107]*The Argus*, 16 January 1894, p. 5.

[108]*The Dubbo Liberal and Macquarie Advocate*, 17 January 1894, p. 3.

the colonial era this eager group of hopeful attendees became more and more out of place on city streets. By 1901 Brisbane's *Evening Observer* wrote that many people 'hurrying to their work' looked at a group of men waiting 'nervously for admittance' outside the gaol with a great deal of curiosity.[109]

The interaction between prison officials and the crowd gathered outside the walls was mediated by mutually understood symbolism. It was common for a black flag to be raised from within the prison to indicate to those waiting outside that the culprit was dead. At Darlinghurst Gaol it was frequently reported that a lengthy bell toll took place at the hour fixed for the execution.[110] In Western Australia, the Private Execution Act stipulated that official documentation confirming the death had to be displayed for a 24-hour period at the entrance gate of the prison.[111] There were some occasional interactions between the official spectators to the hanging and those gathered outside the prison. At one of the earliest private executions in Sydney, of two criminals named Samuel Wilcox and William Rogers, almost two-hundred spectators gathered outside the prison. One account states how the official witnesses to the execution were 'deeply impressed by the melancholy spectacle'.[112] The witnesses then emerged as one group from within the gaol and 'announced' to those waiting outside that the execution had successfully taken place.[113]

Sometimes the signals of a successful execution were not enough to satisfy the curiosity of the crowd outside the gaol. In fact, there were many attempts to peek over the prison walls and view proceedings first hand. Correspondents to William Ryan's private execution in 1855, the first of its kind in Australia, reported how the roofs of tall buildings near Darlinghurst Gaol were covered with spectators.[114] One writer took comfort in the fact that these pariahs could only see but not hear the death so that it was only 'half so great and so pleasurable' as it was under

---

[109] *Evening Observer*, 4 December 1901.

[110] For Darlinghurst, see *The Bird O' Freedom*, 2 June 1894, p. 4.

[111] Western Australia, no. 15 of 1871, *An Act to Provide for Carrying Out of Capital Punishment Within Prisons*, section 9.

[112] *Empire*, 6 July 1855, p. 3.

[113] *Empire*, 6 July 1855, p. 3.

[114] *Colonial Times and Tasmanian Advertiser*, 4 March 1855.

the 'good old system'.[115] In South Australia, at the 1861 execution of the Rainbird Murderers, there was a like-minded group of people attempting to see into the Adelaide Gaol. Before the execution took place a 'considerable concourse of persons' had gathered outside the gaol but all were 'wisely and properly' refused admittance by the Sheriff.[116] Once it was clear that they would not be able to attend the execution *The Advertiser* wrote that:

> A rush was then made to an eminence a little to the westward of the jail, from which we understand that the scaffold was just visible – but a small detachment of the mounted police, who were in attendance under Sergeant-Major Hall, were ordered to clear the ground, and succeeded tolerably in keeping the people back. Among the crowd, which numbered over 50 persons, were a great many youths and children, all anxious to obtain a view of the disgusting scene.[117]

A similar scene occurred in Brisbane at the execution of Thomas Wood in 1860 where excluded spectators, including women, climbed trees to the rear of the prison to watch the spectacle from over the walls.[118] Outside the Old Dubbo Gaol in regional New South Wales there was a large tree that was climbed by enterprising young boys in the late nineteenth century to watch both the everyday workings of the prison as well as the occasional execution. The Prisons Department was so concerned about this intrusion that they had the tree levelled.[119]

The Private Execution Acts made the Sheriff the final arbiter of attendance at colonial executions. For the first time it was possible to actively exclude women, children and the lower classes from viewing the spectacle of death. By law 'adult spectators' were only allowed to watch private hangings so children were, in effect, barred from the outset. Tasmania was the only colonial parliament to, in the actual wording of the Act,

[115] *The Argus*, 5 March 1855, p. 5.

[116] *The Advertiser* reprinted in *The Mercury*, 15 June 1861, p. 2.

[117] *The Advertiser* reprinted in *The Mercury*, 15 June 1861, p. 2.

[118] *The Moreton Bay Courier*, 8 December 1860.

[119] Bill Hornadge, *Old Dubbo Gaol*, Dubbo: Old Dubbo Gaol Restoration Committee, 1974, p. 13.

state outright that the 'adult spectators' be male.[120] Yet, despite the fact that females in the other colonies were technically allowed admittance into the prison, one is hard pressed finding any reference to a female spectator at a private execution. The concern over lower class spectators was easily managed, now the Sheriff could personally discern the status of those asking to attend. Such unwanted spectators were replaced by the press, appropriate officials, select members of the public and even the occasional scientific observer. It was a collection of individuals thought by the Sheriff to conform to the solemnity and tone of the occasion. If enthusiastic members of the public were gathering outside the prison on the day fixed for execution, or even attempting to peek over the walls to see in, it was a comparatively small price to pay for the new-found decorum brought about by private executions.

There is one last aspect of spectatorship that ought to be covered in any discussion on the transition to private executions in Australia. Namely, how the vast majority of colonists became almost fully dependent on newspapers for their information on executions after the passage of the Private Execution Acts. Overnight, reading emerged as the dominant medium through which the death of a criminal could be understood by the public. Newspaper reportage on hangings, it must be noted, was as constant and dependable as before the transition to private executions—there was still comment on the criminal and his crime, the crowd who watched, whether it was conducted in the proper manner, and any other detail that may be relevant to the reader. However, it was now a scene fully processed and communicated via a privileged intermediary, viz. the journalist. The reporters' own beliefs, reasoning and language were always going to colour their description of an important judicial event whether they meant it or not. Moreover, the detail they omitted from their columns, or whatever information the correspondent did not think fit to report due to personal preference, remained forever unknown

[120]Van Diemen's Land, no. 2 of 1855, *An Act to Regulate the Execution of Criminal*, s2. In the consolidated Tasmanian Criminal Code of 1924 this stipulation that members of the public watching private executions must be male was adhered too. See Tasmania, no. 69 of 1924, *The Criminal Code Act*, s397, clause 2.

to their readers. The means to personally attend the hanging and evaluate it on his or her own terms was something reserved for only the very few in the era of private executions.

This was hardly a problem for most readers who felt that the journalist had placed them right there with the criminal at the final scene. As one reader of *The Argus* wrote in a Letter to the Editor in 1859:

> Personally I have never witnessed an execution, and yet I can understand the feelings which are produced by the sight of one. The disgusting details have been heralded forth in the daily papers, and such has been the accuracy with which the proceedings have been described that I am as perfectly acquainted with all the interesting details as if I had stood at the foot of each scaffold.[121]

Despite never witnessing an execution, this reader ('J.W.K.') was convinced that hangings were an affront to the 'refinement of our manners' and the 'increasing delicacy of our sentiments'.[122] It is not to say that such comments were unjustified or illegitimate observations for the reader to make; what should be noted is that J.W.K. could only ever construct their evaluation of executions through the lens of a straight-laced journalist.

As time went by journalists were less likely to write of the gory realities of death by hanging. In part this was a matter of taste. For example, in 1879 the Premier of Queensland stated in Parliament that 'we must condemn any portion of the Press that would seek to put too prominently forward the sickening details connected with an execution'.[123] But, in another way, this was simply because journalists were less able to write about gory realities as time went by—think of the tarp draped below the drop at Melbourne Gaol used to hide the writhing body of the criminal (see Chapter 3). Not being able to personally attend an execution added layers of distance between the general public and the death of

---

[121] *The Argus*, 14 May 1859.

[122] *The Argus*, 14 May 1859.

[123] Instead of 'pandering to the worst feelings of humanity' by providing such details, he thought that, 'A brief mention in the Press to the effect that the execution has taken place is sufficient'. Thomas McIlwraith quoted in *The Darling Downs and General Advertiser*, 13 June 1879, p. 3.

a criminal in ways that were not immediately perceptible. Trapping the image of colonial hangings within the journalist's own viewpoint without any means of recourse was yet another way in which executions were sanitised and refocused. If executions are to be considered a communicative exercise that attempted to convey the consequences of crime to the onlooker then a newspaper report transmitted that intended message far more safely.

* * *

The only spectators to the private hanging of Malachi Martin in December 1862 at the Adelaide Gaol were the press and various government officials—members of the public had been completely excluded from the scene. It was cause for the *South Australian Register* to congratulate the Sheriff on his 'strict adherence' to the 'will of the Legislature':

> There was no crowd of people crushing with heartless curiosity to gain eligible standing ground … no wilderness of upturned faces, expressing pity, disgust, or horror, to distract the thoughts of the doomed man … There was a preternatural stillness in the large and gloomy building. … This certainly must be regarded as a great improvement upon the old system, where the disorder and indecorum of a mob too often perverted the sad and serious lesson which the law intended a public execution to inculcate.[124]

The introduction of private executions allowed for much greater control over who could digest such scenes of violence in the Australian colonies. The Sheriff was granted the power to exclude the troublesome groups that people like Joseph Long Innes (and many others) thought attended public executions—women, children and the lower classes. Once the execution was hidden inside the prison, the vast majority of the public were reduced to gathering outside its walls to wait for an appropriate signal indicating that the criminal had died. Upper class writers like Cunningham, Lang and Kentish could finally rest a little easier knowing that the Sheriff was able to prevent large swathes of the colonial population from viewing an execution. The concern of these writers was predicated

[124] *South Australian Register*, 26 December 1862.

on the cultural belief that scenes of violence demoralised the onlooker and fundamentally transformed their character for the worse. The introduction of private executions sought to remedy these concerns and refocus colonial hangings on the central lesson of capital punishment. As the correspondent to the hanging of Martin pointed out, private executions allowed for the 'sad and serious lesson' of the punishment to come to the fore while thoughts of the 'disorder and indecorum' of the crowd could, at long last, be put to one side.

6

The End of Public Executions

Caught in a reflective mood, South Australia's *Weekly Chronicle* wondered about capital punishment. Looking backwards from 1867 it wrote how the changes to its administration had been dramatic since public executions had come to an end. In fact, it was perplexed as to just how quickly these accepted norms had been upended:

> Among the questions in which we have anticipated reforms in the old country, is that of public executions, years ago abolished throughout Australia. It is strange how suddenly systems that have existed for ages, and have been almost universally cherished, as founded on right and essential to the well-being of society, drop into complete disrepute, all the arguments so seriously and vehemently advanced in their favour being abandoned as scarcely worth a serious thought.[1]

So far in this book we have heard much about how the abolition of public hangings (and the corresponding introduction of private ones)

[1] *The South Australian Weekly Chronicle*, 29 June 1867.

S. Anderson, *A History of Capital Punishment in the Australian Colonies, 1788 to 1900*, Palgrave Histories of Policing, Punishment and Justice,
https://doi.org/10.1007/978-3-030-53767-8_6

impacted upon the punishment in different contexts. Yet, the parliamentary debates, press comment and context of the passage of this legislation have not been fully explored. This Chapter seeks to remedy that by looking into the practicalities around passing the 'Private Execution Acts' through the Australian colonial parliaments during the period 1853 to 1871. The early timing of the Acts in comparison to other jurisdictions within the British Empire tells the historian something about the desires and insecurities of colonial Australians. The trigger for introducing these Acts, especially in New South Wales, came from a culturally loaded desire to appear civilised to the outside world and distance the Australian colonies from their often chequered beginnings. Colonists, after all, were deeply concerned about their tarnished reputation abroad. Satirists in London had long poked fun at the odium of its far-flung penal settlement. A very early cartoon, for example, imagined the future parliament of Botany Bay in action—the speaker was a convict in irons sitting in a tree listening to a rowdy debate below on different hanging techniques.[2] These sorts of jibes at the colonies' reputation were slow to subside in popular memory. Perhaps—so the thought went—by surging ahead in this area of penal policy they could distinguish themselves from the excesses of a blood-stained convict past? That aside, the legislative debates related to this decision, particularly between 1853 and 1858, was a continent-wide airing of grievances about capital punishment as it was then administered in the colonies from which much can be gleaned.

The Private Execution Acts

Acts to abolish the practice of public executions were passed separately among the colonies without any top down direction from Britain or any official dialogue between the colonies to act collectively. It was a case of discreet colonial jurisdictions acting independently to abolish the bloody spectacle of public executions one after the other. The term 'Private Execution Acts' is occasionally used below to refer to these separate

[2]John Hirst, *Freedom on the Fatal Shore: Australia's First Colony*, Melbourne: Black Inc., 2008, p. 176.

pieces of legislation collectively—even though they were titled slightly differently from colony to colony. New South Wales, Victoria and Van Diemen's Land (later called Tasmania) all proclaimed an Act to abolish public executions in 1855.[3] South Australia proclaimed an end to public executions in 1858 while Western Australia waited until 1871 to follow the example set by the colonies to the east.[4] In the case of modern-day Queensland private executions were adopted in 1855 since it was under the administrative jurisdiction of New South Wales until 1859.[5] Though the Act was proclaimed in New South Wales and Victoria in 1855, this hides the fact that the bill actually passed its third reading much earlier. In the Parliament of New South Wales a successful third reading occurred in August 1853, while in November 1854 the bill passed its third reading in the Victorian Parliament.[6] The lengthy delay in proclaiming the bill was due to the fact that, in both cases, it was sent to England for Royal Assent.

Pre-empting England with this reform was a contentious point for the two earliest colonies. At the time the reform was deemed 'so novel', to borrow the words of New South Wales Attorney-General John Plunkett, that it needed to be double-checked by the 'mother parliament'.[7] Plunkett had 'no hesitation' in suggesting that 'the Governor-General [of New South Wales] ought not to give his assent to any such measure until it had been referred home for the decision of the Queen'.[8] After being transmitted to England, *An Act to Regulate the Execution of Criminals*

[3] New South Wales, no. 40 of 1853, *An Act to Regulate the Execution of Criminals*; Victoria, no. 44 of 1854, *An Act to Regulate the Execution of Criminals*; Tasmania, no. 2 of 1855, *An Act to Regulate the Execution of Criminals*.

[4] South Australia, no. 23 of 1858, *Act to Regulate the Execution of Criminals*; Western Australia, no. 15 of 1871, *An Act to Provide for Carrying Out of Capital Punishment Within Prisons*.

[5] Queensland affirmed their position in favour of private executions when they included the measure in the first consolidation of their criminal code, see Queensland, no. 13 of 1865–1866, *Criminal Consolidation Act*, s58–63.

[6] For a record of the bill passing its third reading in the Parliament of New South Wales, see New South Wales, *Votes and Proceedings of the Legislative Council* (hereafter *VPLC*), vol. 1, no. 48 of 1853, 17 August 1853; *The Sydney Morning Herald*, 18 August 1853, p. 2. For evidence that the bill was read a third time and passed in Victoria, see *The Argus*, 15 November 1854, pp. 4–5; *The Argus*, 24 November 1854, p. 4.

[7] *The Sydney Morning Herald*, 21 July 1853, p. 2.

[8] The Colonial Secretary of New South Wales, Edward Thomson, fully endorsed Plunkett's position, *The Sydney Morning Herald*, 21 July 1853, p. 2.

was officially proclaimed in New South Wales on 10 January 1855, a full seventeen months following its initial passage through Parliament.[9] By late November 1854, when the bill had been successfully read a third time in Victoria, news had not yet arrived of New South Wales' success in gaining approval from England. Thus, Victoria joined its northern neighbour in bypassing the Governor's approval and sending the bill to England for Royal Assent.[10] On 10 October 1855, almost a year later, it was announced in the Victorian *Government Gazette* that Her Majesty's Assent had been granted.[11] Conversely, in Van Diemen's Land, South Australia and Western Australia, the resident Governors, not the Queen of England, gave their Assent to the various bills concerning private executions—the precedent of New South Wales and Victoria having already been set.[12]

John Darvall, a former barrister-cum-parliamentarian, was the only person to seriously question the need for Sydney to reserve the Bill for Royal Assent in England:

> What had the Imperial Government to do with the question [of private executions]? Really, after all their struggles for self-government ... it would come to this, that they could not have a gutter cleansed without asking permission from home.[13]

Darvall viewed the alteration of the execution procedure as a 'purely local and municipal' issue that did not require an opinion from the 'Imperial Government'.[14] It was a concern that does have a legitimate legal basis

---

[9]For evidence of Royal Assent being granted in the case of New South Wales see footnote 'a' in New South Wales, no. 40 of 1853, *An Act to Regulate the Execution of Criminals*.

[10]*Portland Guardian and Normanby General Advertiser*, 7 December 1854.

[11]*Victorian Government Gazette*, 9 October, 1855, p. 2561; Victoria, no. 44 of 1854, *An Act to Regulate the Execution of Criminals*.

[12]Despite the fact that Victoria began the legislative process in September 1854, Van Diemen's Land actually beat Victoria by nine days in putting the reform into practice by avoiding the time required to send the bill back and forth between England and Australia. Lieutenant-Governor of Van Diemen's Land, William Denison, proclaimed an end to public executions on 1 October 1855. For details, see *The Hobarton Mercury*, 10 August 1855, p. 4; *Launceston Examiner*, 16 August, 1855.

[13]*The Sydney Morning Herald*, 21 July 1853, p. 2.

[14]*The Sydney Morning Herald*, 21 July 1853, p. 2.

since the precedent throughout the colonial era was to only reserve bills for Her Majesty in England that were of an Imperial concern, rather than that of a local character.[15]

The pioneering legislation of New South Wales came with five specific clauses. As had always been the case, Section 1 of the Act still put the responsibility of running the execution in the hands of the Sheriff or someone to whom he expressly delegated this responsibility. It also declares that the execution must occur 'within the walls of the Prison of the Country City Town or District in which the conviction was had or within the enclosed yard of such Prison'.[16] This is the crucial clause that gave hangings their newly 'private' character. From this point on the gallows across the colonies were mounted differently or covered up in ways that made the scene invisible to those outside the prison. Section 2 of the New South Wales Act outlines who could watch a private hanging. In addition to the usual officers, the key part of this clause (discussed at length in Chapter 5) was that the Sheriff now had the power to admit any 'adult Spectators', chosen from among the general public, to view the execution. Only Western Australia stipulated in the legislation specifically that 'such relatives of the prisoner' were allowed to view the private hanging.[17]

The three remaining sections in the New South Wales Act were largely designed to organise procedural guidelines. The Sheriff is directed not to allow anyone to leave the place of execution until the medical officer signs a form declaring that the criminal's life had expired. Similarly, gaol officers and any public spectators must sign another form stating that they were witness to the death.[18] Any false testimony regarding

[15]This division of power between the centre and the periphery of the British Empire, although sometimes murky, is a good example of what has been viewed as an alternate precursor to the version of Australian Federalism that found full voice after 1901. The more conventional explanation is that Australia's version of Federalism was developed from the practical and constitutional experience of the United States, see Richard Lucy, 'The Division of Powers Between the British Empire and its Australian Self-Governing Colonies, 1855–1900', *Australian Journal of Law and Society*, vol. 6, 1990, pp. 83–96.

[16]New South Wales, no. 40 of 1853, *An Act to Regulate the Execution of Criminals*, s1.

[17]Western Australia, no. 15 of 1871, *An Act to Provide for Carrying Out of Capital Punishment Within Prisons*, s3.

[18]Tasmania has an extensive collection of these official statements signed by public witnesses and medical practitioners ranging from 1856 to 1946, see 'Copies of Declaration by Witnesses

these witness and medical statements came with a maximum penalty of fifteen years transportation. Although penalties for false declarations were present in each of the other colonies, the punishment in New South Wales was the most severe for this kind of transgression. The Sheriff was directed to lodge these documents with the Supreme Court in Sydney for their safekeeping and news of the hanging was to be twice published in the Government Gazette.

The central point of departure between the different Acts passed by the colonies was how to guarantee procedural transparency and make people aware that an execution had occurred. Coronial Inquests following the execution were required by law in every colony except New South Wales and Van Diemen's Land. In these two remaining colonies, the signing of declarations from witnesses to the execution and the medical officer certifying the success of the hanging was deemed suitable enough to satisfy the public mind. Only in Victoria was it possible, upon a clause originally suggested by the Attorney-General, for any person in the colony to be able to view the dead criminal's body within eight hours of the hanging—so long as they had permission from a Justice of the Peace.[19] In the interests of adequately publicising the judicial execution (and in the very rare case that the newspapers avoided comment on the issue), every colony except Western Australia stipulated that news of the death must be published in the colony's Government Gazette.

Western Australia's guarantee of transparency and due process deviated the most from that of other colonies. It was the only colony where the Sheriff and witness declarations as well as the Surgeon's medical certificate had to be displayed 'on or near the principal entrance of the prison' where the execution took place for a minimum of twenty-four hours afterwards.[20] A duplicate of these documents was then sent to the Colonial Secretary's office for safekeeping. Western Australia was also the only colony to allow some room to manipulate the boundaries of the execution ceremony but only in so far as to accentuate the new qualities of the

---

and Doctors of the Execution of Convicted Persons, 1 January 1856 to 31 December 1946', Tasmanian Archives, SC485/1/1.

[19]Victoria, no. 44 of 1854, *An Act to Regulate the Execution of Criminals*, s4.

[20]Western Australia, no. 15 of 1871, *An Act to Provide for Carrying Out of Capital Punishment Within Prisons*, s9.

penalty. In the colony, the Colonial Secretary was given the power 'from time to time' to 'make such rules and regulations to be observed on the execution' that lends 'greater solemnity' to the occasion.[21]

The first criminal in Australia to be hanged in accordance with the newly formed standards of a private execution was William Ryan on 28 February 1855 at Sydney's Darlinghurst Gaol.[22] Found guilty of disembowelling his wife in a drunken stupor, Ryan was led to the newly constructed gallows at the rear of the Gaol and composed himself by shaking hands with the clergymen as the moment of death neared. His final words spoken not long after 9am—'O! Lord have mercy upon my soul!'—echoed around the gaol yard with uncharacteristic clarity in the absence of the usually rowdy Sydney crowd.[23] As soon as the execution ended, the medical officer checked for a pulse, found Ryan dead, and signed the relevant form as stipulated by *An Act to Regulate the Execution of Criminals* which had been proclaimed a month prior. The small number of observers who attended also played their part, signing a witness statement confirming the death.[24] The execution became a simple fact twice printed in the *Government Gazette*, reported through the lens of newspapermen and only witnessed by a select few members of the public. Ryan's death in 1855 was the archetypal example of a private execution ceremony that remained in place until Australia's very last hanging in 1967.

---

[21]Western Australia, no. 15 of 1871, *An Act to Provide for Carrying Out of Capital Punishment Within Prisons*, s9.

[22]John McGuire, 'Judicial Violence and the "Civilizing Process": Race and the Transition from Public to Private Executions in Colonial Australia', *Australian Historical Studies*, vol. 29, no. 111, 1998, pp. 191–192. For primary accounts of Ryan's hanging, see *Empire*, 1 March 1855; *The Sydney Morning Herald*, 1 March 1855, p. 5; *Bell's Life in Sydney and Sporting Reviewer*, 3 March 1855, p. 2; *People's Advocate*, 3 March 1855.

[23]*People's Advocate*, 3 March 1855.

[24]The official documentation is reprinted in *The Maitland Mercury and Hunter River General Advertiser*, 10 March 1855, p. 2.

The Parliamentary Debates

Dr Henry Grattan Douglass, a Member of the Legislative Council of New South Wales from 1851 to 1861, initiated the first Private Execution Act in Australia. Douglass came to New South Wales from Ireland. A young surgeon, he was soon put in charge of the Parramatta General Hospital and appointed superintendent of the Female Factory.[25] He was also a key member of Sydney's Benevolent and Philosophical Societies at different times. Douglass was, briefly during the 1820s, appointed as a magistrate before being forced to resign after an accusation that he had behaved 'improperly' during his time in charge of the Female Factory.[26] Douglass was uniquely positioned throughout his career to analyse criminal behaviour and punitive techniques from many different perspectives; as a medical practitioner, a magistrate presiding over cases, a one-time manager of female prisoners and finally as a lawmaker. He was a man who was, in his own words, 'strongly opposed to capital punishments altogether' but was fully aware that his position was not shared by a majority of the New South Wales Parliament.[27]

The abolition of public executions was something Douglass pursued after a discussion during the Financial Estimates over a faulty set of gallows at Darlinghurst Gaol in Sydney. Since it was last replaced in 1844, the wooden platform of the gallows at Darlinghurst Gaol had surrendered once more to the climate and rotted through.[28] Such a small matter of prison maintenance ought to have been dealt with quickly if not for the need to first discuss the matter on the floor of Parliament. Due process stipulated that the £500 needed to remove the old gallows

---

[25]K.B. Noad, 'Douglass, Henry Grattan (1790–1865)', *Australian Dictionary of Biography* 1966, http://adb.anu.edu.au/biography/douglass-henry-grattan-1987, viewed 20 August 2013; 'Dr. Henry Grattan DOUGLASS (1790–1865)', *The Parliament of New South Wales* 2008, http://www.parliament.nsw.gov.au/prod/parlment/members.nsf/1fb6ebed995667c2ca256ea100825164/8a28df421cb43794ca256e69000968aa?OpenDocument, viewed 20 August 2013.

[26]Noad, 1966; *Parliament of New South Wales*, 2008.

[27]*Empire*, 2 July 1853.

[28]Arthur L. Wintle, 'The Abolition of Public Executions in New South Wales', unpublished B.A. (Hons) thesis, La Trobe University, 1973, p. 23; *People's Advocate*, 9 October 1852.

and erect a new one needed to be included in the Government's Financial Estimates for that year. When the issue of gallows maintenance at Darlinghurst Gaol arose, it soon caught the ire of Douglass who was quick to retort that he would, 'vote any sum to take it down, but not a farthing to set it up'.[29] He then moved to reduce the amount of government money allocated to the reconstruction of the gallows by £200. The remaining £300 Douglass offered for the task was presumably only enough to take down the gallows but not enough to erect a new one.

The incidental defiance of Douglass triggered a discussion on the floor of Parliament that revealed the other Members' disgust at the practice of public executions. The long serving Colonial Secretary of New South Wales, Edward Thomson, offered his view during the Financial Estimates that, 'it was objectionable that the gallows should be constantly exposed; and on the subject of public executions… the American practice of private execution was infinitely preferable on every ground'.[30] Former solicitor George Nichols also advocated for private executions 'under the eye of competent witnesses' rather than the rubbernecking general public. The Attorney-General John Plunkett agreed with the other Members that public executions had a 'demoralising tendency' but suggested that the mood of the general public would be 'greatly against the extreme penalty of the law being carried out privately'.[31] On Plunkett's advice, and after some further discussion on the topic of capital punishment more generally, Douglass removed his amendment. He later said that after the Financial Estimates he continued to have conversations about public executions with many Members of Parliament behind closed doors and found that the majority of lawmakers shared his desire for greater privacy.[32] It was a gap of only a few months before Douglass took leave to introduce a bill with the intention of abolishing public executions in the colony.

---

[29] *The Sydney Morning Herald*, 24 June 1853, p. 2.

[30] *The Sydney Morning Herald*, 24 June 1853, p. 2.

[31] *The Sydney Morning Herald*, 24 June 1853, p. 2.

[32] *Empire*, 2 July 1853.

Douglass formally introduced *An Act to Regulate the Execution of Criminals* in July 1853.[33] It was an action that he thought would indicate to the outside world, and especially to Britain, that New South Wales was now a civilised nineteenth century actor and something more than just a former penal colony. According to the *Empire*'s account of proceedings, Douglass thought that the introduction of private executions 'would be a step in advance for this colony to make, and it would set an example to the mother country, which they might worthily follow, although it emanated from a convict colony'.[34] Douglass continued this theme later in his speech stating that 'this would be a great advance in the civilisation of the criminal laws of the country'.[35] *The Sydney Morning Herald*, another newspaper to offer an account of parliamentary debates in New South Wales, also noted Douglass' motive. *The Herald*'s version of his remarks picks up yet more of this vision for New South Wales to be defined by something other than convicts and punishment:

> No doubt the principle of private execution was new in England, but it was already in practice in Prussia, and also in America; and it was a grave consideration whether this colony, which had originally been a penal settlement, should not take an initiatory step in this matter and show the whole world the progress which had been made in civilisation.[36]

The central concern with the legislation was to safeguard against any possible deception. The Attorney-General John Plunkett put forth his opinion that he 'believed public executions were extremely demoralising; but at the same time he felt that the greatest caution must be exercised in making any change in the present practice, so as not to allow the slightest

---

[33]The key dates of the bill's passage through the Parliament are as follows: 1 July 1853 (Douglass took leave to introduce the bill), 6 July (first reading), 19 July (second reading), 9 and 10 August (committee of the whole), 17 August (third reading). For confirmation, see New South Wales, *VPLC*, vol. 1, no. 26 of 1853, 1 July 1853; New South Wales, *VPLC*, vol. 1, no. 28 of 1853, 6 July 1853; New South Wales, *VPLC*, no. 33 of 1853, 19 July 1853; New South Wales, *VPLC*, vol. 1, no. 43 of 1853, 9 August 1853; New South Wales, *VPLC*, vol. 1, no. 44 of 1853, 10 August 1853; New South Wales, *VPLC*, vol. 1, no. 48 of 1853, 17 August 1853.

[34]*Empire*, 2 July 1853.

[35]*Empire*, 2 July 1853.

[36]*The Sydney Morning Herald*, 2 July 1853.

doubt as to the identity of the criminal'.[37] In an earlier debate on the bill, Plunkett also stated his opinion that public executions were still adhered to in England primarily because of an 'innate hatred of concealment in British law'.[38] That said, he agreed with Douglass that introducing private executions 'was a measure quite in accordance with the great progress daily making in civilisation and enlightenment'.[39] The Solicitor-General, William Manning, agreed that care must be taken in drawing up the bill as, in the new era of private executions, 'the great point was to prevent the possibility of foul play'.[40] James Martin, although not opposed on principle to the reform, thought that with hangings taking place in private it 'would be exceedingly difficult to satisfy the public mind'.[41] It was these types of concerns that demanded witness statements, medical certificates and other legal documentation to be included in the final wording of the Act. Despite initial apprehensions, to hide away the violent spectacle inside the prison yard was a measure generally applauded by the legislators of New South Wales.

An Amendment proposed by George Nichols also tried to exclude women and children from being able to view a private execution. Nicholas stated in a motion that executions had a 'demoralising and hardening influence' on all those who watched and that the Governor of the gaol ought to exclude by law women and children from being admitted to private executions.[42] For Douglass their attendance had been a problem in the public era: 'public execution of criminals was attended by a class of spectators whom they would least like to see present at such a spectacle—women and children—and they were always more impressed with pity for the criminal than with horror at the crime'.[43] That said, the

[37] *The Sydney Morning Herald*, 21 July 1853, p. 2.
[38] *Empire*, 2 July 1853.
[39] *The Sydney Morning Herald*, 2 July 1853, p. 4.
[40] *The Sydney Morning Herald*, 21 July 1853, p. 2.
[41] *The Sydney Morning Herald*, 21 July 1853, p. 2.
[42] For the full wording of this proposed amendment, see New South Wales, *VPLC*, vol. 1, no. 33 of 1853, 19 July 1853.
[43] *Empire*, 2 July 1853.

amendment was narrowly defeated 19 to 18 on the grounds that when a woman was executed it might be desirable to have female witnesses.[44]

The parliamentary debates that took place in the colonies to introduce private executions were also instructive and it was clear that they were looking very closely at Sydney. For instance, during the passage of the private execution legislation in New South Wales, *The Sydney Morning Herald*'s Melbourne correspondent was quick to offer his congratulations: 'Your legislature is right in deciding that executions should be private instead of public… It is very likely that some one of our new members will try his hand on a similar measure in our Council'.[45] As it would turn out, the transition to private executions in Victoria was initiated by the Lieutenant-Governor himself. On 26 September 1854 Lieutenant-Governor Charles Hotham sent a brief communication from the Government Offices directing the Legislative Council to consider a draft of 'A Bill to Regulate the Execution of Criminals'.[46] On the day following Hotham's communication William Stawell, the Attorney-General of Victoria, placed the bill under the consideration of the Legislative Council. To Stawell such scenes were an 'evil' that harmed both spectator and criminal:

> The ATTORNEY-GENERAL in moving the first reading of this bill, observed that much evil attended the present mode of executing criminals. It was injurious and demoralising both to the unfortunate culprit and to the spectators. The former had his thoughts distracted from the awful subject that ought to occupy them, by knowing that he was to die in the presence of a multitude, and the latter were too often attracted to witness the dying struggles of a fellow creature by mere morbid curiosity.[47]

Stawell then noted that executions should take place within the prison walls and listed the type of functionaries that should be compelled to

---

[44]Wintle, 1973, pp. 61–62.

[45]*The Sydney Morning Herald*, 3 August 1853, p. 2.

[46]Victoria, 'Execution of Criminals', *Victorian Parliamentary Papers*, B-no. 7 of 1854.

[47]*The Argus*, 28 September 1854, p. 4.

attend the event. According to *The Argus*, the first reading was met 'without either opposition or discussion' in the House.[48]

In the committee stage the parliamentarian John Myles suggested that some people known personally to the condemned ought to be allowed into private executions to 'sympathise with the criminal and pray for him'.[49] It was a considerate gesture but one that was eventually defeated by the other Members who thought that it was still possible to convey consolation without the need to be physically present at the death. Victoria was a colony where the feeling against capital punishment ran high and many MPs spoke freely about the possibility of abolishing the penalty altogether. However, the Colonial Secretary, John Leslie, stated that this was 'by no means a country in which the experiment of abolishing capital punishment could be tried' and the sole object of the measure before parliament was simply to 'prevent the publicity of… a "necessary evil"'.[50] The Attorney-General reiterated the Colonial Secretary's point, stating that the only question that the House needed to engage in was simply: 'Shall we dispense with the public exhibition of criminals in their very last struggles?'[51]

In July 1855, *A Bill to Regulate the Execution of Criminals* was introduced in the Parliament of Van Diemen's Land.[52] Van Diemen's Land felt itself a step behind the other colonies in initiating this reform. The Solicitor-General remarked that 'The bill had been found sufficient in New South Wales, and he thought it would be found sufficient here'.[53] Like in New South Wales, Members raised concerns over the appropriate safeguards which could prevent any possible corruption. The Colonial Secretary of Van Diemen's Land, William Champ, was someone well placed to judge such concerns being the former Commandant of Port

[48] *The Argus*, 28 September 1854, p. 4. The only opposition occurred at a later reading when the Speaker of the House, James Frederick Palmer, expressed his anxiety that Victoria was not the place to trial private executions because people were so excitable and if they were denied the spectacle of death they might 'flock to the gaol in such numbers as to take possession of the gaol'. For details, see *The Argus*, 3 November 1854, p. 4.

[49] *The Argus*, 3 November 1854, p. 4.

[50] *The Argus*, 19 October 1854, p. 4.

[51] *The Argus*, 26 October 1854, p. 4.

[52] *The Courier*, 19 July 1855.

[53] *The Courier*, 1 August 1855, pp. 2–3.

Arthur but soon erased them believing that 'There was a vast difference between a "private" execution and a "secret" one'.[54]

Three years passed before South Australia decided to adopt legislation mimicking the reforms of the colonies to the east.[55] On 21 September 1858 the Chief Secretary, William Younghusband, rose to give the first reading of the bill in the Legislative Council to abolish public executions. For the Chief Secretary public executions had a tendency to 'demoralise' those who attended, and he questioned the power of the gallows to deter saying that it 'had no beneficial result as an example'.[56] To strengthen his support for the bill, he was quick to tell the Parliament in the first reading that (with ignorance in respect to Western Australia's predicament) 'A similar law was in force in all the other Australian colonies'.[57] The Commissioner of Public Works, Arthur Blyth, raised a similar point saying that South Australia needed to become 'assimilated' with the other colonies who had already adopted private executions.[58] Public executions were maligned in Adelaide for encouraging misbehaviour on the part of the criminal while corrupting the innocent. William Townsend remarked that at public executions 'the man who was to die went up to the scaffold with courage he was a hero, his likeness was taken, and his form was embodied in waxwork for the public gaze'.[59] William Burford remarked how 'the love of notoriety and the pride of dying game would be done away with' which would finally lead criminals to receive punishment in the 'proper spirit'.[60] As for the crowd at public executions in South Australia, Arthur Blyth stated that, 'They were attended by a greater proportion of the female portion of the community than of the male, and even children and infants were taken to view them'.[61]

---

[54] *The Courier*, 1 August 1855, pp. 2–3.

[55] It should be noted that South Australia is the first colony where an official Hansard exists for the debate over private executions in the 1850s. Previous to that colonial newspapers had dutifully copied down the speeches of Members and reprinted them for public consumption in varying degrees of detail and length.

[56] *South Australian Parliamentary Debates* (hereafter *SAPD*), 21 September 1858, p. 173.

[57] *SAPD*, 21 September 1858, p. 173.

[58] *SAPD*, 7 October 1858, p. 331.

[59] *SAPD*, 7 October 1858, p. 331.

[60] *SAPD*, 7 October 1858, p. 332.

[61] *SAPD*, 7 October 1858, p. 331.

Interestingly, South Australia was the only Parliament to suggest that prisoners, like members of the general public, ought to be shielded from the spectacle of executions. If the prevailing logic was that the general public were 'demoralised' by the hanging of a criminal, it should follow that lawmakers would be keen to hide the spectacle from convicted criminals as well. Thus, the proposed solution of William Burford, a man well-known in Adelaide for his strong religious convictions and desire to abolish capital punishment, was to establish a separate gaol, 'specially set apart for the execution of criminals, in order not to run the risk of contaminating other prisoners'.[62] However, the Treasurer, Boyle Finniss, opposed the construction of a so-called 'public slaughterhouse' because it was not only costly but 'indecorous and improper to have a building of this kind'.[63] After some further cajoling over how news of private executions might be distributed, the legislation eventually passed the second and third reading with little trouble.[64] The only real opposition encountered in the colony was due to their attachment to hanging Indigenous offenders at the scene of the crime but that is better discussed elsewhere (see Chapter 7).

It was not until January 1871 that the Parliament of Western Australia passed a bill to abolish public executions. This was almost two decades after the New South Wales legislature had mooted the possible introduction of a new and more discreet mode of capital punishment in its parliamentary chambers. Unfortunately the primary documents surrounding the passage of the private execution legislation are reserved in providing an explanation for the delay. After being read a first time at the Western Australian Legislative Council on 7 December 1870, the second reading took place on 19 December 1870. But instead of a lengthy discussion

---

[62] *SAPD*, 7 October 1858, p. 333. William Burford was a fervent opponent of capital punishment which I have written about in another context, see Steven Anderson, 'Twentieth Century Dreams, Ninetieth Century Realties: Reframing the Abolition of Capital Punishment in South Australia', in C. Collins and P. Sendziuk (eds), *Foundational Fictions in South Australian History*, Adelaide: Wakefield Press, 2018, pp. 165–176.

[63] *SAPD*, 7 October 1858, p. 333.

[64] William Townsend suggested an amendment compelling at least two South Australian newspapers to publish news of a private hanging. It was dismissed on the grounds that an execution would be newsworthy enough for newspapers to write about, without having to be compelled to do so by law. For details, see *SAPD*, 7 October 1858, pp. 333–334.

on the bill that usually takes place upon the second reading (as was the case in the other Australian colonies), Hansard simply states: 'The bill was read a second time, and passed through Committee, without discussion'.[65] *The Perth Gazette and Western Australian Times*' version reads almost identically but adds that it was 'passed without amendment'.[66] As for the third reading of the bill, it took place on 28 December 1870 and was assented to five days later on 2 January 1871.[67] The complete lack of newspaper comment surrounding the Act suggests support for the measure rather than division. As evidence for such a view, there were some calls in the newspapers before 1871 urging the authorities to abolish public executions and align themselves with the example found in the other colonies.[68]

The Reaction of the Colonial Newspapers

The response of the colonial newspapers to the Private Execution Acts as they were under the consideration of the colonial parliaments was overwhelmingly supportive. To the newspapers, capital punishment as a whole was acceptable to the majority but the 'barbarous' manner in which it was being carried out needed fundamental reform. To start with New South Wales, its newspapers had a lot to comment on as the Bill passed through the legislature. *The Sydney Morning Herald* offered its cautious support, stating that the current mode of execution was beyond repair. As a whole, public executions needlessly excited 'morbid passions' and often struck the tone of 'cold-blooded revenge', rather than that of a solemn punishment.[69] The newspaper came down exceptionally hard on the 'criminal rabble' who insisted on attending with an attitude not appropriate to the occasion: 'Brutalising, public executions certainly are;

[65] *Western Australian Parliamentary Debates*, 19 December 1870, p. 54.

[66] *The Perth Gazette and Western Australian Times*, 28 December 1870, p. 4.

[67] *The Inquirer and Commercial News*, 4 January 1871, p. 3; Western Australia, no. 15 of 1871, *An Act to Provide for Carrying Out of Capital Punishment Within Prisons*.

[68] See, for example, *The Perth Gazette and Western Australian Times*, 15 October 1869; *The Inquirer and Commercial News*, 17 July 1867.

[69] *The Sydney Morning Herald*, 12 July 1853, p. 2.

and, in as far as example is concerned, it may be doubted whether the terror they are intended to inflict is equal in force to the disgust or the pity they generate'.[70] For *The Sydney Morning Herald*, the death penalty was still very much necessary to deter crime but the current mode of execution was simply not hitting the right notes.[71] The newspaper also cautioned against the growing secrecy of the punishment ensuring that it must still 'meet the just and stern requirements of public justice'.[72] In its public comment, the newspaper was at pains to protect the transparency of the punishment in this new era of private executions.

The *Freeman's Journal*, another Sydney publication supporting the bill before Parliament, was surprised that no one in the colony had thought of this reform earlier: 'It appears somewhat strange in an age of such maudlin sentimentalism and spurious humanity as the present, that no philanthropist or statesman has taken up the question before now'.[73] It also thought the crowd who came to watch was a blight on the age: 'We do sincerely hope that public executions will be abolished, and the shameful spectacle taken away, of women and children, prentice boys and older fools running with all speed from their respective occupations to witness the last convulsive movements of a fellow mortal, as if it were a matter of public rejoicing or some exhilarating scene of innocent amusement'.[74] There was concern from *The Sydney Morning Herald* over the transparency of private executions and the capacity for corruption but the *Freeman's Journal* was unfazed by the possibility. With characteristic acerbity it advised its rival publication to 'discard all such old womanish apprehensions' and 'frightful nursery maids' tales'.[75]

Regional newspapers appeared to be in agreement with those of the city on the issue of public executions. *The Maitland Mercury*, for example, thought it was time that women and children were shielded

[70] *The Sydney Morning Herald*, 12 July 1853, p. 2.

[71] *The Sydney Morning Herald* was very much in favour of retaining capital punishment. It was even called the 'gibbet-loving *Herald*' by a rival publication only a few years earlier, see *Bell's Life in Sydney and Sporting Reviewer*, 23 September 1848.

[72] *The Sydney Morning Herald*, 12 July 1853, p. 2.

[73] *Freeman's Journal*, 23 July 1853, pp. 7–8.

[74] *Freeman's Journal*, 23 July 1853, pp. 7–8.

[75] *Freeman's Journal*, 23 July 1853, pp. 7–8.

from proceedings and saw very little 'beneficial purpose' that public executions could serve.[76] The *Bathurst Free Press and Mining Journal* was very much disgusted at the spectacle and those who attended saying that, 'A raree show, a horse race, bull bait, or man fight will not excite half the curiosity in the vulgar and unfeeling which is stirred up by the spectacle of a dying wretch struggling out his last breath at the rope's end'.[77] As for moving before England in this reform, the paper offered some words of encouragement to any nervous MPs:

> Whilst but too happy to borrow all that is excellent or praiseworthy in the institutions of the mother country, we protest against the folly of copying her errors. And it will be highly credible to the enlightenment and public feeling of New South Wales, if the first step be taken by her legislature towards the reform of an abomination which has long been a scandal to civilisation.[78]

Moving from New South Wales to the other colonies and their newspapers, the proposal caused a large discussion. Upon hearing the news of the Victorian Parliament's success in gaining Royal approval for the introduction of private executions, *The Argus* of Melbourne published a strongly worded piece entitled 'The Private Gallows'. It offered unconditional support for the reform as well as outlining the benefits privacy might bring to the overall decorum of the spectacle. First of all, the 'crowds of scum' who ritually assembled at the base of the scaffold would henceforth be a relic of Victoria's barbarous past.[79] Thankfully, in the absence of a crowd, it thought the criminal would feel no obligation to act like a hero or a martyr as had been the case in the era of public hangings:

> The heroism of the gallows will be destroyed; and the convict, instead of being elevated by the sympathy of the spectators to the dignity of the martyr, or by his own morbid self-esteem to that defiant position which

---

[76] *The Maitland Mercury and Hunter River General Advertiser*, 30 July 1853, p. 2.

[77] *Bathurst Free Press and Mining Journal*, 9 July 1853, p. 2.

[78] *Bathurst Free Press and Mining Journal*, 9 July 1853, p. 2.

[79] *The Argus*, 19 October 1855, p. 4.

> has been supposed to be attained by those who 'die game,' will part from the world under the eye of the few authorised to witness his departure better fitted to meet that Presence into which he is to be so suddenly thrust.[80]

The Argus labelled public executions 'horrid', 'degrading' and 'demoralising' while looking forward to a future where capital punishment was stripped of its festive tone.[81] Given the subdued nature of the private gallows, the newspaper hoped that 'depravity will no longer have excuse for holding holiday on occasions when the circumstances ought to suggest fasting and humiliation rather than a festival'.[82] The article was also careful to put the Act on a grander plane, seeing it as evidence of enlightened progress occurring in the colony of Victoria and one step before the abolition of capital punishment as a whole: 'We are now about to put in practice a law which, though a startling innovation upon English precedent, may fairly be considered a sign and proof of an advancing civilisation, destined, we trust, in time, wholly to supersede death punishments'.[83]

The newspapers of Van Diemen's Land were similarly supportive of the push towards private executions. An impatient *Hobarton Mercury* thought that the reform was overdue:

> It is quite time that the disgusting exhibitions, which have so long pampered the morbid curiosity of the ignorant and the vicious, should come to an end... Every essayist now-a-days has something to say on such subjects, until we are wearied to death of the theme, and our only wonder is how people have tolerated public executions so long. They ought to have gone out with bear-baiting, thirty years ago.[84]

The *Colonial Times* viewed the disappearance of public death from Hobart's streets as much needed: 'Nothing can be more opposed to the

---

[80] *The Argus*, 19 October 1855, p. 4.
[81] *The Argus*, 19 October 1855, p. 4.
[82] *The Argus*, 19 October 1855, p. 4.
[83] *The Argus*, 19 October 1855, p. 4.
[84] *The Hobarton Mercury*, 25 July 1855, p. 2.

philosophy of punitive discipline; or so injurious, in the main, to the interests of society'.[85] *The Courier* also praised the move stating that it was, 'in consonance with that spirit of improvement of the law which has so creditably distinguished England of late years'.[86] As news of the legislation travelled north to Launceston, *The Cornwall Chronicle* was similarly relieved by the thought of a calm, contemplative criminal on the drop: 'instead of being diverted from the solemnity of their eternal preparation by the presence of ancient comrades of their own stamp, who come to see whether they die craven, or game... will find in the presence of a few staid men, only an additional incentive... to a reverential, penitent, and submissive demeanour'.[87]

The South Australian press rejoiced at the prospect of introducing private executions into the colony. The *South Australian Register* was quick to offer its best wishes for the success of the bill thinking it conducive to cultivating an improvement in 'public morals'.[88] For the newspaper, public executions were linked to the old tyrannical regimes of Europe, not the quickly civilising colony on Australia's southern shores:

> The advancement of society in Europe generally has tended to eradicate the odious practices which subjected the criminal to torture as a precedent of death. We believe that breaking on the wheel, the rack, and other medieval inventions for prolonging the sufferings of those doomed to death are now banished from those States which belong to the great European family; if they linger at all, it is among those nations who yet groan under the worst tyrannies. In our native land these practices never took root, and disappeared with the light and freedom which accompanied the Reformation.[89]

An added bonus for the *Register* was that volatile interactions between crowd and criminal could be tempered: 'There will be no inducement to cultivate a spirit of bravado – no encouragement to "die game;" there

---

[85] *Colonial Times*, 24 July 1855, p. 2.

[86] *The Courier*, 3 August 1855, p. 2.

[87] *The Cornwall Chronicle*, 28 July 1855, p. 4.

[88] *South Australian Register*, 2 October 1858, p. 2.

[89] *South Australian Register*, 2 October 1858, p. 2.

will be the consciousness that those who witness the scene, are either the cold, official functionaries of the law, or those whose emotions vibrate between abhorrence of the criminal and pity for the man'.[90]

Unusually, *The South Australian Advertiser* took a similar stance to its counterpart in both tone and content. It believed that the 'virtuous recoil with disgust' at public hangings whereas only the 'profligate and abandoned attend an execution as they would a race, a fair, or a play'.[91] In the *Advertiser*'s opinion public hangings were:

> [A] rallying point for the outcasts of society … a fruitful harvest-field for pickpockets, ruffians, and harlots; it is a region of fearful moral contagion to the idle and the curious, who follow apathetically in the course of the stream, or are led by morbid inquisitiveness to see a man die; it is, in fact, precisely the place where the better qualities of human nature run great risk of defilement, and where vice discovers the most fruitful and congenial field of action.[92]

Furthermore, it also believed that the imagery of violent death emanating from the scaffold was one that created more criminals than it deterred. The newspaper thought that public hangings were a 'seed-time' from which many 'crime-harvests' would soon follow.[93] It continued: 'The lesson which the hangman teaches is not of an ameliorating, not of a refining, not of a reformatory, not even of a terrifying character'.[94] Instead, the paper viewed the public scaffold as 'purely a lesson in crime, a lesson in demoralisation, a lesson in the downward series, terminating in the abysses of shame, crime, and ruin'.[95] Like the *Register* though, it too saw this legislation as proof of the advancing civilisation of the age: 'We think that the friends of humanity will rejoice in this triumph of

---

[90] *South Australian Register*, 2 October 1858, p. 2.
[91] *The South Australian Advertiser*, 8 October 1858, p. 2.
[92] *The South Australian Advertiser*, 8 October 1858, p. 2.
[93] *The South Australian Advertiser*, 8 October 1858, p. 2.
[94] *The South Australian Advertiser*, 8 October 1858, p. 2.
[95] *The South Australian Advertiser*, 8 October 1858, p. 2.

reason and civilisation over the degrading relics of a barbarous age'.[96] *The Advertiser* continued that public hangings are 'one of the last lingering vestiges of a barbarous *regime*, and, thank God, it is about to disappear'.[97] Clearly, there was a build up of perceived problems that colonial parliaments and the press identified in the 1850s that could be solved with the introduction of private executions. However, it is now time to return to a discussion of the specific trigger for this penal reform which, as it turns out, was deeply rooted in the popular memory of colonists.

The Legacy of Convictism and the Timing of the Transition

The proclamation of the Private Execution Acts through Australian Colonial Parliaments beginning in 1855 was early in the context of the British Empire. It anticipated the United Kingdom itself while comparable settler colonies like New Zealand, Canada and the Cape of Good Hope were similarly delayed. New Zealand was the first to follow the example of New South Wales by abolishing public executions in 1858.[98] Lawmakers were convinced of the 'demoralising tendency' of public executions and were prompted to act on the issue by a Memorial from the Auckland Provincial Council suggesting that reform was needed.[99] Canada and the Cape of Good Hope waited until 1869 to abolish public executions, both within a year of Britain passing the reform in 1868.[100] In the Canadian Parliament a bill advocating private executions was first suggested by an MP named Alexander Morris as early as December 1867 but it took until 1869 for it to be included in a much larger

[96] *The South Australian Advertiser*, 8 October 1858, p. 2.

[97] *The South Australian Advertiser*, 8 October 1858, p. 2, emphasis original.

[98] New Zealand, no. 10 of 1858, *Act to Regulate the Execution of Criminals*.

[99] *Hawke's Bay Herald*, 5 June 1858, p. 6.

[100] Canada, Chapter 29 of 1869, *An Act Respecting Procedure in Criminal Cases, and Other Matters Relating to Criminal Law*, sections 106–124; Cape of Good Hope, no. 3 of 1869, *For Regulating the Execution of Capital Punishment*.

Act pertaining to procedure in criminal cases.[101] The central motivation for Morris appeared to be that Britain and some substantial jurisdictions in Europe and America had already introduced private executions, though the Australian colonies were not mentioned among his examples.[102] Uncovering the motivations of lawmakers in the Cape of Good Hope becomes difficult upon learning how scarce official records are for the 1869 parliamentary debates owing to an economic depression.[103]

Whatever the individual justification of each far-flung parliament, the fact that the Australian colonies were the pacesetter in the British Empire regarding private executions requires further investigation. A cursory knowledge of colonial history is enough to know that the key difference between the Australian colonies and the other substantial British settlements is their long association with convicts. Indeed, Australia's convict past explains why Henry Grattan Douglass originally felt the need to prove to the world that New South Wales was fast becoming civilised through the introduction of private executions. The comparatively early introduction of private executions in the Australian colonies ought to be understood by reference to this broader narrative. Moreover, private executions were an affirmation of a 'civilised' sense of self, a reminder of their worldly advancement against the backdrop of a penal past and the challenges of frontier society.[104]

Australia Imagined (2005) is a primary source compendium examining how the British periodical press constructed Australia during the colonial era and provides written evidence for the colonies' image problem abroad. In the introductory essay Judith Johnston and Monica Anderson acknowledge that before the discovery of gold, the 'general

---

[101] *Canadian Parliamentary Debates*, House of Commons, 13 December 1867, p. 271; *Canadian Parliamentary Debates*, House of Commons, vol. 2, 28 April 1869, p. 95.

[102] *Canadian Parliamentary Debates*, House of Commons, vol. 2, 28 April 1869, p. 95.

[103] Peter Ralph Coates, 'Cape Colonial Parliamentary Publications, 1854–1910, with Special Reference to Documents in the Dutch language', unpublished Information Science M.A. Thesis, University of South Africa, 2009, p. 93.

[104] A similar idea to this—that private executions were a performative affirmation of civilised identity—is pursued by Jürgen Martschukat in the context of Hamburg, Germany, a jurisdiction that introduced private executions in 1854. For his perceptive essay, see Jürgen Martschukat, 'Nineteenth-Century Executions as Performances of Law, Death, and Civilization', in Austin Sarat and Christian Boulanger (eds), *The Cultural Lives of Capital Punishment: Comparative Perspectives*, Stanford: Stanford University Press, 2005, pp. 49–68.

tone' of the British press towards Australia was 'one of disparagement, due solely to the transportation of convicts'.[105] It is hard to disagree with such an assessment upon further examination of the printed extracts they provide. Sydney Smith's work published in the *Edinburgh Review* of 1819 viewed New South Wales as a 'sink of wickedness' and a place where convicts go to 'become infinitely more depraved'.[106] Smith then compared New South Wales to a sunken marsh that 'may be drained and cultivated' but, in the meantime, 'no man who has his choice, would select it … for his dwelling-place'.[107] In a separate extract from 1849 written by William Smith O'Brian, a prominent Irish nationalist turned transportee himself, Britain is squarely blamed for creating in Australia a 'school of sin', 'nurseries of depravity' and a collection of colonies 'drowned with the flood of her own wickedness'.[108] Another example comes from the London publication *Leisure Hour* which conducted a five part overview of the Australian colonies in 1852. Despite being generally hopeful for their future, it began by remarking how: 'Persons of mature age can well remember the time when Australia, the "great south land", was invested with no pleasing associations, and would have been regarded as the last spot on the surface of the globe to be voluntarily selected as a home'.[109]

Insecurities over the standing of the Australian colonies in the civilised world were perceptible on the continent itself. As the authors of *Australia Imagined* rightly point out, the disparaging views of the British press were being 'overheard' by the colonists themselves, since many of these periodicals were circulated, purchased and read in Australia very soon after publication.[110] Commenting on Australia's lack of renown abroad,

---

[105] Judith Johnston and Monica Anderson, *Australia Imagined: Views from the British Periodical Press: 1800–1900*, Perth: University of Western Australia Press, 2005, p. 3.

[106] Sydney Smith, 'Botany Bay', *Edinburgh Review*, vol. 32, 1819, pp. 28–48, as reprinted in Johnston and Anderson, 2005, p. 36.

[107] Smith quoted in, Johnston and Anderson, 2005, p. 37.

[108] William Smith O'Brian, 'Transportation as It Now Is', *Edinburgh Review*, vol. 90, 1849, pp. 1–39 as reprinted in Johnston and Anderson, 2005, p. 28.

[109] 'Australia I—Its General Features and Resources', *Leisure Hour*, vol. 1, 1852, pp. 497–501 as reprinted in Johnston and Anderson, 2005, pp. 43–44.

[110] Johnston and Anderson, 2005, p. 2.

The Courier of Hobart printed an article in 1851 entitled 'The Reputation of the Colony'.[111] It regretted how the British public would never consider 'penal colonies as fields of national glory' and thought that the reputation of both New South Wales and Van Diemen's Land had been 'very much injured by the uses to which they have devoted them'.[112] It continued by stating that: 'Every judge, in pronouncing the sentence of the law, makes a point to allude to this country in no very flattering terms'.[113] When the London correspondent for *Bell's Life in Sydney and Sporting Reviewer* in 1849 said to, 'Thank your kind stars that you are living far away from civilised life', the newspaper did not take kindly to the intended compliment. Such an accusation was labelled a 'slur' as the newspaper asked 'Why should it be that this vast country be marked out by them as a blot upon the map of the world, and its sons held up as but one degree removed from the dusky savages whom civilisation has displaced?'[114] A senior figure in the early Australian Catholic Church, William Ullathorne (see Chapter 4), was another keenly aware of Australia's reputation abroad. If the standing of the colonies was not quickly remedied, he thought that the 'nation of crime' would soon become 'a by-word to all the peoples of the earth'.[115]

With a need to transform the image of Australia abroad, and with the insecurities perceptible among the colonists themselves, a natural correlation emerges between the introduction of private executions and the legacy of convictism. For the three colonies that proclaimed an end to public executions in 1855—New South Wales, Victoria and Van Diemen's Land—all had recent experiences with convicts to varying degrees. New South Wales ceased transportation in 1840 (ignoring a brief resumption in 1848), Van Diemen's Land accomplished the same in 1853 whereas the experience with convicts in the Port Phillip District

[111] *The Courier*, 22 February 1851, p. 2.
[112] *The Courier*, 22 February 1851, p. 2.
[113] *The Courier*, 22 February 1851, p. 2.
[114] *Bell's Life in Sydney and Sporting Reviewer*, 18 August 1849.
[115] William Ullathorne quoted in James Boyce, *Van Diemen's Land*, Melbourne: Black Inc., 2008, pp. 236–237.

(later Victoria) was miniscule by comparison and over by 1849.[116] Between 1850 and 1868 Western Australia accepted almost 10,000 British convicts before it too abolished public executions only three years later in 1871.[117] South Australia was unique in that the adoption of Edward Gibbon Wakefield's plan for 'Systematic Colonisation' circumvented the need for convict labour, although the convict-free status of the colony (and its gallows) has recently been challenged in the historiography by Paul Sendziuk and me.[118]

Executions were not the only physical punishment profoundly affected by the memory of the convict era. In comparison with other British settler societies and the United Kingdom itself, Australia was comparatively reluctant to use the whip after the 1850s. For example, the two oldest penal colonies in Tasmania and New South Wales had all but finished with the punishment by 1900.[119] Mark Finnane in *Punishment in Australian Society* (1997) briefly explores the connection between this relatively early demise in usage by reference to the convict past:

> To what extent was the memory of the convict era a factor in the demise of flogging after the 1850s? To argue that it was a significant factor would be consistent with what we know of the larger history of changes in modern Western penality. In the last resort, those changes have to be explained not in terms of changing economic modes or the preferences of the judiciary, but in terms of an altered cultural connotation attached

[116]Of the approximately 160,000 convicts that were shipped to the Australian continent between 1788 and 1868 the vast majority were sent to New South Wales and Van Diemen's Land for punishment, Victoria only accepted around 1750 'Pentonvillians' between 1843 and 1849 from Van Diemen's Land, see Marian Quartly, 'Convicts', in G. Davison, J. Hirst, and S. Macintyre (eds), *The Oxford Companion to Australian History*, revised edition, Melbourne: Oxford University Press, 2001, pp. 156–157; Helen Doyle, 'Pentonvillians', in Davison, Hirst, and Macintyre, 2001, p. 504.

[117]Quartly, 'Convicts', in Davison, Hirst, and Macintyre, 2001, pp. 156–157.

[118]Steven Anderson and Paul Sendziuk, 'Hang the Convicts: Capital Punishment and the Reaffirmation of South Australia's Foundation Principles', *Journal of Australian Colonial History*, vol. 16, 2014, pp. 83–111; Paul Sendziuk, 'No Convicts Here: Reconsidering South Australia's Foundation Myth', in R. Foster and P. Sendziuk (eds), *Turning Points: Chapters in South Australian History*, Adelaide: Wakefield Press, 2012, pp. 33–47.

[119]Mark Finnane, *Punishment in Australian Society*, Melbourne: Oxford University Press, 1997, pp. 124–125.

> to punishments of the body … The relatively early demise of whipping in Australia may demonstrate a particular cultural context's peculiar power to change decisively the possibilities of punishment.[120]

For Finnane, it was not simply the mere fact of convictism that provoked the decline of whipping in Australia, but also the way the period was remembered and sustained by Marcus Clarke's widely read book *For the Term of His Natural Life* (1874).[121] The image of the 'lash' was used by Clarke in his fiction to highlight the 'brutality and brutalising effects of the convict system'.[122] The book was not just a 'reflection of opinion' but it became an 'agent of political and cultural formation' during the late nineteenth century.[123] Whether it was an execution or a whipping, the use of bodily punishments in the colonies were clearly influenced by the cultural legacy of the convict era.[124]

The timing of the Private Execution Acts in Australia is a reminder that punishment is intimately connected to the society it resides within. David Garland wrote that 'designing penal policy' is an exercise in 'defining ourselves and our society in ways which may be quite central to our cultural and political identity'.[125] If Australian colonists like Henry Grattan Douglass were insecure in their civilised standing in the world because of a penal past, the introduction of private executions went some way to assuaging that concern. It was, to repeat his words one last time, an opportunity to 'show the whole world the progress which had been made in civilisation'.[126]

---

[120] Finnane, 1997, p. 125.

[121] Marcus Clarke, *For the Term of His Natural Life* [1870–1872], Adelaide: Rigby Limited, 1977.

[122] Finnane, 1997, p. 109.

[123] Finnane, 1997, pp. 109–110.

[124] In an interesting aside Finnane notes that, in contrast to the other Australian jurisdictions, the two largely convict free colonies of Victoria and South Australia still had whipping as a sentencing option well into the mid-twentieth century. See Finnane, 1997, p. 125.

[125] David Garland, *Punishment and Modern Society: A Study in Social Theory*, Oxford: Clarendon Press, 1990, p. 276.

[126] *The Sydney Morning Herald*, 2 July 1853, p. 4.

* * *

Between the years following the successful passage of the Private Execution Acts through the Australian colonies and Britain passing a similar law, there was more than enough time for self-congratulation. In an article entitled 'The Model Colony' there were three things that *The Argus* thought Britain could learn from Victoria: the secret ballot, the extension of male voting rights and, not least of all, the practice of private executions. To repeat its chosen metaphor: 'While she stands shivering on the bank we have plunged boldly into the stream'.[127] It was through the success of these three measures that colonists had given 'substance, progress, and character to the land of our adoption' and hoped that it would be possible to 'suggest new strides upon the path of freedom to countries older, larger, and infinitely more powerful than our own'.[128] When reporting on one of Hobart's first private executions in 1856, *The Courier* thought it should 'rejoice' that the colony was 'in advance of the mother-country'.[129] In 1867 a Western Australian newspaper, lamenting that its own colony was still yet to adopt the practice, was philosophical in supporting the foresight of its colonial neighbours in moving before Britain on private executions:

> In the Mother Country the old system is doomed ... Australia can take credit for having already, in practice, solved questions, that for generations had formed subjects of discussion among the thinkers and writers in England, and which have been the battle-ground of many debates in the British Parliament. And not among the least of the questions in which the sister colonies have anticipated reforms in the old country, are these public executions.[130]

These types of sentiments, combined with Henry Grattan Douglass' initial motivation for introducing the first Private Execution Act in New South Wales, demonstrate that this was something more than just

---

[127] *The Argus*, 1 July 1856, p. 4.

[128] *The Argus*, 1 July 1856, p. 4.

[129] *The Courier*, 17 April 1856, p. 2.

[130] *The Inquirer and Commercial News*, 17 July 1867.

another penal reform. To first recognise and then abolish something as stereotypically 'barbarous' and 'savage' as public executions before the 'Mother Parliament' was significant given the foundation history of New South Wales and Van Diemen's Land in particular. There appears a deep, underlying desire to publicise to Britain that the Australian colonies were civilised and refined, so much so that their actions should be an example for others to copy. The need to transform the image of the Australian colonies from a collection of penal societies to a collection of civil societies was a unique situation that was not present in Britain or any of its other substantial possessions. Their early adoption affirmed a nervous colonist's 'civilised' sense of self in light of a colonial culture that was often fearful of a scornful imperial gaze.

7

Race and the Reprisal of Public Hangings

Like the other colonial legislatures to the east, South Australia and Western Australia abolished public executions in 1858 and 1871 respectively—the westernmost colony being the later of the two. However, only a few years after their abolition, both colonies reprised the practice of public executions but only for Indigenous offenders. For European criminals, the basic tenet of a private execution within the walls of the prison held true for as long as capital punishment remained on the statute books. In complete contrast are the colonies of New South Wales, Victoria and Tasmania which never contemplated the formal reintroduction of public executions once they were abolished. Queensland sits somewhere in the middle since it occasionally allowed for a controlled number of spectators at the execution of non-Europeans but only if they were of the same ethnicity as the criminal. The early settlers of South Australia and Western Australia valued Indigenous executions for the role they played on the frontier. The 'terror' of a public execution, preferably enacted at the scene of the crime, was perceived to pacify

S. Anderson, *A History of Capital Punishment in the Australian Colonies, 1788 to 1900*,
Palgrave Histories of Policing, Punishment and Justice,
https://doi.org/10.1007/978-3-030-53767-8_7

Indigenous resistance to colonisation.[1] In the vast untamed frontiers of these two colonies, public executions broadcasted a decipherable symbol of settler law and power to an Indigenous audience who did not share the colonisers' culture or language. Their perceived efficacy was based on a disparaging cultural construction of Indigenous intellect, habit and temperament. While privacy was prized after the mid-nineteenth century for European offenders, the opposite held true for Indigenous ones. Only from a public execution, so the thought went, could Indigenous Australians on the frontier fully digest the example capital punishment had to offer.

The 'Value' of Indigenous Executions to South Australia and Western Australia

In the formative years of South Australian settlement it was very clear what purpose Indigenous executions were to perform in the colony. In 1840 twenty-six Europeans were killed in the Coorong after their brig, the *Maria*, ran aground in the area. The survivors had fallen foul of the local Milmenrura clan, a group of the Ngarrindjeri people, who were engaged by the Europeans to guide them back to Adelaide.[2] The 'Maria Massacre', as it became known, was the single largest murder of Europeans by Indigenous people in Australian colonial history.[3] The South Australian Police Commissioner, Major Thomas O'Halloran, was dispatched by the Governor to 'apprehend, and bring to summary justice, the ringleaders in the murder, or any of the murderers (in all not to exceed three)'.[4] The speech he gave at the subsequent double hanging at the scene of the massacre articulates the rationale of Indigenous executions in the colony thereafter:

[1]Steven Anderson, 'Punishment as Pacification: The Role of Indigenous Executions on the South Australian Frontier, 1836–1862', *Aboriginal History*, vol. 39, 2015, pp. 3–26.

[2]Robert Foster, Rick Hosking, and Amanda Nettelbeck, *Fatal Collisions: The South Australian Frontier and the Violence of Memory*, Adelaide: Wakefield Press, 2001, p. 13.

[3]Foster et al., 2001, p. 13.

[4]*The South Australian Register*, 19 September 1840, p. 4.

> Black men, this is the white's punishment for murder, the next time white men are killed in this country more punishment will be given. Let none of you take these bodies down, they must hang till they fall in pieces. We are now friends, and will remain so, unless more white people are killed, when the Governor will send me, and plenty more policemen, and punish much more severely. All are forgiven except those who actually killed the wrecked people, who, if caught, will also be hung. You may go now, but remember this day, and tell what you have seen to your old men, women, and children.[5]

From the earliest days of the colony, it was clear that the role of frontier hangings was to pacify the Indigenous threat to the colonial project. It was a need most pressing for settlers residing on the Eyre Peninsula. The resistance offered in the region by local Indigenous peoples was at its highpoint in the early 1840s—for instance, the population of the major settlement of Port Lincoln fell from 270 in 1840 to 128 in February 1842. The remaining settlers even began to flirt with the idea of abandoning the township altogether in the worst days of 1842.[6] To combat the violence, the *Southern Australian* demanded that the response at Port Lincoln echo the one taken by O'Halloran at the Coorong in 1840. That is, an execution at the site of the crime where the Indigenous offender's people were gathered to watch. Moreover, the newspaper thought that, since the perpetrators were difficult to locate, perhaps any member of the 'tribe' could serve as the hangman's example in such turbulent times:

> [There] are few acquainted with Encounter Bay who would know the good effect which this proper example had. Would not the same judicious step do good at Port Lincoln, on any of a tribe who were known to be at a murder, instead of waiting till the identical one is taken who threw the

---

[5]Thomas O'Halloran as quoted in Alexander Tolmer, *Reminiscences of an Adventurous and Chequered Career at Home and at the Antipodes, Volume 1* [1882], facsimile edition, London: Gilbert and Rivington Ltd., 1972, p. 190.

[6]Neville Wanklyn and Margaret Wanklyn, *The Early History of the City of Port Lincoln 1802–1971*, Port Lincoln: The Corporation of Port Lincoln, 1971, p. 7.

fatal spear, of which there is as much chance of catching the crow which stole the seed of wheat?[7]

As the colonisation of South Australia's west coast persisted, hangings were a frequent fixture. In fact, 13 of the 23 Indigenous Australians to be executed in the history of South Australia were for crimes committed on the Eyre Peninsula.[8] These executions were instrumental in calming settler anxieties about the 'outrages' being perpetrated on settler bodies and property. One story emerged after the execution of Kulgulta and Mingulta in 1849 which would have assured many colonists on the Eyre. After 'some exertion' by the police to round up an audience of 'natives' to watch the scene, only the attendance of one Indigenous boy was secured. Still, word of the scene spread quickly:

> The boy went away and was next heard of at Mr Dunkin's station, about five miles to the west of Taunto [the place of execution], where by that time a number of natives had assembled. To them he went through in pantomime the whole scene of death, erecting a mimic gallows and imitating even the last struggles of the murderers. It is the opinion of the settlers of the district, many more of whom would have been present but that they were in the midst of the shearing, that the example will have a beneficial effect.[9]

The support for the public execution of Indigenous offenders at the scene of the crime was long lasting. It was heard again at the colony's last ever Indigenous hangings in 1861 and 1862 on the west coast of the Eyre Peninsula. For *The South Australian Register*, it was the 'expressed belief' of those living near the troubled district that, 'the effect of these executions will be good, and that no other means would have been so effectual in preventing the reoccurrence of such outrages'.[10]

[7] *The Southern Australian*, 29 March 1842 quoted in Robert Clyne, *Colonial Blue: A History of the South Australian Police Force*, Adelaide: Wakefield Press, 1987, pp. 75–76.

[8] Alan Pope, *One Law for All? Aboriginal People and the Criminal Law in Early South Australia*, Canberra: Aboriginal Studies Press, 2011, pp. 175–178.

[9] *The Southern Australian*, 16 November 1849, p. 2.

[10] *The South Australian Register*, 19 September 1861, p. 2.

Western Australians were also convinced that the heightened publicity of an Indigenous execution had benefits for settler safety. One newspaper correspondent who claimed to be 'well acquainted with the habits of the aborigines', praised the efficacy of the gallows:

> I conscientiously believe … that for every life that is taken by sentence of the law, a dozen is preserved by the terror instilled by the execution of such sentence. When Kanyan was hung [for the murder of another Indigenous man in 1850], I know, from personal experience, that thereby four murders were prevented in the districts of Northam and Toodyay. In the settled districts I believe murder to be nearly at an end, in consequence of the late executions; I mean among aborigines inhabiting the settled districts. Among the bushmen it still exists, and naturally will continue, until the terror of the law shall reach them.[11]

The *Perth Gazette* agreed with the *Inquirer*'s correspondent on this subject. The following year it wrote that capital punishment had an 'awe-inspiring effect'.[12] Through the lesson of the gallows, 'the aborigines are beginning to feel that life is worth clinging to, and that they will be less given to their death dealing propensities, at least where the influence of our laws is known and experienced'.[13] In 1862 it was said that the example of executions would have, 'such an effect upon the natives as will in future deter them from again committing acts of hostility upon the settlers'.[14] Reporting on another Indigenous hanging in 1865 the *Perth Gazette* stated its opinion that: 'we are, in reality, dealing with people who are but children in reasoning power, moved and swayed by a savage impulse as entirely now as on the day when they first came into contact with the white man thirty-six years ago'.[15]

Western Australia occasionally displayed Indigenous bodies on the frontier after an execution to enhance the deterrent effect. At the colony's first legal execution in July 1840, Doodjep and Bunaboy (sometimes

---

[11] *Inquirer*, 16 April 1851, p. 2.

[12] *The Perth Gazette and Independent Journal of Politics and News*, 11 April 1851.

[13] *The Perth Gazette and Independent Journal of Politics and News*, 11 April 1851.

[14] *The Inquirer and Commercial News*, 17 January 1866, p. 2.

[15] *The Perth Gazette and West Australian Times*, 21 July 1865, pp. 2–3.

written as Barrabong) were hanged at York for the murder of a mother and child.[16] As a lasting warning the bodies were left hanging long afterwards for the local Indigenous population to contemplate the consequences of crime. That said, a disturbing letter to the Editor of the *Inquirer* appeared two months later detailing the mutilation of the deceased bodies by local Europeans:

> The ears of one of these unhappy natives have been cut off, and are now preserved in the house of a small farmer in the district. Others have gone out, *and fired at the bodies* – stretching out their legs by the insertion of sticks between them, and committing other disgusting acts of brutality…[17]

At the aforementioned execution of Kanyan in 1850 the authorities transported his dead body to St. Aubyn's where it was 'hung in chains'.[18] The gibbetting of an Indigenous criminal happened on at least one other occasion. When Yandal and Goologol were hanged in Perth for two separate murders in 1855 their bodies were then transported to York. Displayed in a 'conspicuous part of the district', it was hoped that the example might quell recent Indigenous-settler violence.[19] In the aftermath of South Australia's 'Maria Massacre' the two dead bodies remained displayed indefinitely on the sands of the Coorong where they were hanged but that was the only time such a practice took place in the colony.[20] The gibbetting of Indigenous criminals in Western Australia occurred long after New South Wales and Tasmania had abolished the practice of 'hanging in chains' by 1837 (see Chapter 2). It was, for the record, never once practised on European offenders in South Australia or Western Australia.

---

[16]As mentioned in Chapter 2 the earlier 1833 execution by firing squad of the Indigenous male, Midgegooroo, is not tallied in Brian Purdue's final count of Western Australian executions, see Brian Purdue, *Legal Executions in Western Australia*, Perth: Foundation Press, 1993, pp. iv–vi.

[17]*Inquirer*, 23 September 1840, p. 31 emphasis original.

[18]*Inquirer*, 17 April 1850, p. 3.

[19]*The Perth Gazette and Independent Journal of Politics and News*, 20 July 1855, p. 2.

[20]Tolmer, 1972, p. 190.

The display of Indigenous bodies after death is the logical extension of the idea that the 'terror' of public executions could pacify resistance to colonisation on the frontier. For a people who did not share British culture and language the easily decipherable symbolism of the gallows was seen as a useful aid to the isolated colonist. The practice of hanging Indigenous Australians at the scene of the crime and forcing the offender's people to watch the execution was designed to teach the traditional owners of the land that British law was now omnipotent. In a frontier unable to be properly policed, the ability to scare compliance into Indigenous people by planting the image of the scaffold in their mind was something to be welcomed rather than banished in the eyes of many.

The Selective Reintroduction of Public Executions

In both colonies the original decision to abolish public executions for Indigenous Australians as well as Europeans came under direct criticism—though most detectably in South Australia. At the second reading in Adelaide of the 1858 Act abolishing public executions, Thomas Strangeways anticipated the consequences of the proposed legislation:

> The Act would entirely prevent the execution of the aborigines in the usual manner. If any of the white population committed a crime, it was perhaps desirable they should be executed under the provisions of that Act, but it had hitherto been considered necessary in the case of an aborigine that he should be executed in the place where the crime was committed, in order that the associations connected with the crime should be connected with the punishment. If that Bill were passed, however, the supposed sentence of death on aborigines would be practically abolished.[21]

[21] *South Australian Parliamentary Debates* (hereafter *SAPD*), 7 October 1858, p. 331.

Consequently, Strangeways suggested a special clause be inserted into the 1858 legislation that would allow the Governor, upon his written consent, to propose a place of execution other than the Adelaide Gaol for Indigenous offenders. The success of Strangeway's clause would have, in effect, facilitated the continuation of public executions for offenders of Indigenous background. Two other Members supported the clause but it was eventually voted down by a majority of the House who thought that, 'such scenes did no credit to our civilisation in the eyes of savages'.[22]

The will of Parliament to banish public executions for Indigenous offenders was strongly tested over the next three years, beginning at the execution of Manyella in 1860. At trial the twenty-year-old Indigenous male was found guilty of wilfully murdering John Jones, a hutkeeper, near Mount Joy on 13 May 1860.[23] Having been sentenced to death two years after the introduction of private executions, the law dictated that Manyella be executed in private or, in the wording of the legislation, 'within the walls of the Gaol'.[24] However, in conflict with the original intention of the 1858 Act, Manyella was taken on a long journey back to a police station at Streaky Bay, the closest to the scene of the murder, and hanged in the public gaze. The restrictions of the 1858 legislation were overcome by proclaiming the existing Police Station at Cherriroo, Streaky Bay, a Public Gaol.[25] After making this decision public in the *Government Gazette*, John Morphett was quick to raise the issue in the Legislative Council stating that the colony's newest gaol was nothing more than a hut.[26] This new 'prison' did not have high walls like those enclosing Adelaide Gaol so the execution was performed in full view of the town, but technically still 'within the walls of the Gaol', which avoided any accusations that the hanging was illegal.

Manyella's execution was a creative solution to a problem that highlighted how this new legislation found itself in complete opposition to the presumed needs and desires of those settling South Australia's outlying districts. While explaining the Government's actions in the

---

[22]William Younghusband quoted in, *SAPD*, 7 October 1858, p. 332.

[23]*Adelaide Observer*, 18 August 1860, p. 4.

[24]South Australia, no. 23 of 1858, *Act to Regulate the Execution of Criminals*.

[25]*South Australian Government Gazette*, 20 September 1860.

[26]*SAPD*, 25 September 1860, p. 920.

Legislative Council, the Chief Secretary began by stating that the government had been requested by the settlers in the district to 'make an example of the murderers in the vicinity of this crime, so that his tribe might receive a salutary lesson'.[27] He continued by positing that, given the previous success with public executions on the Eyre Peninsula, 'he trusted they would need no more executions at Streaky Bay'.[28]

Even more pronounced than in the case of Manyella was the outrage directed at South Australia's first truly private Indigenous execution. It was conducted in June 1861 inside the Adelaide Gaol following the murder of Mary Ann Rainberd and her two children by four Indigenous males. 'We have been cheated', stated an incensed *The Northern Star*, 'the fellows should be hanged up here [in Kapunda, the town where the murders took place], or they should have been placed at the rifle target for the volunteers to shoot at, so they would have a lingering death'.[29] Employing a more restrained prose *The Advertiser* questioned the logic of private Indigenous executions. It felt as though the ability of the punishment to communicate a 'salutary lesson' to its Indigenous inhabitants was severely reduced:

> What effect will this private execution have upon the aboriginal natives? What practical result will follow it? Where is the salutary lesson of terror that it was intended to teach other would-be murderers? The mere destruction of four murderers was surely not *all* that was contemplated by the jury who convicted them; we will venture to say it was not the *principal* idea.[30] Of course, the law inflicts vengeance; and in a still more emphatic sense it holds forth salutary warnings; but what warning to the native tribes is there in the private hanging of these four men?

The private execution of the 'Rainberd Murderers' was clearly a waste in the eyes of the early settler. In the seclusion of the prison yard, the gallows was shorn of its additional functions that had proved so

[27] *SAPD*, 25 September 1860, p. 920.

[28] *SAPD*, 25 September 1860, p. 920.

[29] *The Northern Star* quoted in Peter Liddy, *The Rainberd Murders: 1861*, Adelaide: Peacock Publications, 1993, pp. 82–83.

[30] *The Advertiser*, 8 June 1861, p. 2 [original emphasis].

useful in dealing with disobedient Indigenous groups on a vast frontier. The didactic potential of the execution to communicate the authority of settler law had been neutered—so much so that the young colony's legislature sought to remedy the situation.

In 1861 the disharmony between the laws of South Australia and the will of the people was corrected when an amendment to the 1858 Act was passed along racial lines. The amendment stipulated that a sentence of death passed over 'any aboriginal native' could be 'publicly carried into execution at the place at which the crime … was committed, or as near to such place as conveniently may be'.[31] The Indigenous offender's body was also to be buried at the place of execution or close by that site. It signalled the partial reinstatement of public executions in South Australia but only for Indigenous offenders. The existing system of private executions for non-Indigenous offenders was not altered by the 1861 amendment.

Justification for South Australia's amendment came from two sources; the past efficacy of Indigenous hangings and the cultural and linguistic differences of the Indigenous population. From the 'example' provided at the Coorong in 1840 to subsequent Indigenous executions on the Eyre Peninsula, MPs expressed their belief that the gallows had proven itself a valuable friend of the isolated settler. John Bagot was one Member who expressed his fear of future Indigenous violence if denied access to the pacifying qualities of public hangings. Referencing the recent Rainberd murders he thought that, 'If some steps were not taken to check such horrible crimes upon women and children, the remote districts would be again given up to savage tribes'.[32] There was even the suggestion by Edward Grundy that Indigenous bodies be left hanging from the gallows indefinitely following the execution. Given that 'mildness and kindness' had failed to civilise Indigenous people, the government must resort to a 'system of terror' to persuade such 'unsophisticated creatures' from future delinquency.[33] The return of gibbetting alongside public executions was deemed a step too far and his suggestion was subsequently voted down.

[31] South Australia, no.1 of 1861, *Act to Amend an Act, no. 23 of 22nd Victoria, Intituled 'An Act to Regulate the Execution of Criminals'*, s1.

[32] *SAPD*, 28 May 1861, p. 111.

[33] *SAPD*, 28 May 1861, p. 112.

In 1871 Western Australia introduced private executions for all criminals, regardless of race, but by 1875 they had passed an amendment altering this original position. Like South Australia before it, the Western Australian legislation stipulated that the 'Execution of aboriginal natives [was able] to take place as if the said Act [of 1871] had not been passed'.[34] When introducing the amendment to Parliament the Attorney-General, Robert John Walcott, clearly explained the aim of reinstating public executions for Indigenous offenders: 'The object of this measure was to strike terror into the heart of other natives who might be collected together to witness the executions of a malefactor of their own tribe'.[35] Walcott insisted that the bill was not conceived in a 'vindictive spirit' but as a means to deter Indigenous wrongdoers from committing 'outrages' among themselves and against the settlers.[36] A number of Members speaking at the second reading of the amendment also expressed their support, commenting on the previous capacity of the gallows in preventing Aboriginal crime. The amendment was passed by a majority of Members and assented to in December 1875.[37]

The very idea that the 'terror' of public executions could deter Indigenous offenders from crime had a strong basis in colonial culture. There is a long documented history of viewing Indigenous people through the lens of the 'savage' that can be traced back as far as William Dampier in the late seventeenth century. His comment about Indigenous people on the west coast of the continent as being 'the miserablest [*sic.*] People in the World' is well known.[38] The idea of the 'savage' was not the

---

[34]Western Australia, no. 1 of 1875, *An Act to Amend 'The Capital Punishment Amendment Act, 1871'*, the quote is taken from the sidebar.

[35]*The Inquirer and Commercial News*, 15 December 1875.

[36]*The Inquirer and Commercial News*, 15 December 1875.

[37]Western Australia, no. 1 of 1875, *An Act to Amend 'The Capital Punishment Amendment Act, 1871'*.

[38]For the full quote, see William Dampier quoted in Glyndwr Williams, 'Reactions on Cook's Voyage', in I. Donaldson and T. Donaldson (eds), *Seeing the First Australians*, Sydney: Allen & Unwin, 1985, p. 37. For historical accounts of how early Australian settlers read Indigenous bodies and habits through various conceptual apparatus brought with them from Europe, see Kay Anderson, *Race and the Crisis of Humanism*, London: Routledge, 2007; Shino Konishi, *The Aboriginal Male in the Enlightenment World*, London: Pickering & Chatto Publishers, 2012; Penny Russell, *Savage or Civilised? Manners in Colonial Australia*, Sydney: The University of New South Wales Press, 2010, pp. 19–52.

only category of analysis that colonists carried with them from Europe, particularly when concepts like that of the 'noble savage' are also taken into account. If Dampier was the archetype for one school of thought, then another early figure in Australian exploration history, Captain James Cook, embodies the other. On first impression he wrote that Indigenous Australians were 'far more happier than we Europeans', live in the 'Tranquillity' of nature and 'set no Value' upon the materialism of European life.[39] However, when Indigenous peoples appeared to fall prey to the 'vices of civilisation'—drink, dice and venereal disease—rather than excel in the areas of bodily propriety, habit, dress and biblical instruction, an increasingly disparaging account of Indigenous people became dominant among settlers as the colonial era matured.[40]

Such cultural stereotyping led to further assumptions about effective ways of carrying out punishment on the Indigenous population. In Moreton Bay, Libby Connors also noticed how the 'theatre of justice' was used to express the 'power and terror' of British law to Indigenous peoples.[41] Moreover, in the Queensland Parliamentary debates on maintaining rape as a capital crime, Ross Barber quotes many MPs who believed death to be one of the few punishments that actually deterred Indigenous wrongdoers. One MP quoted in 1860, for instance, said that Indigenous people 'could not be deterred by any other punishment than that of death'.[42] As an analogue to the retention of public executions, Western Australia also banished the punishment of whipping in 1883 and reintroduced it in 1892 but only for Indigenous criminals. The Attorney-General of Western Australia justified the amendment by

[39]For the full quote, see Captain James Cook quoted in Williams, 1985, p. 35.

[40]Russell McGregor, 'The Doomed Race: A Scientific Axiom of the Late Nineteenth Century', *Australian Journal of Politics and History*, vol. 39, no. 1, 1993, pp. 14–22, quote on p. 17.

[41]Libby Connors, 'The Theatre of Justice: Race Relations and Capital Punishment at Moreton Bay 1841–59', in R. Fisher (ed.), *Brisbane: The Aboriginal Presence 1824–1860*, Brisbane: Brisbane History Group, 1992, pp. 48–57, quote on p. 50.

[42]Ross Barber, 'Rape as a Capital Offence in Nineteenth Century Queensland', *Australian Journal of Politics and History*, vol. 21, no. 1, 1975, pp. 31–33.

likening 'black fellows' (as well as those of other non-European backgrounds) to naughty children: 'Give them a little stick when they really deserve it, and it does them a power of good'.[43]

Colonial culture ordered and categorised Indigenous people in such a way that rendered violent, public and bodily punishments commensurate with their assumed 'savagery'. The selective reinstatement of public executions in Western Australia and South Australia is just another example of how culture—operating completely separate from the penal sphere—had direct implications for choices in punishment in the colonial period. The practice of executions was materially altered in such a way as to maximize the lesson of the gallows on a specific population that was interfering with the goals of colonial society to expand into new frontiers. To inculcate a feeling of 'awe' and 'terror' in the Indigenous onlooker was, in the eyes of the coloniser at least, necessary for the example to be properly received. As an aside, it is worth briefly pointing out that these two administrations were also trying to communicate to nervous colonists as well. Strengthening the symbolism of capital punishment for Indigenous Australians was a means through which lawmakers could show that they were listening and responding to the concerns of colonists. For a simple legislative amendment there certainly were many layers of meaning, both implicit and explicit, to unpick.

Indigenous Executions After the 1861 and 1875 Amendments

The long held view in South Australia and Western Australia that the 'terror' of public hangings could pacify Indigenous resistance on the frontier made their selective reintroduction particularly attractive to lawmakers. Yet, the question must be asked, how widespread were these spectacles of frontier intimidation in the years following the passage of the amendment? For South Australia there is only a small number of

[43]The Attorney-General of Western Australia quoted in, Mark Finnane and John McGuire, 'The Uses of Punishment and Exile: Aborigines in Colonial Australia', *Punishment and Society*, vol. 3, no. 2, 2001, p. 284.

cases to discuss. On the Eyre Peninsula in late 1861, two Indigenous men were publically hanged at Fowler's Bay and another two at Venus Bay, on both occasions for the murder of a European settler.[44] In September 1862, the hangman returned to Venus Bay to execute Meengulta who speared a hutkeeper after a dispute over rations.[45] Meengulta was the last Indigenous Australian to hang in the history of South Australia.[46] This means that only on five occasions were Indigenous offenders executed in the post-amendment era and all within two years of it being passed. Thus, despite the rhetoric of the colonists and the push for legislative changes, a public execution in South Australia was never seen again after 1862.

Curiously, Western Australia hanged many more Indigenous offenders after 1875 but the sites of these executions were, more often than not, the colony's gaols rather than the frontier. After the amendment's assent in December 1875 until the last Indigenous execution in Western Australia in May 1900, a total of eighteen Indigenous people were executed.[47] Only on one occasion—at the triple execution of Terribie, Corrondine and Tchawada in February 1892—was the hanging held at the scene of the crime. It was reported that around seventy 'able-bodied natives' saw the execution at Mount Dockrell, near Halls Creek in the north of Western Australia.[48] The correspondent thought that the triple execution successfully communicated 'the penalty they risk in attempting the lives of white men'.[49] Otherwise, Indigenous executions after the

[44] *The South Australian Register*, 16 August 1861, p. 3; *The South Australian Register*, 19 September 1861, p. 2.

[45] Pope, 2011, p. 103. This execution was missed by the otherwise accurate *Hempen Collar*. See David Towler and Trevor Porter (eds), *The Hempen Collar: Executions in South Australia: 1836–1964*, Adelaide: The Wednesday Press, 1990.

[46] A.R.G. Griffiths states that in 1906 an Indigenous person was executed in South Australia but, on closer inspection, the hanged man was in fact a Muslim immigrant by the name of Natalla Habbibulla. See A.R.G. Griffiths, 'Capital Punishment in South Australia 1836–1964', *Australian & New Zealand Journal of Criminology*, vol. 3, no. 4, 1970, p. 218; *Adelaide Times*, 17 November 1906.

[47] Purdue, 1993.

[48] *Western Mail*, 26 March 1892, p. 26; *The Inquirer and Commercial News*, 26 March 1892, p. 6.

[49] *Western Mail*, 26 March 1892, p. 26; *The Inquirer and Commercial News*, 26 March 1892, p. 6.

1875 amendment were performed in Rottnest Island (5), Roebourne (5), Derby (3) and Perth (2)—all in that particular location's gaol precinct.[50]

Despite the decision of the authorities to execute Indigenous criminals within the prison setting rather than at the scene of the crime, these Western Australian executions were still viewed by a great number of Indigenous inmates detained in these locations. At the dedicated prison for Indigenous offenders established on Rottnest Island off the coast of Perth, there are accounts in 1879 and 1883 of every resident prisoner being forced to watch the hangings.[51] On another occasion at Roebourne Gaol in 1893, the 'native prisoners' and 'town natives' witnessed the execution of Cooperabiddy.[52] As suggested by the wording of the 1875 amendment, public executions at the scene of the crime were an option for the Governor, not an obligation. Perhaps it was an option less readily taken up after a prison system was established in Western Australia that was already heavily populated with Indigenous peoples. Displaying the consequences of crime in front of a contained audience of Indigenous prisoners may have been just as effective as a public hanging in front of their own people in public in the eyes of the authorities.

In Western Australia the 1875 amendment was wholly repealed in 1952, after surviving two substantial consolidations of the Criminal Code in that jurisdiction in 1902 and 1913.[53] In South Australia the right of the Governor to hang an Indigenous offender at the scene of the crime was not officially revoked until 1971.[54] It survived both the 1876 and 1935 Criminal Law Consolidation Acts, the latter being (notwithstanding on-going revisions) the primary legislative vehicle in South Australian criminal law that codifies crimes and penalties to this

[50] Purdue, 1993.

[51] *The Western Australian Times*, 22 June 1883, p. 3; *The Inquirer and Commercial News*, 20 June 1883, p. 3; *The Inquirer and Commercial News*, 23 July 1879, p. 3; *The Western Australian Times*, 18 July 1879, p. 2.

[52] *The Inquirer and Commercial News*, 31 March 1893, p. 28; *The West Australian*, 22 March 1893, p. 2.

[53] For the incorporation of the 1875 amendment into the 1902 and 1913 Western Australian Criminal Codes, see Western Australia, no. 14 of 1902, *The Criminal Code of Western Australia*, 1902, s663; Western Australia, no. 28 of 1913, *Criminal Code Act Compilation Act*, s678. For its eventual repeal in 1952, see Western Australia, no. 27 of 1952, *Criminal Code Amendment Act*.

[54] South Australia, no. 96 of 1971, *Criminal Law Consolidation Amendment Act*, s4.

very day.[55] Nevertheless, the amendment was a dormant feature of South Australian and Western Australian criminal law following the last Indigenous executions many years earlier and it remains unlikely that a subsequent Governor would have exercised the option, especially in the twentieth century.

Indigenous Executions and the Colonies to the East

The move to reintroduce public executions for Indigenous criminals was isolated to Western Australia and South Australia with the remaining colonies to the east never formally contemplating their reprisal. It is strange considering disparaging cultural constructions of Aboriginality and the threat of frontier violence was prevalent in the other colonies. To start with Victoria, the difference in that colony lies with the leadership of Charles La Trobe, Superintendent of the Port Phillip District (1839–1851) and later Lieutenant-Governor of Victoria (1851–1854). Victoria never once hanged an Indigenous offender at the scene of the crime. An explanation for this position came in 1842 with the execution of an Indigenous male named 'Roger' who was found guilty of the murder of a settler at Mount Rouse. The presiding judge, John Walpole Willis, wrote in a letter to La Trobe stating that there were 'no mitigating circumstances' in the case of 'Roger' and believed that, 'if the sentence is to be carried out the example would have a better effect if the execution took place at Mt Rouse rather than at Melbourne'.[56] La Trobe's responded that his preferred site for Indigenous executions had always been the colony's capital.[57] La Trobe explained his position to Judge Willis this way:

---

[55]South Australia, no. 38 of 1876, *Criminal Law Consolidation Act*, s14; South Australia, no. 2252 of 1935, *Criminal Law Consolidation Act*, s307.

[56]Judge Willis as quoted in Ian MacFarlane, *1842: The Public Executions at Melbourne*, Melbourne: Public Records Office of Victoria, 1984, p. 53.

[57]Two Indigenous men had been executed in Melbourne earlier in 1842 despite their murders being committed in Port Fairy. See Edmund Finn (pseudonym 'Garryowen'), *The Chronicles of Early Melbourne 1835 to 1852: Historical, Anecdotal and Personal* [1888], centennial edition, Melbourne: Heritage Publications, 1976, p. 295.

> I think it exceedingly doubtful whether, from what we know of their temper, it would be productive of the good effect intended upon the natives in that part of the country. It would possibly not only disgust them with the spot which has been chosen for their future location, but might arouse feelings which it is of the greatest importance to avoid exciting…[58]

La Trobe was the key figure that determined the location of executions from the earliest days of the colony until he gave up his position of Lieutenant-Governor in May 1854. Given the colony's Private Execution Act was proclaimed the following year, there was hardly any time to establish a new convention for Indigenous executions outside of his administration. Thus, La Trobe's conviction that public executions at the scene of the crime would actually encourage rather than pacify Indigenous violence is central to understanding why Victoria diverged from South Australia and Western Australia in this regard.[59] As an aside, it is interesting to see La Trobe's mind at work in this passage. He is clearly trying to reconcile his view of the Indigenous 'temper' (as he puts it) with what he knows of the practice of executions to see whether they would connect to achieve the intended ends of punishment. Not only does he hint at the didactic function of punishment but also that, within the same cultural milieu, a different conclusion can be reached about the 'right' punitive technique to employ.

Queensland occupies an interesting middle ground in this discussion of race and the reprisal and public executions. The timing of private executions in Queensland was tied to New South Wales since it did not separate from that colony until after Sydney proclaimed its Private Execution Act in 1855. Queensland was certainly not exempt from its share of late nineteenth-century frontier violence—or racial tension for that matter. These factors put the merits of fully private executions to the

---

[58]Charles La Trobe quoted in, MacFarlane, 1984, p. 54.

[59]La Trobe's logic was not unheard of in Western Australia with one Member, William Marmion, basing his opposition to the 1875 amendment on this line of reasoning. Noting the 'revengeful nature of the Aborigines', Marmion thought public hangings might inflame tensions and encourage reprisal attacks on Europeans. See *The Inquirer and Commercial News*, 15 December 1875.

test. In 1865, for example, one MP stated during a debate on Queensland's first consolidation of the criminal law since becoming a colony: 'for the aborigines, I believe, hanging is the only thing that brings home to them the terrors of the law'.[60] When an Indigenous criminal named Dugald was sentenced to death for rape in 1872 it was suggested that his execution take place where Brisbane's Indigenous inhabitants collect their blankets rather than in the private confines of the prison.[61] As John McGuire has already demonstrated, Queensland occasionally allowed for a controlled number of spectators of the same ethnic group to attend Indigenous, Pacific Islander and Asian hangings well into the 1890s.[62] John McGuire labelled these hangings 'semipublic' to get across the sense that Queensland's private executions were sometimes modulated owing to the race of the offender.[63]

Australia's two oldest colonies, New South Wales and Van Diemen's Land, never contemplated the reintroduction of public executions of Indigenous offenders once abolished. The reason for this difference is complex but can be put down to two important factors. First, by the 1850s the frontiers of New South Wales and Van Diemen's Land were more stable in comparison to South Australia and Western Australia. The two older colonies had already overcome the most acute Indigenous resistance in the decades preceding the abolition of public executions and thus did not have a convincing reason to reintroduce them.[64] Second, as mid-century humanitarianism swept through the Colonial Office in London, the later settling colonies of South Australia and Western Australia were obliged to deal with Indigenous resistance through the

---

[60] *Queensland Parliamentary Debates*, 2 August 1865, p. 396.

[61] A more palatable compromise was reached whereby Indigenous prisoners on St Helena were transferred to Brisbane Gaol to watch the hanging. For the circumstances of Dugald's execution, see John McGuire, 'Judicial Violence and the "Civilizing Process": Race and the Transition from Public to Private Executions in Colonial Australia', *Australian Historical Studies*, vol. 29, no. 111, 1998, pp. 203–204.

[62] McGuire, 1998, pp. 203–208.

[63] McGuire, 1998, p. 187.

[64] Tasmania's 'Black War' that transpired under the Governorship of George Arthur is one major example of European settlers dealing with Indigenous resistance through violent and often unsanctioned means. See Robert Hughes, *The Fatal Shore: A History of Transportation of Convicts to Australia, 1787–1868*, London: Vintage Books, 1986, pp. 414–424; Nicholas Clements, *The Black War: Fear, Sex and Resistance in Tasmania*, Brisbane: University of Queensland Press, 2014.

judiciary, or with at least some semblance of due process. It was an obligation much weaker in the earliest days of colonising the Australian continent where widespread settler reprisals and military skirmishes were often conveniently overlooked.[65] Public executions on the frontier presented Western Australia and South Australia with an opportunity to legally 'terrify' the Indigenous population who resisted colonisation. A need already satisfied for the established colonies of Tasmania and New South Wales by the 1850s.

* * *

At first glance, the evidence presented above suggests something contrary to the nineteenth-century narrative that executions were on the path to greater privacy. However, when one understands how nineteenth-century colonial culture viewed Indigenous bodies, beliefs and intellect the reprisal of public executions makes perfect sense. Settlers were, in fact, altering the practice of capital punishment in such a way whereby they thought it might be better equipped to communicate the lesson of the gallows to a troublesome target population. In South Australia and Western Australia this task was deemed more urgent than in the older colonies where the frontier was under greater control. Still, only a limited number of Indigenous offenders were actually executed in accordance with the amendments after their successful passage through both legislatures. In Queensland, the 'terror' public hangings could induce in non-European onlookers was also seen as valuable to the administration's penal goals. Indigenous offenders, Pacific Islanders as well as some Asian offenders occasionally underwent a 'semi-public' execution after private executions were officially introduced. To twenty-first-century readers the outward utterances of colonists towards Indigenous Australians are jarring, to say the least. However, this development—when properly contextualised—fits neatly into a penal regime that was framed with settler interests in mind.

---

[65] In Castles' overview of Australian legal history he states that as a 'general rule' those colonists who wronged Indigenous peoples in the first fifty years of European settlement were never prosecuted. See Alex C. Castles, *An Australian Legal History*, Sydney: The Law Book Company Limited, 1982, p. 521.

8

The Push to Abolish Capital Punishment

For a rounded analysis of the death penalty in the Australian colonies it is necessary to explore one last aspect of it—namely, those people who passionately disagreed with the practice entirely. Prior to the 1840s it was a voice only faintly heard in the public sphere. Capital punishment was questioned for its use in specific cases or crimes but the idea that it should disappear completely was rarely countenanced. That said, by the mid-point of the nineteenth century, opposition to the penalty as a whole was a concept growing in prominence. General community debate was accompanied by the appearance of dedicated abolitionist publications and, sometimes, short-lived organisations. From these records, the arguments and actions of key abolitionist figures can be deciphered. Bills introduced in Parliament with the aim to abolish the punishment were common in New South Wales but not elsewhere. Moreover, only one of these bills, introduced in 1896, reached the committee stage. Thinking about the abolitionists as a group managing penal change is an interesting proposition. They certainly contributed to the public debate, reminded everyone of the death penalty's contradictions, and spruiked the benefits of non-capital punishments. However, in reality, abolitionists were only

S. Anderson, *A History of Capital Punishment in the Australian Colonies, 1788 to 1900*, Palgrave Histories of Policing, Punishment and Justice,
https://doi.org/10.1007/978-3-030-53767-8_8

a minority voice in the colonial period. Retentionists (i.e. those in favour of retaining capital punishment) held the balance of power—not just on the floor of colonial parliaments where it mattered the most—but also in the wider court of public opinion. Changes to penal policy were sanctioned and shaped by those who believed in the efficacy of the death penalty in at least some circumstances. The custodians of the colonial gallows were, ultimately, those who wished for it to continue. Though it seems that nineteenth-century legislators were willing to approve radical reform in the area of labour relations, racial policy and the extension of democratic rights, they were ultimately unwilling to part with the example an execution could provide.

The Abolitionists and Their Arguments

Nathaniel Lipscomb Kentish; Benjamin Suggitt Nayler; Edward Wardley; W. H. Burford; John Camille Weale; David McLaren; Alfred Joseph Taylor; Frederick Lee—these names barely appear in the Australian historical record yet, collectively, they make up the most visible nineteenth-century abolitionist figures that existed outside of the colonial parliaments. In fact, each man had published something of a treatise of varying length and form against capital punishment in the nineteenth century.[1] These individuals tended to be pious (both

[1]W.H. Burford, *Lecture on Capital Punishment, Viewed in Its Social, Political, and Scriptural Aspects*, Adelaide: William Kyffin Thomas Printer, 1864; Nathaniel Lipscomb Kentish, *Essay on Capital Punishment*, Hobart Town: S.A. Tegg, 1842; Fredrick Lee, *Abolition of Capital Punishment: A Lecture, Delivered in the School of Arts, Sydney, New South Wales, on Thursday, May 26, 1864*, Sydney: Hanson and Bennet Printers, 1864; David McLaren, *Lecture on the Abolition of Capital Punishments Delivered by David McLaren to the Literary and Scientific Association and Mechanic's Institute, at Adelaide, December 18, 1840*, Hobart Town: S.A. Tegg, 1842; Benjamin Suggitt Nayler, *An Appeal from the Prejudices, to the Judgements, of the Inhabitants of Melbourne; on the Capital Punishment Question*, Melbourne: Robert Bell, Machine Printer, 1866; Alfred Joseph Taylor, *Capital Punishment: Reasons Why the Death Penalty Should Be Abolished; with Suggestions for an Efficient Substitute*, Hobart Town: Davies Bros., Printers 'Mercury' Steam Press Office, 1877; Alfred Joseph Taylor, *Additional Notes on Capital Punishment*, Hobart Town: Printed at the 'Mercury' Steam Press Office, 1878; Alfred Joseph Taylor, *The Death Penalty: A Plea for the Abolition of Capital Punishment*, Hobart: Printed at The Daily Post, 1912; Edward Wardley (pseudonym 'Fiat Justitia'), *The Abolition of Capital Punishment Considered by 'Fiat Justitia'*, Sydney: Gibbs, Shallard, & Co., Machine Printers, 1869; John Camille Weale, *The*

McLaren and Burford were lay preachers), highly educated (Hardley trained as a surgeon, Kentish as an engineer) and affluent (Lee was a successful merchant, Taylor the head of the Tasmanian Library). Moreover, their published pleas for abolition were accessible across Australia. Excluding Western Australia, at least one of these men had their work published in each colony. Of course, abolitionists were not identical to one another in all facets of life. For instance, William Burford was remembered for selflessly donating his time and money to help establish Churches of Christ in South Australia. By contrast, an unflattering biographical account of Nathaniel Kentish's life summarised him as 'egotistical and pedantic', and 'obsessed with the worth of his own achievements'.[2] There is, therefore, variation to be found in the nature of their argumentation. Abolitionist figures had slightly different reasons and emphases that informed their fervent dislike of the death penalty.

This section will closely follow the life and works of Alfred Joseph Taylor in Tasmania and Frederick Lee in New South Wales. Not only does it ensure our understanding of the abolitionist case can be made with greater precision but, in many ways, these two men should be elevated above the other names for their prominence and longevity in pursuit of total abolition. Fredrick Lee (c.1815–1898) was a long-lived colonist who came to New South Wales in his thirties and found success primarily as a mercantile broker. He was a well-known figure in Sydney's mid-century business circles—for example, he was very active in the Sydney insurer, and later bank, the A.M.P. Society. His obituaries note strong ties to local charitable causes in addition to the Jewish and Masonic communities of his adopted home.[3] Alfred Joseph Taylor (1849–1921) eschewed the world of trade and finance for one of books and bureaucratic formality. He ran the Tasmanian Public Library for a staggering 47 years after he was first appointed as chief librarian in

---

Calvary of Superstition or the Downfall of the Scaffold: An Essay on Capital Punishment, Brisbane: A. Keith, Leader Office, Albert Street, 1886.

[2]L.J. Blake, 'Kentish, Nathaniel Lipscomb (1797–1867)', *Australian Dictionary of Biography* 1967, http://adb.anu.edu.au/biography/kentish-nathaniel-lipscomb-2302, viewed 10 October 2019.

[3]For Frederick Lee's obituaries, see *Australian Star*, 25 August 1898, p. 5; *Hebrew Standard of Australasia*, 26 August 1898, p. 8; *Evening News*, 25 August 1898, p. 5.

1874 while still in his twenties. The son of a transported convict sent to Tasmania from New South Wales for forgery, he was a self-made scholar whose passion for intellectual life was spurred by a boyhood incident that confined him to a wheelchair.[4] His opposition to the gallows competed with a number of other public issues that caught his attention—secular education, trade unionism and sexual purity among them.

Both the ideas of Lee and Taylor were captured for the historical record via the publication of their ideas in pamphlet form. Taylor's most substantial work on the issue was *Capital Punishment: Reasons Why the Death Penalty Should Be Abolished; with Suggestions for an Efficient Substitute* (1877). It was printed in Hobart and dedicated to the Speaker of Tasmania's House of Assembly. Something of a postscript appeared the following year with his *Additional Notes on Capital Punishment* (1878). A twentieth-century work by Taylor, *The Death Penalty: A Plea for the Abolition of Capital Punishment* (1912), has been excluded from this analysis. Lee, meanwhile, published his *Abolition of Capital Punishment* (1864) to announce his ideas on the issue. It was a published version of a lecture he delivered in person to the School of Arts in New South Wales in May of that year. These works represent nothing less than a fully formed exposition on the death penalty by two leading abolitionist figures.

From the outset of their publications, Lee and Taylor both stress that capital punishment was not in lockstep with the progress of 'civilisation'. Taylor, in his preface, informs the reader that this central idea is pursued in his work. Capital punishment, suggests Taylor, was once needed when man was obliged to 'defend by force of arms and personal prowess his possessions, his family, his life' but not anymore.[5] He writes:

> I do not deny that there was a time when the infliction of a death penalty was a stern necessity … But as civilization has advanced—and still advances—with giant strides, so have our opportunities increased for providing other and more effectual means for the protection of society – means more efficient … more certain and attended with better results to mankind because [they are] less brutal and so less demoralising and

[4]Michael Roe, 'Taylor, Alfred Joseph (1849–1921)', *Australian Dictionary of Biography* 1976, http://adb.anu.edu.au/biography/taylor-alfred-joseph-4691, viewed 10 October 2019.
[5]Taylor, 1877, p. 3.

> debasing in their influence upon society ... And I hold that it can be shown that the death penalty is no longer adapted to the present condition of society and that it is no longer expedient to enforce it.[6]

Lee, early on in his work, makes a very similar point. Once upon a time, he writes, 'mankind was almost in a state of nature' where the principles of *lex talionis* ('an eye for an eye; a tooth for a tooth') made perfect sense.[7] Lee suggests that such forms of justice, like those found in the Hebrew Scriptures, 'could not be tolerated in the nineteenth century, nor be upheld by any benevolent or civilised individual'.[8] Later in his publication he repeats at length the familiar criticisms of the behaviour of the scaffold crowd (borrowing examples from London) and numerous reports of bungled hangings. He thought these accounts were akin to reading the tales of James Fenimore Cooper, a dramatist of American pioneer life: '[W]e might almost imagine we were listening to the romantic tales by Cooper, of barbarities committed by North American Indians instead of atrocities perpetrated under the sanction of law, by a civilized nation in the nineteenth century'.[9]

In addition to questioning the hangman's place in the 'civilized' world, both sought to challenge the default assumption that capital punishment was sanctioned by the Bible—important given the centrality of religion in colonial life. Lee (likely relying on a personal knowledge of Hebrew) argued that the stark endorsement of the death penalty in Genesis 9:6 ('Whoso sheddeth man's blood, by man shall his blood be shed') was poorly translated into English. He thought that it ought to have read 'Whoso sheddeth man's blood by man *will* his blood be shed'.[10] By reinterpreting this key passage Lee inferred that—although the death penalty was certainly permissible—it did not amount to the status of a biblical command. Lee supported his position by recounting the punishment given by God after the 'first homicide'—that of Cain against his

[6]Taylor, 1877, p. 3.

[7]Lee, 1864, p. 5.

[8]Lee, 1864, p. 5.

[9]Lee, 1864, p. 30.

[10]Lee, 1864, pp. 3–4.

brother Abel (Genesis 4:1–18).[11] God punished Cain's murder not with death but to a life of restless wandering, even setting a mark upon him ('the mark of Cain') to protect him from being killed by others seeking vengeance. If the death penalty was indeed a divine command for murder, then 'the Almighty would *surely* have exacted the extreme penalty' the first time it was committed.[12] Taylor, though a committed Unitarian, made theological argumentation secondary to his analysis. Yet he too, for the record, questioned the accepted translation of Genesis 9:6 while also cautioning against literal interpretations of Bible passages in general.[13]

Both men shared a keen interest in international developments. Taylor, for instance, claimed that high mercy rates in Austria had caused a decrease in crimes; France's supposed reduction of capital crimes to just 13 (from a high of 113) saw no increase in murder, and; Tuscany's experiment with total abolition had been a great success.[14] Similarly glowing reports from places as far as Russia, Prussia, Belgium, Switzerland, Portugal and Sweden were all incorporated into his analysis. Lee, meanwhile, added examples from Michigan, New York and Saxe-Weimer (in modern-day Germany) as success stories. Lee goes on to quote the well-known English abolitionist MP, John Bright, who believed that in '*no* country where capital punishment has been abolished has there been an increase of crime'.[15] What is curious about this line of argument, other than their insistence that the colonies have nothing to fear from total abolition, is that it shows Australian abolitionists had access to international news and information. Taylor proudly displayed on the title page of his *Additional Notes on Capital Punishment* (1878) that he was an 'Honorary and Corresponding Member' of the Howard Association, a leading penal reform organisation formed in London in 1866. Lee also acknowledges his debt to 'abler pens than mine [and] many philanthropic and talented writers on the subject'.[16]

[11]Lee, 1864, p. 4.
[12]Lee, 1864, p. 4.
[13]Taylor, 1877, p. 30.
[14]Taylor, 1877, pp. 15–19.
[15]Lee, 1864, p. 11.
[16]Lee, 1864, p. 3.

Both Lee and Taylor harboured concerns that innocent people had their lives cut short by the executioner—a fact that clearly motivated them to action. Lee's account is most interesting in this respect as he reprints personal correspondence with John Joseph Therry—one of the most prominent and high-ranking Catholic priests in New South Wales.[17] Therry wrote that, over his four decades in the colony, he personally knew of 'several cases' where innocents had been executed.[18] However, Therry insisted that, through his endeavours, he had helped attain mercy for innocent men on at least two occasions.[19] One of these men even sent Therry a deathbed letter thanking him for saving him from the gallows—Lee's pamphlet reprinted this note in full. Taylor uses similar examples gleaned from a dialogue he recently had with another well-travelled Catholic Priest, Julian T. Woods.[20] While pursuing missionary work in Australia, Woods claimed that he had counselled two old dying men who had confessed to crimes for which other innocent men had suffered at the gallows in their place.[21] In his *Additional Notes* Taylor offers another four accounts from European jurisdictions, some of which detail exonerating evidence attained after the hanging had taken place.[22] The wrongly imprisoned can regain their reputation and be compensated, says Taylor, but for the wrongly executed, 'not all the riches which society commands' could remedy the mistake.[23]

Lee and Taylor both spend long passages arguing how capital punishment fails to address the root causes of crime and, in doing so, reveal just what they thought of the criminal 'type' in Australia. To speak in broad brushstrokes, they stereotyped the typical Australian criminal as uneducated, poor, idle, vice-ridden, impulse-driven, irrational and immoral;

---

[17] J. Eddy, 'Therry, John Joseph (1790–1864)', *Australian Dictionary of Biography* 1967, http://adb.anu.edu.au/biography/therry-john-joseph-2722, viewed 11 October 2019.

[18] Lee, 1864, p. 30.

[19] Lee, 1864, pp. 30–31.

[20] For more on J.T. Woods, see D.H. Borchardt, 'Tenison-Woods, Julian Edmund (1832–1889)', *Australian Dictionary of Biography* 1976, http://adb.anu.edu.au/biography/tenison-woods-julian-edmund-4700, viewed 10 October 2019.

[21] Taylor, 1877, p. 8.

[22] Taylor, 1878, pp. 5–12.

[23] Taylor, 1877, p. 23.

so indifferent to living that their actions were almost suicidal by intent. Take Lee's explanation for murder as one example:

> In many cases the homicide is committed in consequence of a morbid craving for blood, an overwhelming impulse to take life, frequently combined with a suicidal tendency; probably an inflammatory action upon the brain, an *irresistible* influence, which impels the criminal to commit the crime, *totally regardless* of the consequences. Now, in dealing with the minds of men who generally commit crime, we must not measure them by *our own* standard.[24]

Or, Taylor's summation of the criminal mind:

> They are really and truly slaves to controlling passions, and placed in circumstances which will stimulate the most active impulses of their nature, will commit crimes of the deepest dye, having no thought at the time of the consequences to themselves of such actions. Hanging fifty such would not deter others governed by the same impulses…[25]

Taylor later speculates that the desire for crime 'borders upon disease and insanity' and is possibly a consequence of hereditary: 'Do we think it unnatural that a bad tree should bear bad fruit?'[26] Lee uses the term of 'moral insanity' at one point to describe the desire to commit crime.[27] They suspect that if the causes of wrongdoing are not environmental but hardwired into the criminal's very constitution then executions were ineffective at preventing crime. The punishment had to go deeper than mere spectacle. In fact, in both their works, they praise punishments that, above all else, aimed to reform the character of the individual. 'I believe this idea of reformation to be a truly Divine idea,' writes Lee, 'one that should pervade all punishments'.[28]

---

[24]Lee, 1864, p. 13.

[25]Taylor, 1877, p. 10.

[26]Taylor, 1877, p. 12.

[27]Lee, 1864, p. 14.

[28]Lee, 1864, p. 7.

Taylor and Lee, following their portrayal of the common criminal, saw the logical alternative to the death penalty as life imprisonment without release. But, to view abolitionists as soft-hearted humanitarians because of this suggestion is somewhat misleading. Abolitionists make the case that prison is a more effective punishment precisely because it was more miserable than hanging. Here is Lee sharing his thoughts on lifetime incarceration:

> Why, in such an imprisonment there is a gibbet for every hour: no hope, reminding me of the Hell of Dante, over whose dread portals that sublimes of geniuses inscribes in his immortal poem, 'Here Hope never enters'. No escape, a terrible doom which comprehends the forever, to wake day after day a hopeless captive … and at the close of each day's work locked up like a wild beast in his den for twelve weary hours in a dark cell, a prey to his gloomy thoughts…[29]

Both Lee and Taylor invoked the ideal of the nineteenth-century penitentiary in their texts—a place of strict discipline, endless labour, bouts of solitary confinement and enforced sobriety. Only such an enforced shift in lifestyle from vice to virtue could mend the 'criminal class' in Australia they contended. At different moments, they also anticipate the central criticism of this alternative—namely, that prison is more expensive than death. Lee laments that placing a cost/benefit analysis on a criminal's life makes him 'blush for humanity' while Taylor goes out of his way to make the case that prisons are actually profitable institutions.[30]

A key argument for abolitionists in the colonial period harks back to some of Beccaria's famous axioms. Namely, the death penalty, owing to its very severity, was unenforceable—or, at the very least, uncertain in its application. Lee and Taylor point to juries who have failed to convict on capital offences 'in the very teeth of law and evidence'.[31] Taylor writes: '[C]an anyone blame the man who would hesitate before returning a verdict, the penalty attached to which, if enforced, is unalterable?'[32]

---

[29]Lee, 1864, p. 23.

[30]Lee, 1864, p. 36; Taylor, p. 24.

[31]Taylor, 1877, p. 8.

[32]Taylor, 1877, p. 7.

Both men go on to provide evidence of jurymen who are hesitant in their duty. Lee, for example, relays a case in New South Wales where the criminal was indicted on two counts—one capital, the other not. Prior to delivering the verdict the head juror explicitly asked the judge if he would recommend mercy should the criminal be found guilty on the capital count. When the Judge did not grant him any assurances the foreman announced him guilty on the non-capital count alone.[33] Given their confidential nature, abolitionists' assertions of jury deliberations will always be speculative. Lee himself, in an interesting aside, actually excused himself from jury duty when he was empanelled to sit on a capital case.[34]

Taylor and Lee's agitation did not start and stop with the publication of these pamphlets. As two leading abolitionists of the colonial period, they were very active in their own ways. It is likely that Taylor was first spurred to action in his twenties while following the case of the rapist Job Smith.[35] Thereafter he wrote compulsively to his local newspapers about the ills of the death penalty. In 1879, for example, he provided Tasmanians with specific information on wrongful convictions in England, the reimposition of capital punishment in Switzerland and a troubling capital case in New South Wales.[36] He also antagonised other people sending in letters to the local newspapers on criminal cases, disagreeing with them on points of logic or fact.[37] This constant barrage of letters was too much for Hobart's *Mercury*. In 1879 it declared that Taylor was misusing their columns and aggravated their readership by 'inflicting on them arguments from which their souls revolted'.[38] The *Mercury* determined that it would no longer allow 'such dangerous doctrines' and 'distorted views' to be published in its columns.[39] It even blamed Taylor

---

33 Lee, 1864, p. 34.

34 *Empire*, 21 February 1866, p. 2.

35 Taylor wrote in private to the Colonial Secretary arguing for a commutation of his sentence which he believed aligned with public sentiment on the matter, see Richard P. Davis, *The Tasmanian Gallows: A Study of Capital Punishment*, Hobart: Cat and Fiddle Press, 1974, p. 79.

36 *Tribune*, 20 October 1879, p. 2; *Tribune*, 4 June 1879, p. 3; *Tribune*, 5 June 1879, p. 3.

37 *Mercury*, 24 May 1875, p. 2; *Mercury*, 31 May 1875, p. 3; *Mercury* 10 August 1877, p. 2.

38 *Mercury*, 26 March 1879, p. 2.

39 *Mercury*, 26 March 1879, p. 2. Taylor had been warned two years earlier that they were reluctant to publish his ideas, see *Mercury*, 30 March 1877, p. 3.

for the fact that a criminal (guilty of a capital crime in the newspaper's opinion) had recently been released back into society. Unfazed, Taylor found other periodicals willing to carry his letters. Hobart's *Tribune*, for one, was happy to oblige. The *Tribune*'s Editor wrote the following note after Taylor's falling out with the *Mercury*: 'We are induced to insert Mr. Taylor's communication, in the belief that no cause suffers through free discussion'.[40] After the 1870s and early 1880s his correspondence on capital punishment slowed down but never entirely stopped. In 1915 he publicly advocated for the reprieve of a criminal—much to the chagrin of the Library of Tasmania's Trustees. According to the historian Michael Roe, Taylor's refusal to be silenced represented something of a test case for the ability of Australian civil servants to advocate for private beliefs in the public sphere.[41]

In New South Wales Lee, less of a writer than Taylor, was a central figure in anti-capital punishment action in the last half of the nineteenth century. During the mid-1860s he gave many well-attended lectures in locations like temperance and church halls.[42] It was common for notable citizens to come in person to listen to his talks. Lee's published account of his lecture to the School of Arts examined above, for example, had two Members of the Legislative Assembly seated on stage while he delivered it.[43] Between 1868 and 1872 he was involved in a dedicated abolitionist society in New South Wales (see below). During the 1880s, Lee helped organise petitions for mercy in the cases of William Rice (1884), Robert Hewart (1888) and Louisa Collins (1889).[44] On each of these occasions he formed part of a deputation to the Governor to advocate for clemency in person. To a lesser extent, through letters to Government Ministers and/or comments in the newspapers, he pressed for leniency in the cases of Ernest Buttner (1889), John Buttner (1889), John Makin (1893) as

[40] *Tribune*, 27 March 1879, p. 3.

[41] Roe, 1976.

[42] See *Empire*, 19 April 1864, p. 5; *Sydney Morning Herald*, 27 May 1864, p. 4; *Sydney Mail*, 1 July 1865, p. 2; *Empire*, 7 August 1865, p. 5.

[43] *Sydney Morning Herald*, 27 May 1864, p. 4.

[44] For Lee's involvement in Rice's case, see *Sydney Morning Herald*, 19 April 1884, p. 8. For Hewart's case, see *Evening News*, 10 September 1888, p. 5. For Collins' case, see *Daily Telegraph*, 4 January 1889, p. 6.

well as for Charles Montgomery and Thomas Williams (1894).[45] He had mixed success in his endeavours. For instance, he advocated for clemency to be shown to the perpetrators of the infamous gang-rape of Mary Jane Hicks at Mount Rennie in Sydney's then bushland in 1886.[46] Owing in part to his agitation, only four of the original nine youths originally sentenced to death were actually executed.[47] The first time he advocated on behalf of an individual criminal—that of Henry Manns in 1863—it was less successful. A total of 16,000 people signed a petition for mercy but to no effect. 'I used every possible exertion' Lee recalled, but the Governor was fixated on making an example.[48]

Abolitionist Organisations and Community Debates

Outside of the actions of abolitionist figures some dedicated anti-capital punishment groups emerged during the nineteenth century—in South Australia and New South Wales specifically. The Society for the Abolition of Capital Punishment—hereafter S.A.C.P. (SA)—was a small organisation started in 1844 that had eight founding members. If not for the existence of the private records of William Anderson Cawthorne, at one point Secretary of the organisation, details would be even more elusive than is already the case. At the very back of one of Cawthorne's personal notebooks that documents local Indigenous manners and customs, and in between his own hand sketches on that same subject, the Minutes of the South Australian Society for the Abolition of Capital Punishment

---

45 For Lee's involvement in Buttner's case, see *Australian Star*, 4 June 1889, p. 3. For Makin's case, see *Australian Star*, 3 August 1893, p. 3. For Montgomery and Williams' case, see *Australian Star*, 22 May 1894, p. 2.

46 *Sydney Morning Herald*, 16 December 1886, p. 3.

47 Helen Doyle, 'Mount Rennie Rape', in G. Davison et al. (eds), *The Oxford Companion to Australian History*, Melbourne: Oxford University Press, 1998, p. 441.

48 Lee, 1864, p. 32.

between 26 September 1844 and 25 April 1845 can be found.[49] The diligent note-taking of Cawthorne, a schoolmaster and stationer for most of his life, sheds rare light on the internal workings of an abolitionist organisation in the nineteenth century. William Burford was another founding member whose involvement is notable. He became, as the nineteenth century progressed, South Australia's equivalent to Frederick Lee and Alfred Taylor—a prominent abolitionist figure lecturing against the death penalty, corresponding with the local press, and advocating for mercy in particular cases.[50]

Cawthorne's Minutes reveal that the Society was, during 1844 and 1845, involved in a number of different activities, including: lobbying the government for mercy on behalf of two condemned criminals; preparing anti-capital punishment material for circulation in the colony; and, inquiring into the local newspaper editors' position on the issue. In its short existence the Society also made an enemy of the local retentionist publication the *Southern Australian* who had mounted an attack on the infant Society in one of its articles.[51] The Minutes of the early meetings depict an organisation in its embryonic stages—Crawford notes the need for the Society to purchase a transaction book and to design a seal. Yet, in the last batch of meetings included in Cawthorne's Minutes (April 1845), resolutions were passed to fix regular monthly meetings, for members' annual subscriptions to be paid in advance, and elect key offices (Treasurer and Secretary, etc.) for the coming year. It is curious then that, save for some rare mentions in the newspaper in mid-1845, S.A.C.P. (SA) rarely leaves traces in the historical record in later years. The last that is heard of the group in the newspapers was in March 1847

[49]William Anderson Cawthorne, 'Minutes of the Society for the Abolition of Capital Punishment, 26 September 1844–25 April 1845', in 'Rough Notes on the Manners and Customs of the Natives', State Library of South Australia, PRG 489/3.

[50]Other than Cawthorne and Burford the other Members listed are James Nicholson, Henry Downer, James White, J.H. Pace, Charles Catton and S.R. Hall. See also, Steven Anderson, 'Nineteenth Century Dreams, Twentieth Century Realities: Reframing the Abolition of Capital Punishment in South Australia', in C. Collins and P. Sendziuk (eds), *Foundational Fictions in South Australian History*, Adelaide: Wakefield Press, 2018, pp. 165–176.

[51]*The Southern Australian*'s criticism prompted a written response from two of its Members, see *The South Australian Register*, 29 March 1845, p. 3; *The South Australian Register*, 3 May 1845, p. 3.

when an advertisement was placed in the *South Australian* for the Society to meet on 'urgent business' at a hotel in Port Adelaide.[52]

Another anti-capital punishment 'Committee' emerged briefly in South Australia during the year 1874. Interested citizens met after an anonymous newspaper advertisement ran for several days with the hope of bringing like-minded people together.[53] William Burford came to the meeting and suggested that it would be best to form a Committee and successfully passed the motion, 'That a Committee be formed for the purpose of bringing this matter of capital punishment prominently before the public'.[54] Out of the nearly fifty people in attendance, a Committee of nine men was elected.[55] At the second meeting a few months later the group resolved to correspond with the Literary Societies and to form sub-committees throughout the colony. The group hosted two public lectures on capital punishment, one by William Burford and another by James Jolly. Burford's lecture was published and widely circulated with financial help from the Committee.[56] In September 1874 the Committee appears to have sought the statistics from the latest criminal returns from a sympathetic MP.[57] Yet, this is the last the newspapers note about the activities of this group. Like its precursor that was established in the mid-1840s, it too appears to have been a short-lived effort.

In New South Wales a group named 'The Society for the Abolition of Capital Punishment'—hereafter S.A.C.P. (NSW)—was active between 1868 and 1872. Despite the similar name, it had nothing to do with the South Australian abolitionist group. The genesis for a society came out of a meeting hosted in the 'President's Room' in the Legislative Council chaired by Terence Aubrey Murray in late 1867.[58] They called for memberships and subscriptions in both city and country newspapers.

---

[52] *South Australian*, 19 March 1847, p. 3.

[53] *Evening Journal*, 7 January 1874, p. 2.

[54] *South Australian Advertiser*, 9 January 1874, p. 2. In a lengthy talk to those gathered, Burford lamented the failure of the earlier S.A.C.P. (S.A.): 'Some years ago–about 30 years ago–several gentlemen, amongst whom was himself, associated together in a similar movement to the present, but they could not make headway'.

[55] *South Australian Advertiser*, 9 January 1874, p. 2; *South Australian Register*, 9 January 1874, p. 6.

[56] *The South Australian Register*, 28 February 1874, p. 2.

[57] *The South Australian Register*, 10 September 1874, p. 6.

[58] *Sydney Morning Herald*, 24 December 1867, p. 5.

Two months later they had a provisional committee consisting of no less than six parliamentarians, four doctors and ten clergymen—in addition to a number of other members of the public.[59] None other than Frederick Lee acted as Secretary for the Society. *The Sydney Morning Herald* raised its eyebrow when the name of a former lawyer and current MP, John Plunkett, appeared as one of a number who had joined the 'craze'.[60] Plunkett was, according to the newspaper, Attorney-General for nearly twenty years, 'in the good old times when the lash and the gallows were the implements of punishment'. From 'ripe experience' it chirped, he should know something of the subject.[61] When the formation of the group was reported in newspapers, some questioned if the Parliament of New South Wales could ever be daring enough to move 'from being a step behind, to take a step in advance of the law of Great Britain, as well as of most European States?'[62]

Without doubt the group's most controversial moment was their intervention in the case of the Irishman, Henry O'Farrell, who attempted to assassinate the touring English royal Prince Alfred, the Duke of Edinburgh. They advocated for mercy in his case on two grounds. First, medical evidence suggested he was insane; a recent mental breakdown had caused strange public behaviour and delusional thoughts. Second, O'Farrell's charge of wounding with intent to murder was only a capital offence in New South Wales but not England.[63] However, speculation was rife as to whether it was a Fenian conspiracy. In the middle of the furore, Terence Aubrey Murray—the MP instrumental in establishing the S.A.C.P. (NSW) at a meeting earlier in the year—declared that he now 'discarded any connection with such a society'.[64] A report on his speech stated that Murray, 'hoped that the foul assassin would be hanged fifty

[59] *Sydney Morning Herald*, 15 February 1868, p. 8.

[60] *Sydney Morning Herald*, 25 February 1868, p. 3.

[61] *Sydney Morning Herald*, 25 February 1868, p. 3.

[62] *Sydney Morning Herald*, 25 September 1869, as quoted in, James Gregory, *Victorians Against the Gallows: Capital Punishment and the Abolitionist Movement in Nineteenth Century Britain*, London: I. B. Tauris, 2012, p. 42.

[63] *Freeman's Journal*, 27 March 1869, p. 9.

[64] *Queensland Times, Ipswich Herald and General Advertiser*, 28 March 1868.

cubits high, so that everybody could see him, and that the gallows would remain standing till the last Fenian was exterminated out of the colony'.[65] As the fanfare around the case continued to grow, one member of the opposition asked for Lee's correspondence with the government regarding O'Farrell's sanity to be tabled for all to see. The government declined the invitation, citing the confidentiality of the Executive Council's deliberations. Lee, on the other hand, did not share those concerns and furnished the public with his correspondence via the newspapers.[66] In the end, the group's agitation was unsuccessful—O'Farrell was hanged at Darlinghurst Gaol on 21 April 1868.

After the O'Farrell case the New South Wales group continued to agitate for change, despite some jeers from the local press. The satirical *Sydney Punch*, for example, published a mock meeting of the Society that was attended by famous murderers. The fictional meeting ended with a resolution that gave 'all noble murderers a further opportunity of slaking their thirst for blood'.[67] From 1868 and into 1870 the S.A.C.P. (NSW) remained active as an organ for discussion and agitation on specific cases. The group's actions were again punctuated in 1870 when they had a hand in preparing a thwarted capital punishment abolition bill that was presented to the Legislative Assembly on their behalf by William Brookes (see below).[68] Records of dedicated abolitionist organisations, outside of New South Wales and South Australia, remain elusive. When hearing about the formation of Lee's Society one correspondent recalled that if 'our memory be not treacherous' a similar group emerged in Sydney during the early 1860s.[69] The historian of the Tasmanian gallows, Richard Davis, also alludes to a group of abolitionists active in Launceston during the 1860s as well but he does not offer much detail about them.[70]

In the last decades of the nineteenth-century diverse opinions about the death penalty could be heard in the press. Often the same colony had

---

[65] *Queensland Times, Ipswich Herald and General Advertiser*, 28 March 1868.

[66] *Freeman's Journal*, 27 March 1869, p. 9.

[67] *Sydney Punch*, 5 June 1869, p. 7.

[68] *Evening News*, 16 July 1870, p. 2.

[69] *Sydney Morning Herald*, 25 February 1868, p. 3.

[70] Davis, 1974, p. 79.

opposite views represented: Tasmania had Hobart's *Mercury* favouring retention while Launceston's *Examiner* was firmly opposed to capital punishment.[71] During the 1850s, the Adelaide reading public could follow the duels between the *South Australian Register* and the *Adelaide Times* against the enthusiastically pro-gallows *Southern Australian*.[72] Sydney's *Empire*, *People's Advocate*, *Chronicle* and the short-lived weekly *Atlas* were all among the publications that identified with abolitionist views at one time or another.[73] The firmly retentionist *Sydney Morning Herald* (called the 'gibbet-loving Herald' by some) often teased these smaller competitors for being 'mock philanthropists' who harboured a 'diseased sympathy' towards malefactors.[74] Perhaps, though, *The Argus* of Victoria was a more typical story. Though regarded as a conservative newspaper for most of its 111-year existence, it flirted with both sides of the debate over the years. For instance, it defended an abolitionist stance during a lengthy three-year exchange during the 1850s in its columns with its own 'Geelong Correspondent' who supported death punishments.[75] Yet, two decades later, when a Victorian MP asked whether the government would consider abolition, *The Argus* editorialized in favour of the death penalty, at least in cases of deliberate murder.[76]

Often the stance of a newspaper could be traced down to its proprietor or editor. Edward Wilson, joint-proprietor of *The Argus* from 1849,

[71] Davis, 1974, p. 63.

[72] For a brief discussion on abolitionist debates and action in South Australia see Gregory, 2012, pp. 40–41. See also, Andrew Russ and Bianca Zanatta, 'The Application and Eventual Abolition of the Death Penalty in South Australia', South Australian Parliamentary Research Library, 2017.

[73] Arthur L. Wintle, 'The Abolition of Public Executions in New South Wales', unpublished BA (Hons) thesis, La Trobe University, 1973, pp. 30–31 and 43–44; Gregory, 2012, p. 41.

[74] Wintle, 1973, pp. 33–34.

[75] The debate *The Argus* had with its Geelong Correspondent lasted three years between 1851 and 1853. For the report that set off this discussion see *The Argus*, 22 October 1851, thereafter see *The Argus*, 22 November 1851; 14 April 1852; 30 March 1853; 1 April 1853; 2 April 1853; 14 April 1853; 20 April 1853; 28 April 1852. For Letters to the Editor commenting on this discussion see 'Seneca', *The Argus*, 21 April 1853; 'R', 6 May 1852; 'Geelong Subscriber', 3 December 1851.

[76] *The Argus*, 18 October 1879, p. 7.

was a known abolitionist with an interest in penal systems.[77] Henry Parkes, also an abolitionist, was the founding editor-proprietor of *Empire* on his way to becoming one of the New South Wales most prominent statesmen. The Rev. Dr J. D. Lang ran three news publications in Australia beginning with the *Colonist* (1835–1840), the *Colonial Observer* (1841–1844) and then the *Press* (1851).[78] While serving as a Member of New South Wales Parliament as the Member for Port Philip during the 1840s Lang had declared his total abolition to capital punishment.[79] The co-founder of Launceston's *Examiner* was John West, an early historian of Tasmania and well-known anti-transportation campaigner who occasionally expressed his belief in the futility of hangings.[80] Although the sheer volume of periodicals in the nineteenth century inevitably led to diverse opinions, the default position was that the gallows had a role to play in the penal system of the Australian colonies. Whatever their position, however, every publication had no issue keeping the reading public abreast of developments in England. British parliamentary debates, prominent criminal cases and dissenting opinions on the issue (Dickens's letters, for example) were all closely monitored in the Australian newspapers.

Dissenting newspaper voices and dedicated abolitionist groups served to unsettle accepted opinion—something that filtered down to local levels. Nineteenth-century colonial life was dotted with community groups of all shapes, sizes and interests. Hosting a discussion or organised debate to work through the merits and drawbacks of capital punishment was one of many topics they touched upon. For instance, records show organisations as diverse as the Australian Natives Association and local literary societies hosting debates and talks on the matter.[81] However,

[77]Geoffrey Serle, 'Wilson, Edward (1813–1878)', *Australian Dictionary of Biography Online* 1976, http://adb.anu.edu.au/biography/wilson-edward-4866, viewed 14 July 2015.

[78]D.W.A. Baker, 'Lang, John Dunmore (1799–1878)', *Australian Dictionary of Biography* 1967, http://adb.anu.edu.au/biography/lang-john-dunmore-2326, viewed 10 July 2015.

[79]Wintle, 1973, pp. 28–29.

[80]John Reynolds, 'West, John (1809–1873)', *Australian Dictionary of Biography Online* 1967, http://adb.anu.edu.au/biography/west-john-2784, viewed 1 July 2015.

[81]See, for example, *Northam Advertiser*, 9 October 1897, p. 3; *Albany Advertiser*, 21 August 1897, p. 3.

mock parliaments (often called Parliamentary Associations or Parliamentary Classes) and ordinary debating societies found a natural home for such discussions.[82] A window into this world can be found in a handwritten essay by an eighteen-year-old William Ponder in 1873 at the Young Men's Mutual Improvement Society in Kapunda (a small town north of Adelaide). Ponder wrote in favour of the abolition of capital punishment thinking it fitted neatly with other legislative improvements enacted by 'philanthropists and legislators' that had improved the 'tone of society'.[83] At the end of the year, he submitted his piece to an essay competition alongside twenty-eight competing entries but without success. The following year he tried again but this time it was an essay on the merits of trial by jury.

The final area where an opposition to capital punishment manifested was in public petitions to abolish the death penalty. As early as 1842 Nathaniel Kentish, an early abolitionist active in South Australia and Tasmania, organised a petition that encouraged all of her 'Her Majesty's Dominions' to stop engaging in the 'barbarous, anti-Christian, sacrilegious, murderous, and illegal' practice of capital punishment.[84] Other attempts, less ambitious in scope, came from other parts of society. For example, Adelaide's fledgling Quaker community sent the South Australian Parliament two petitions in the 1890s asking for total abolition.[85] In 1869, 443 residents of Sydney signed a petition that said capital punishment was 'a relic of a barbarous age, and quite unsuited to the present advanced state of civilization'.[86] Whether it was dedicated abolitionist organisations, newspaper debates, local community discussion or various petitions, it was clear that capital punishment was a topic

---

[82]The 'Ipswich Parliamentary Class', for example, debated the merits of capital punishment at different times from the 1870s to the 1890s, see *Queensland Times, Ipswich Herald and General Advertiser*, 11 June 1872; *Brisbane Courier*, 22 September 1887, p. 7; *Brisbane Courier*, 2 August 1894, p. 5. For a debating society discussing capital punishment, see *Mercury*, 9 June 1890, p. 2.

[83]William David Ponder, 'Essays', State Library of South Australia Archival Collection, 1879, D 5218 T, pp. 5–6.

[84]Kentish, 1842, pp. 56–58.

[85]*South Australian Parliamentary Debates* (hereafter *SAPD*), House of Assembly, 12 August 1891, p. 715; *SAPD*, House of Assembly, 26 September 1894, pp. 1529–1530.

[86]New South Wales Parliament, *Sessional Papers*, 1869, p. 353.

that provoked debate in the nineteenth century. The true test of the acceptability of these beliefs, however, would come when they were presented to lawmakers.

Colonial Parliaments and the Push for Abolition

All this talk about the efficacy of capital punishment that existed in the public sphere mattered little unless action was taken on the floor of colonial parliaments. Once responsible government was granted to the Australian colonies in the 1850s (though Western Australia waited until 1890) the abolition of capital punishment was, theoretically, made more possible than ever before. It finally tilted the lawmaking power of each colony away from the appointed Governors and toward elected representatives. The appetite for abolition could be tested in parliaments in different ways. Motions and questions probing the Members' position on the topic were common across all jurisdictions. In Tasmania, for instance, one MP moved a motion (later withdrawn) to encourage the government to abandon death punishments. The 1876 motion read: '[T]hat the almighty having an interest in every human life, in the opinion of this Honourable House, the death sentence is unwarrantable by any earthly tribunal'.[87] Victorian MPs around the same time were active during the sittings of 1861, 1876 and 1879 when specific criminal cases provoked different MPs to ask whether abolition was on the government's legislative agenda.[88] During the 1890s South Australian MPs—Cohen, Solomon, Brooker and Wood, respectively—moved multiple motions in favour of abolition that inquired into the government's position on the issue.[89]

---

[87]Tasmania, *Journals of the Tasmanian House of Assembly*, 1876, p. 40.

[88]*Victorian Hansard*, Legislative Assembly, 19 March 1861, p. 518; *Victorian Hansard*, Legislative Assembly, 7 December 1876, pp. 1684–1691; *Victorian Hansard*, Legislative Assembly, 16 October 1879, pp. 1496–1497.

[89]These questions and motions were in the 1891 (twice), 1892, 1894, and 1895 sittings, see *SAPD*, House of Assembly, 11 June 1891, p. 50; *SAPD*, House of Assembly, 12 August 1891, pp. 717–720, see also pp. 1361–1362, 1652–1657, and 1869–1870; *SAPD*, House of Assembly,

Outside of these passing discussions on the issue, it is telling that the vast majority of colonial parliaments in the era of responsible government—in fact, every jurisdiction barring New South Wales—did not witness a fully fledged abolitionist bill pass a first reading. The closest moment occurred during the years 1861 and 1862 when Louis Lawrence Smith twice attempted to introduce a bill into the Victorian Parliament.[90] During his first attempt, in November 1861, Smith was chastised by the then Chief Secretary of the colony who complained that it would be a 'waste of money to have the bill printed' and accused Smith of misreading the 'temper of the House and the country' in relation to the issue.[91] The follow-up attempt made by Smith in January 1862 was again opposed by a government who believed the measure would 'imperil the well-being of society' citing problems 'unknown in older countries' like bushranging and relatively isolated townships.[92] As hinted at above New South Wales is the exception when talking about abolitionist legislation. In contrast to the other colonial jurisdictions, clusters of bills aiming to completely abolish capital punishment received a first reading and one (in 1896) even made it past the committee stage. In fact, one can identify three different waves of legislative attempts in New South Wales that are worth exploring further—1859 to 1862, 1870 to 1873, and a decade long effort from 1889 to 1900.

The first wave of abolitionist bills in New South Wales Parliament was led by Terence Aubrey Murray. He introduced a bill that explicitly advocated for complete abolition in 1859, four years following responsible government being granted to the colony in 1855. In Murray's brief speech he told his fellow lawmakers that it was high time colonial parliaments discussed an issue that had occupied their British counterparts for many years.[93] A first reading was permitted but the second reading

23 August 1891, p. 663; *SAPD*, House of Assembly, 26 September 1894, pp. 1531–1535, see also 2000; *SAPD*, House of Assembly, 3 July 1895, pp. 400–402, see also pp. 502–509 and 2974–2976.

[90] *Victorian Hansard*, Legislative Assembly, 31 October 1861, pp. 240–243, see also p. 192; *Victorian Hansard*, Legislative Assembly, 16 January 1862, pp. 411–413.

[91] *Victorian Hansard*, Legislative Assembly, 31 October 1861, p. 241.

[92] *Victorian Hansard*, Legislative Assembly, 16 January 1862, p. 413.

[93] *Sydney Morning Herald*, 28 September 1859, p. 3.

was repeatedly postponed until the formal parliamentary sitting had ended.[94] Over the following two years (1860 and 1861) Henry Parkes, the 'Founding Father' of Federation as he is now known to schoolchildren, introduced an identical measure to Parliament. Parkes stated in his 1860 address that this effort was nothing more than an attempt to revive Murray's ignored bill from the previous year.[95] However, yet again, Parliament finished sitting without turning its attention to the matter.

Henry Parkes' second attempt in 1861 made more headway than the previous attempts. In fact, a lengthy parliamentary debate was sparked as to whether it should be given a second reading. Parkes began the discussion by stating how the taking of life by the state was a matter of the 'highest interest' in civil society.[96] An older Member of the House was quick to point out that New South Wales was full of men who had once escaped the English gallows. These men had 'completely reformed' and 'became exemplary citizens' he argued.[97] Others who supported Parkes' bill followed a line of argumentation not dissimilar to those found in the writings of Frederick Lee and Alfred Taylor outlined above. Retentionist MPs offered a spirited defence of their position during the proceedings. To narrow the focus to just one parliamentarian alone, Charles Cowper argued that the most hardened criminals could not reform and the threat of death, for such offenders, was still the best deterrent. Although the 'mother parliament' had discussed the issue for many years, continued Cowper, they had never concluded that it was the right course of action. Safeguards were always in place to prevent miscarriages of justice—whether it took the form of the judge, jury, executive or the prying eyes of the general public. He also noted that private executions were working just as Parliament had intended. In uttering the following statement, Cowper was reflecting the dominant view of the legislature at the time:

[94]New South Wales Parliament, *Votes and Proceedings*, 1859, pp. 105, 191, 243, 273, 475, 504, 543, 596, 617, and 640.

[95]*Sydney Morning Herald*, 13 October 1860, p. 5.

[96]*Sydney Morning Herald*, 26 January 1861, pp. 4–6.

[97]John Robertson as quoted in, *Sydney Morning Herald*, 26 January 1861, pp. 4–6.

> [T]he time had not yet arrived when this alteration of the law ought to take place. (Hear, hear.) It was quite true that this colony had been in advance of the mother-country in legislation on more than one occasion. This was perhaps to our credit, but he thought that before we determined to make any alteration in so important a branch of our jurisprudence as this we ought to feel that we were proceeding on safe grounds and consider well the conclusions at which we might arrive.[98]

For a legislature that had taken the bold decision to abolish public executions a handful of years earlier, the abolition of capital punishment entirely was simply a step too far. The vote to approve the second reading was eventually lost by Parkes—16 votes to 25.[99] Though a well-known abolitionist throughout his career (Parkes had a local abolitionist pamphlet dedicated to him as late as 1880) he never acted on his conviction as a matter of government business in his successive stints as Premier.[100] Later that year a different MP, Samuel Gray, tried again to push ahead with an abolitionist bill but quickly saw there was no appetite for further discussion in the aftermath of the debate Parkes had inspired. Gray withdrew the bill before a first reading was even moved.[101]

A decade passed in the New South Wales legislature before another wave of abolitionist bills were proposed, likely sparked by the anti-capital punishment Society that Frederick Lee was involved in at the time. William Brookes led the charge in 1870 with a new abolition bill. With the public furore over O'Farrell's attack on the Duke of Edinburgh so recent in their minds, one senior MP said to Brookes that these 'periodical addresses' on the ills of capital punishment were interfering with government business.[102] Henry Parkes defended Brookes'

---

[98] *Sydney Morning Herald*, 26 January 1861, pp. 4–6.

[99] *Sydney Morning Herald*, 26 January 1861, pp. 4–6.

[100] The abolitionist pamphlet called Parkes 'Eastern Australia's most profound Statesman' and a man of 'progressive knowledge', see 'Iota', *Crime: Its Causes: Is Death Punishment Deterrent?* West Maitland: T. Dimmock, Printer and Publisher, High Street, 1880, held at the Mitchell Library, State Library of New South Wales.

[101] New South Wales Parliament, *Votes and Proceedings*, 1861, pp. 157 and 387.

[102] James Martin quoted in, *Sydney Morning Herald*, 9 March 1870, p. 2.

measure saying that the merits of the death penalty were discussed year on year in England and therefore it should not be 'pooh-poohed' out of the House.[103] Though the bill was introduced, Brookes eventually dropped it soon afterwards. In the next parliamentary sitting which straddled 1870 and 1871, Brookes again tried to introduce the same bill but it too was a non-starter.[104] On each of these occasions in the early 1870s, many MPs foreshadowed their opposition to the bill should it proceed any further through Parliament. This second wave of failed abolitionist legislation came to a close at the 1872–1873 sitting when the newspaperman-cum-MP Edward Grenville introduced yet another abolition bill. The second reading debate, however, was repeatedly postponed until Parliament ran out of sitting days.

The final wave of abolitionist legislation occurred in New South Wales around the 1890s. Two abolition bills were moved in Parliament by Thomas Walker, in 1889 and 1890, respectively though neither were granted a first reading (nor did they generate any substantial commentary in the House).[105] However, John Haynes' attempts to do the same in 1895, 1896, 1898, 1899 and 1900 were altogether different.[106] Haynes, a former newspaper journalist and proprietor, proved to be an astute politician—enjoying nearly three decades as a sitting Member.[107] The progress these abolition bills made were, in large part, due to Haynes' political tact. Haynes, outwardly at least, always appeared willing to compromise on the final outcome of his abolition legislation—perhaps

---

[103] *Sydney Morning Herald*, 9 March 1870, p. 2.

[104] New South Wales Parliament, *Votes and Proceedings*, 1870–1871, pp. 37, 147, 292, 328, 487, and 668.

[105] New South Wales Parliament, *Votes and Proceedings*, 1889, p. 161; New South Wales Parliament, *Votes and Proceedings*, 1890, p. 26.

[106] New South Wales Parliament, *Votes and Proceedings*, 1895, pp. 122, 158, 183, and 192; New South Wales Parliament, *Votes and Proceedings*, 1896, pp. 20, 80, 151, 407, 429, and 441; New South Wales Parliament, *Votes and Proceedings*, 1898, pp. 37, 42, 124, 165, 216, and 236; New South Wales Parliament, *Votes and Proceedings*, 1899, pp. 83, 90, and 235; New South Wales Parliament, *Votes and Proceedings*, 1900, pp. 15, 20, and 143.

[107] Heather Radi, 'Haynes, John (1850–1917)', *Australian Dictionary of Biography* 1972, http://adb.anu.edu.au/biography/haynes-john-3738, viewed 14 October 2019; Parliament of New South Wales, 'Mr John Haynes (1850–1917)', *Parliament of New South Wales Website* 2019, https://www.parliament.nsw.gov.au/members/formermembers/Pages/former-member-details.aspx?pk=931, viewed 20 October 2019.

the result could be a simple reduction of the capital code that everyone could agree upon. However, through his actions, it was clear that Haynes would steadfastly refuse anything less than total abolition. His 1896 bill to abolish capital punishment was, in particular, a landmark moment for Australian abolitionists. It was the first time an abolition bill successfully passed its second reading to continue to be considered clause by clause in the committee stage. I will spare the reader a tedious account of the other bills from the 1890s and now discuss the 1896 attempt in depth given its relative importance.

While introducing his 1896 abolition Bill, Haynes encouraged MPs, rather than to simply dismiss it out of hand, to discuss it clause by clause in committee instead. Only that way, he argued, could a pragmatic bargain be struck between committed abolitionists (like himself) and those who supported the whittling of the capital code to just the bare minimum. Haynes' speeches in support of abolition articulated a desire for New South Wales to keep up with the march of 'civilisation' and try out an 'experiment' with the radical reform. Consider this extract from Haynes where he took aim at the supposed piety of his fellow legislators:

> I cannot understand that men claiming to have, living in themselves, a personage who was the model of life, and whose every word was charity and forgiveness, being the last to give up their attachment to this barbaric practice – while they raise their voices to God, crying aloud still for the slash of the lash on the backs of unfortunate men; crying aloud still for the vengeance of the executioner. The day has come in New South Wales when we may deliberately make an experiment. If it should be attended with this result, that murder is on the increase it will be easy for us to go back … We have established the case, I think, beyond dispute when we can legitimately ask for an experiment. Surely it is a thing which no man can object to on behalf of humanity.[108]

To encourage action Haynes, throughout his speech, compared the penal code of New South Wales to countries that were supposedly lower down on the scale of civilization. 'The time has arrived', Haynes claimed,

---

[108] *New South Wales Parliamentary Hansard* (hereafter *NSWPH*), Legislative Assembly, 9 June 1896, p. 667.

'when we ought to say that New South Wales is not on all-fours with Persia, Abyssinia, China, and other countries which have little regard for human life'.[109] Members should not hold onto such 'cast-iron principles' adopted by other countries and instead be proud to show that 'we have given up the barbaric principle of hanging people'.[110] Other abolitionist MPs supported Haynes in his position. One said that the colony, by hanging its criminals, was engaging in something which was 'not creditable to us'.[111] One of the last Members to speak suggested that should the bill become law that he would feel as though New South Wales 'had at last made a step out of the old bloodthirsty days'.[112] Haynes himself was confident in the bill: 'From what I can see it is going to be carried, and it will be one of the grandest accomplishments ever achieved by the House. We cannot do very much wrong by making an experiment in this direction'.[113]

The other colonies were, once again, caught looking at the New South Wales example regarding capital punishment. For example, around the time of this debate a cartoon was published in *The Free Lance*, a short-lived periodical from Melbourne, about New South Wales' efforts (see Illustration 8.1). It depicts a determined woman (representing New South Wales) taking an axe to the gallows while 'Nosey Bob' (the colony's long-time executioner) is drying his eyes in the background. In the caption it mentions how a judge, fond of handing out the death sentence, had recently retired. Moreover, the memory of convictism was again raised as a motivating factor. *The Free Lance* wrote of how 'the baleful shadow of Botany Bay has a chance of at last being lifted from that too long-tainted mother province'. The publication did, however, wrongly report that the bill had managed to pass through the House of Assembly. In fact, a flock of MPs were determined to argue fiercely with Haynes on these key ideas and the others forwarded by the abolitionists. Under no circumstances did they want to see this radical idea made into a legal reality.

---

[109] *NSWPH*, Legislative Assembly, 9 June 1896, p. 667.
[110] *NSWPH*, Legislative Assembly, 9 June 1896, p. 667.
[111] William Affleck as quoted in *NSWPH*, Legislative Assembly, 9 June 1896, p. 669.
[112] Francis Cotton as quoted in, *NSWPH*, Legislative Assembly, 9 June 1896, p. 686.
[113] *NSWPH*, Legislative Assembly, 9 June 1896, p. 686.

AT LAST!

N.S.W. PASSES SENTENCE OF DEATH ON THE GALLOWS

Illustration 8.1 An 1896 cartoon in Melbourne's *The Free Lance* related to the push to abolish capital punishment in New South Wales (*Source The Free Lance*, 12 September 1896, p. 9, held by the National Library of Australia)

The MPs who led the defence of capital punishment in 1896 were Albert Gould, Thomas Waddell and Henry Copeland. Gould, the Minister for Justice at the time, believed in limiting the capital code to murder and rape alone, but would go no further than that. The scaremongering around innocent men being hanged was ill-founded in his view; Gould's personal experience on the Executive Council was evidence enough for him that the reexamination of each capital case was undertaken thoroughly. His other concern was that lifetime incarceration without hope of release was detrimental to the ends of reform. It would make a 'brute of him' and create a prison inmate infinitely more difficult to 'control'.[114] Waddell was another MP who believed strongly in the merits of capital punishment. He restated that the 'function of parliament' was to 'interpret, as nearly as possible, the feelings of the people'.[115] Yet, he did not see an overwhelming groundswell of support for the measure—despite the claims of the abolitionists to the contrary. Moreover, by trying to 'save life in one way' abolitionist MPs were actually 'sacrificing life in other ways' since no deterrent to crime was as effective as the hangman's noose.[116] Waddell also took a swipe at the supposed humanitarianism of abolitionist MPs. The law should not be altered 'simply because a few sentimental, soft-hearted, well-meaning people clamour for it'.[117] He claimed that the 'maudlin sympathy' of abolitionists was with the perpetrators, not the victims or bystanders. The final vocal opponent was Henry Copeland, someone who proved obstructive throughout the entire debate. Copeland was a military man and suspicious of the glowing statistics quoted to him by abolitionists. These statistics could be 'read in all manner of ways' he grumbled.[118]

Common to Gould, Waddell and Copeland's arguments was that New South Wales was simply not the right place to try out the 'experiment' Haynes wished for. The example of death was necessary, they believed, in a colony that had a pattern of settlement very different from that of Europe where abolitionists drew their inspiration. Since the colony

[114] *NSWPH*, Legislative Assembly, 9 June 1896, p. 672.

[115] *NSWPH*, Legislative Assembly, 9 June 1896, p. 676.

[116] *NSWPH*, Legislative Assembly, 21 October 1896, p. 4259.

[117] *NSWPH*, Legislative Assembly, 9 June 1896, p. 676.

[118] *NSWPH*, Legislative Assembly, 21 October 1896, p. 4253.

was only sparsely settled, the gallows was the only protector of the men, women and children that bravely populated the interior. As Copeland put it: 'In a comparatively thinly-populated country like this, where men in thousands of instances had to leave their homes and their wives and daughters unprotected in the bush, it was absolutely necessary that we should have some punishment that would act as a deterrent'.[119] The death penalty was 'absolutely essential' according to Gould since the 'chastity and purity of our women' needed safeguarding.[120] For Waddell, women and children were certainly part of his consideration but not the only people in need of protection. The itinerant bushman was, to his mind, also in desperate need of security:

> [I]t was the nomadic class in this colony who were most liable to be murdered – men who had the least protection, owning to their manner of life. This was a measure to withdraw the protection that now existed to human life in the scattered districts of the colony. The great proportion of the murders committed occurred in the far interior among the poorer classes.[121]

After providing a series of examples from the press that supported the above assertion, Waddell concluded that it was precisely these men who 'ran the most risk from the assassin's knife and bullet'.[122] Waddell and Copeland could speak from some personal experience on the matter of crime in the interior since both had financial interests in country districts either in the mining or pastoral industries.[123] Gould, meanwhile,

[119] *NSWPH*, Legislative Assembly, 21 October 1896, p. 4251.

[120] *NSWPH*, Legislative Assembly, 7 July 1896, p. 1357.

[121] *NSWPH*, Legislative Assembly, 21 October 1896, p. 4256.

[122] *NSWPH*, Legislative Assembly, 21 October 1896, p. 4257.

[123] Parliament of New South Wales, 'Mr Thomas Waddell (1854–1940)', *Parliament of New South Wales Website* 2019, https://www.parliament.nsw.gov.au/members/formermembers/Pages/former-member-details.aspx?pk=975, viewed 20 October 2019; Parliament of New South Wales, 'The Hon. Henry Copeland (1839–1904)', *Parliament of New South Wales Website* 2019, https://www.parliament.nsw.gov.au/members/formermembers/Pages/former-member-details.aspx?pk=751, viewed 24 October 2019.

gained his experience of criminal cases as a lawyer.[124] Abolitionists, however, rebutted this key point by claiming that crime was actually an urban problem, not a country one.

As both sides of the debate continued their discussion, the 1896 abolition bill progressed steadily through the New South Wales Parliament. The first reading on 19 May was followed by a successful vote at the second reading on 9 June. At the committee stage (discussed on 7 July and then 21 October) the abolitionists stared down an amendment from retentionists that would have maintained murder and rape as capital offences in the colony.[125] The bill had emerged from the committee stage with its central goal to completely abolish capital punishment still intact. However, it was at this point that Parliament chose to drag its feet. With just over a week left on the sitting calendar for the year a vote was needed in the lower house to adopt the committee's report and proceed to a third reading. As it turns out Henry Copeland was the one who took it upon himself to filibuster any further discussion on the bill. Rather than proceed smoothly to a vote, Copeland interrupted with a twenty-minute speech where he, eventually, moved for it to return to the committee for yet further discussion on its individual clauses. Haynes did his best to hurry Copeland during the speech. At first he did so through heckling, and later, by moving that Copeland no longer be heard. Other abolitionists also tried to shout him down—challenging him to take the vote on the committee's report if he was so confident that the will of Parliament was against the measure. Copeland's long-winded speech continued right until the clock struck 8 p.m. and the Speaker directed the House that the time had come to handle government business. It was the last time this iteration of Haynes' bill was discussed before Parliament was dissolved again.

Even though the vote on the committee's report was never taken due to Copeland's obstruction, it is hard to tell whether it would have passed. The earlier debates on the 1896 abolition bill quoted above occurred late at night after busy sitting days, with only a very small number of

[124]Parliament of New South Wales, 'Sir Albert John Gould (1849–1936)', https://www.parliament.nsw.gov.au/members/formermembers/Pages/former-member-details.aspx?pk=897, viewed 23 October 2019.

[125]New South Wales Parliament, *Sessional Papers*, 1896, p. 623.

interested Members present. In fact, less than thirty MPs were in the chamber when the 1896 bill was being discussed in committee. It was the last matter of business before the Legislative Assembly was adjourned just before 2 a.m.[126] Given it would have been reviewed and debated in the upper house, it was a long way from being welcomed as law in New South Wales. Still, Haynes did not give up his fight. Prior to Federation, the same bill was introduced in 1898, 1899 and 1900. Copeland, however, was always on standby to prevent Haynes from achieving his dream of a colony free from the death penalty. For example, Copeland insisted that an amendment be made to insert the words 'in certain cases' into the title of Haynes 1898 'Capital Punishment Abolition Bill'.[127] Though debates ensued, familiar arguments were heard, and the same people came to support their side, none of these subsequent efforts would make it as far through Parliament as the 1896 attempt.

* * *

When Australian historians remember the great movements of the colonial period, female suffrage and trade unionism will be high on their list; perhaps they will place the anti-transportation movement and the desire for Federation on the same plane with them. However, the push to abolish capital punishment does not register in these same discussions. And, in the final analysis, that conclusion is not an unfair one to reach. Abolitionist figures like Alfred Taylor in Tasmania and Frederick Lee in New South Wales did their best to try and create a groundswell of opposition to the gallows. Chatter in the columns of newspapers and among community groups was a constant feature of the colonial period, especially in the second half of the nineteenth century. Dedicated abolitionist 'societies' emerged in Adelaide in the 1840s and in Sydney in the late 1860s which aimed to formally organise opposition. Yet, these groups were short-lived and ultimately ineffectual in achieving their central goal. Indeed to call it an anti-capital punishment 'movement' is something of a misnomer since that label implies a continuity of effort and something that threatened to gain mainstream acceptance. Rather, agitation against

126 *NSWPH*, Legislative Assembly, 21 October 1896, p. 4264.

127 *NSWPH*, Legislative Assembly, 30 August 1898, pp. 312–314.

capital punishment tended to come in fits and spurts and differed in strength from colony to colony. The degree of action and effort was intimately linked to the enthusiasm of a single person, or a small group of people, in a specific time and place. Despite the progress of John Haynes' 1896 abolition bill, the majority of colonial lawmakers were simply unwilling to 'experiment' with a society that only locked up—rather than hanged—its worst criminals. When it came to parliamentary action, it was those who wanted to retain the death penalty that had the loudest voice and the last say. It would have to wait until the twentieth century for committed abolitionists to finally win over the majority of lawmakers to their side of the debate.

9

Conclusion: Death of a Spectacle

In Centennial Park in Sydney the Commonwealth of Australia was proclaimed on 1 January 1901. Among the festivities at the ceremony was a 10,000-strong school choir providing a full-throated rendition of *Federated Australia*, *Advance Australia Fair* and *Rule Britannia*. The colonial period was sung to a close; the six colonies of Great Britain were now the states of Australia. As for what that meant for capital punishment, it carried on much as before since most matters of criminal law remained the residual responsibility of the states. However, as the twentieth century passed, each Australian jurisdiction moved to abolish capital punishment entirely. They did so in the following order: Queensland (1922), Tasmania (1968), the Commonwealth (1973), Victoria (1975), South Australia (1976), Australian Capital Territory (1983), Western Australia (1984) and New South Wales (1985).[1] Yet, these dates tend to hide the perennial underuse of the punishment. New South Wales, for example, had its last execution in 1939 and had

[1] Sam Garkawe, 'The Reintroduction of the Death Penalty in Australia?—Political and Legal Considerations', *Criminal Law Journal*, vol. 24, no. 2, 2002, pp. 101–108.

S. Anderson, *A History of Capital Punishment in the Australian Colonies, 1788 to 1900*, Palgrave Histories of Policing, Punishment and Justice,
https://doi.org/10.1007/978-3-030-53767-8_9

removed the death penalty for murder by 1955; in 1985 it was treason and piracy that were made non-capital offences. As for the practice of executions themselves, the spectacle of it all was well and truly dead. At Australia's last execution, that of Ronald Ryan inside Pentridge Prison in 1967 for murder, there was a large tarpaulin draped below the drop to prevent anyone from viewing the scene. When one journalist present stooped low to the ground in an attempt to see under it a nearby prison guard chastised him—'None of that!'—he was reported as saying.[2]

From the very first execution onwards, the idea that crime had consequences needed to be communicated by those in positions of authority to grease the wheels of a functioning society. It was crucial that the 'lesson' of the gallows be made crystal clear to colonists through the perfect performance of an execution. But, at every turn, popular memory and cultural beliefs interfered with its proper transmission. The memory of convictism, the desire to be viewed as 'civilised' within the British Empire, a nineteenth-century understanding of race, a wish to die 'game'—anything and everything could intersect with the operation of the death penalty. The practice of executions as it existed at the time of Federation, and the space afforded to capital punishment within the overall penal regime, certainly put it in a stronger position to properly communicate the intended meaning of punishment. Still, how the lesson of the gallows was received was never fully in the control of the colonial authorities: a botched execution was still always possible; criminals might become folk-heroes; and journalists had it in their power to publish a scathing account of the scene. Moreover, the Governor-in-Council might extend or restrict mercy without knowing how its decision would play out while lawmakers could alter the capital statutes in unpopular ways. Nevertheless, it was in this striving to perfect the lesson of the gallows and systematically remove any distractions to it that drove change in this area of colonial punishment. Along the way these alterations had to accommodate and respect the unique and ever-changing cultural norms of colonial society.

[2]Mike Richards, *The Hanged Man: The Life and Death of Ronald Ryan*, Melbourne: Scribe, 2002, p. 388.

A long-standing distraction from the example of an execution was just how frequently they were botched. Amateur hangmen, faulty equipment and uncorrected flaws in technique caused a great deal of avoidable pain for the condemned and outrage on the part of the onlooker. In the interests of 'humanity and decency' the Colonial Office in London attempted to standardise execution procedure in 1880 by circulating a Memorandum to the Australian colonies on proper technique. It signalled how a more fundamental aversion to pain and suffering was developing in colonial culture during the 1850s, even when applied to the body of a deserving criminal. New modes of execution (like electrocution in America) or old ones (like the guillotine in France) were occasionally talked about in the colonies and lauded for their supposedly painless and foolproof design. However, colonial authorities never abandoned hanging as their method of choice. Instead, they looked to fix their techniques and find new ways to conceal the pain felt by the criminal to those watching.

A penitent criminal was desired for those administering the execution but the allure of 'dying game' was a powerful cultural expectation working against this outcome. It was often left to a diligent clergyman to direct the condemned away from bravado and toward a more remorseful and dignified exit from this world. On the day of execution the sheriff and hangman also worked to manufacture some kind of penitence from the criminal. Though acting 'game' gave the condemned an opportunity to construct the narrative of the execution, the behaviour of dying criminals could often be subsumed into larger cultural contexts. This was most obvious in the aftermath of Ned Kelly's hanging. He died displaying very little resistance at the gallows, uttering a seemingly innocuous statement in front of no one other than official witnesses—it was as close to a perfect execution for which the authorities could hope. However, as Kelly's legacy demonstrates, even the actions of a compliant criminal were able to produce a narrative that was contrary to the administration's wishes.

To behold large numbers of women, children and members of the lower class gathering enthusiastically at the foot of the public scaffold was a cause of great concern. Elite writers thought that witnessing scenes of violence actively demoralised and hardened the onlooker. It was the key reason that more respectable colonists tended to avoid public executions and chastise those who did attend. The Private Execution Acts guaranteed that spectators would only attend executions in a strictly professional capacity; everyone else now required the personal approval of the sheriff to witness the scene. This fundamentally altered the way colonists interacted with the gallows since it forced them to read about the death rather than view it firsthand. By trapping the experience of an execution within the description provided by journalists, it sanitised the death penalty and refocused attention on the example it could provide.

The transition to private executions in Australia was an interesting chapter in the history of capital punishment on the continent. When Henry Grattan Douglass introduced the first Private Execution Act in 1853 he did so as a means to publicise to Britain that New South Wales was becoming a little more civilised and refined. It was a desire deeply rooted in the cultural legacy of convictism and a wish to distance the colony from its penal past. The trigger for reform was impossible to replicate in Britain's other substantial possessions and it propelled the Australian colonies to move quickly in the context of the Empire. Underpinning this unique desire was a public execution spectacle that had, for a long time, been the subject of concern for all of the colonies. It was not lost on legislators that an execution in private would correct many of the distractions to do with the crowd, criminal and execution procedure.

At first glance the decision of South Australia and Western Australia to selectively reintroduce public executions for offenders of an Indigenous background appears to counter a nineteenth-century narrative that was said to appreciate more discreet forms of execution. However, in the eyes of legislators, the changes made it more likely for the message of punishment to be successfully communicated to Indigenous Australians. On the untamed and newly established frontiers of these two latter settling colonies, the 'terror' that public executions could evoke in local Indigenous populations was viewed as immensely valuable. Belief in their efficacy was deeply rooted in disparaging European cultural constructions of Indigenous intellect, temperament and habit. The colonies to the east avoided amending their own legislation, though Queensland was more flexible in tailoring the private execution audience to match the ethnicity of the criminal hanged. Despite the sentiments of South

Australian and Western Australian lawmakers, Indigenous hangings on the frontier were never widespread after the amendments were passed.

Abolitionist voices started to be heard more frequently in the colonies by the middle of the nineteenth century. Prominent pamphleteers were often independently wealthy men, piously minded and comparatively well-educated. Their arguments drew from the work of European intellectuals, the Bible, contemporary examples of capital punishment's failures as well as a desire to keep pace with 'civilization' abroad. In practical terms, abolition was not a cause pursued like an intercolonial 'movement' nor was a dedicated organisation active for more than a handful of years in any given colony. The New South Wales legislature stands out due to the disproportionate amount of abolition bills it dismissed, most often at the first reading. However, the failure of abolition bills showed, again and again, that the majority of the legislature was actually in favour of the death penalty being administered. From this numerical dominance we can deduce that the transformations capital punishment underwent in the colonial period were actually sanctioned by those who favoured the retention of hangings and believed very much in the example they set.

Surrounding all of these debates and changes were generations of governors and lawmakers ensuring that the parameters of capital punishment matched the context within which it operated. Too extensive a capital code and they were overly cruel; too limited and they were not doing enough for a frontier society with a strong criminal element. The capital statutes were modulated according to a number of uniquely colonial anxieties—over bushranging, the safety of frontier women and the gender imbalance—to name a few. Similarly, the prerogative of mercy allowed the Executive to carefully vet each candidate before they shook hands with the hangman. It allowed them to double-check that the punishment was suitable for the crime and that an egregious error was not being committed by sending the condemned to their death. Even so, external beliefs related to age, gender and race all played their part as to whether the execution should actually go ahead. While the majority of lawmakers and the general public favoured the use of capital punishment in at least some circumstances, the days of hanging a criminal over a petty crime were long gone by the time of Federation.

This book has borrowed freely from the sociologically-informed literature on penal change to produce an historical study that looks at capital punishment with a new lens in Australia. The central dynamic of penal messaging and reception, passing through the external filter of culture, has been a productive one for this study to pursue. The practice of executions in Australia changed in dramatic ways throughout the nineteenth century. It went from being public to private, amateur to professional and haphazard to standardised. Meanwhile, the capital statutes were narrowed, mercy was wielded more freely and the hangman was called upon for only the very worst criminals. To preserve the central lesson of the gallows—that crime has consequences—the British punishment that arrived in Australia with the First Fleet in 1788 was forced to alter its course. Those who chose to navigate at different moments had to plot a route that respected the unique contours of Australian colonial culture and memory. The passage taken ended up killing the spectacle of capital punishment but allowed it, for better or worse, to pass safely into twentieth-century waters.

Bibliography

Primary Sources

Parliamentary Material

Acts of Parliament

Australian

New South Wales, no. 17 of 1883, *An Act to Consolidate and Amend in Certain Respects the Criminal Law.*
New South Wales, no. 40 of 1853, *An Act to Regulate the Execution of Criminals.*
New South Wales, no. 2 of 1837, *Imperial Acts Adoption Act.*
New South Wales, no. 24 of 1835, *An Act to Provide for the Conveyance and Postage of Letters.*
New South Wales, no. 3 of 1832, *Offenders Punishment and Justices Summary Jurisdiction.*
Queensland, no. 13 of 1865–1866, *Criminal Consolidation Act.*
South Australia, no. 96 of 1971, *Criminal Law Consolidation Amendment Act.*
South Australia, no. 2252 of 1935, *Criminal Law Consolidation Act.*
South Australia, no. 532 of 1891, *An Act to Amend 'The Northern Territory Justice Act, 1875'.*

S. Anderson, *A History of Capital Punishment in the Australian Colonies, 1788 to 1900*, Palgrave Histories of Policing, Punishment and Justice
https://doi.org/10.1007/978-3-030-53767-8

South Australia, no. 38 of 1876, *Criminal Law Consolidation Act.*
South Australia, no. 35 of 1872, *Juvenile Offenders Act.*
South Australia, no. 1 of 1861, *Act to Amend an Act, no. 23 of 22nd Victoria, Intituled 'An Act to Regulate the Execution of Criminals'.*
South Australia, no. 23 of 1858, *Act to Regulate the Execution of Criminals.*
Tasmania, no. 69 of 1924, *The Criminal Code Act.*
Tasmania, no. 16 of 1885, *The Defence Act.*
Tasmania, no. 6 of 1875, *An Act for the More Effectual Punishment of Juvenile Offenders.*
Tasmania, no. 5 of 1863, *An Act to Consolidate and Amend the Legislative Enactments Relating to Offences Against the Person.*
Tasmania, no. 2 of 1855, *An Act to Regulate the Execution of Criminals.*
Tasmania, no. 1 of 1845, *An Act to Remove Doubts in Certain Cases of Arson.*
Tasmania, no. 5 of 1840, *An Act to Amend the Laws of This Colony Relating to Robbery and Stealing from the Person.*
Tasmania, no. 14 of 1838, *An Act for the More Perfect Constitution of Courts of General Quarter Sessions and to Provide for the More Effectual Punishment and Control of Transported and Other Offenders.*
Tasmania, no. 1 of 1837, *An Act for Extending to This Colony Sundry Statutes Passed for the Amendment of the Criminal Law.*
Tasmania, no. 17 of 1836, *An Act for the Prevention of Sheep and Cattle Stealing, and for Abolishing the Punishment of Death in Such Cases.*
Tasmania, no. 2 of 1835, *An Act to Consolidate and Amend Certain of the Laws Relating to the Courts of General Quarter Sessions and to the More Effectual Punishment and Control of Transported and Other Offenders.*
Tasmania, no. 6 of 1834, *An Act to Extend to Van Diemen's Land Certain Statutes Passed in England for Amending the Laws Relating to Forgeries—To Embezzlements by Public Officers—And to Offences Against the Coin—And for Abolishing Capital Punishments in Certain Cases.*
Victoria, no. 1079 of 1890, *The Crimes Act.*
Victoria, no. 951 of 1887, *The Juvenile Offenders Act.*
Victoria, no. 44 of 1854, *An Act to Regulate the Execution of Criminals.*
Western Australia, no. 27 of 1952, *Criminal Code Amendment Act.*
Western Australia, no. 28 of 1913, *Criminal Code Act Compilation Act.*
Western Australia, no. 14 of 1902, *The Criminal Code of Western Australia.*
Western Australia, no. 1 of 1875, *An Act to Amend 'The Capital Punishment Amendment Act, 1871'.*
Western Australia, no. 15 of 1871, *An Act to Provide for Carrying Out of Capital Punishment Within Prisons.*

Western Australia, no. 9 of 1868, *An Ordinance to Make Better Provision for the Suppression of Violent Crimes committed by Convicts.*

Western Australia, no. 7 of 1854, *An Ordinance for the Suppression of Violent Crimes Committed by Convicts Illegally at Large.*

International

Canada, Chapter 29 of 1869, *An Act Respecting Procedure in Criminal Cases, and Other Matters Relating to Criminal Law.*

Cape of Good Hope, no. 3 of 1869, *For Regulating the Execution of Capital Punishment.*

New Zealand, no. 10 of 1858, *Act to Regulate the Execution of Criminals.*

United Kingdom, Chapter 24 of 1868, *Capital Punishment Amendment Act.*

United Kingdom, Chapter 59 of 1850, *An Act for the Better Government of Her Majesty's Australian Colonies.*

United Kingdom, Chapter 56 of 1841, *An Act for Taking Away the Punishment of Death in Certain Cases, and Substituting Other Punishments in Lieu Thereof.*

United Kingdom, Chapter 26 of 1834, *An Act to Abolish the Practice of Hanging the Bodies of Criminals in Chains.*

United Kingdom, Chapter 62 of 1832, *An Act for Abolishing the Punishment of Death in Certain Cases, and Substituting a Lesser Punishment in Lieu Thereof.*

United Kingdom, Chapter 48 of 1823, *An Act for Enabling Courts to Abstain from Pronouncing Sentence of Death in Certain Capital Felonies.*

Parliamentary Debates

Australian

New South Wales Parliamentary Hansard (NSWPH), Legislative Assembly, 30 August 1898; 21 October 1896; 7 July 1896; 9 June 1896; 14 September 1882.

Queensland Parliamentary Debates, 2 August 1865.

South Australian Parliamentary Debates (*SAPD*), House of Assembly, 3 July 1895; 26 September 1894; 18 November 1891; 23 August 1891; 12 August 1891; 11 June 1891; 28 May 1861; 7 October 1858; 21 September 1858.

Victorian Hansard, Legislative Council, 2 September 1890; 16 October 1879; 7 December 1876; 16 January 1862; 31 October 1861; 19 March 1861.

Western Australian Parliamentary Debates, Legislative Assembly, 19 December 1870.

International

Canadian Parliamentary Debates, House of Commons, 28 April 1869; 13 December 1867.

Parliamentary Papers, Reports, Votes and Proceedings

Australian

New South Wales Parliament, *Sessional Papers*, 1896; 1869.

New South Wales Parliament, *Votes and Proceedings*, 1900; 1899; 1898; 1896; 1895; 1890; 1889; 1870–1871; 1861; 1859; 1853.

Tasmania, 'Gaol Discipline: Report from the Select Committee, with Minutes of Proceedings and Evidence', *Tasmanian Parliamentary Papers*, no. 177 of 1884.

Tasmania, *Journals of the Tasmanian House of Assembly*, 1876.

Victorian, 'Execution of Criminals, Report of the Sheriff, Relative to Recent Executions at Her Majesty's Gaol, Melbourne', *Victorian Parliamentary Papers*, no. 32 of 1858.

Victorian, 'Execution of Criminals', *Victorian Parliamentary Papers*, B-no. 7 of 1854.

International

United Kingdom, 'Report of the Capital Punishment Commission: Together with the Minutes of Evidence and Appendix', London: Printed by George E. Eyre and William Spottiswoode, 1866.

Unpublished Colonial Material

Art Gallery of South Australia (AGSA)

Frome, E. C., '"Pilgaru"—Two Natives Hung for Murder, September 1840', Watercolour on Paper, 11.1 × 19cm, AGSA.

Skipper, John M., 'Early Execution, South Australia', Pencil on Paper, 16.3 × 20.1 cm, c.1840, AGSA, 367D3.

Skipper, John M., 'Execution of George Hughes and Henry Curran, Adelaide, 16 March 1840', Pencil on Card, 15.0 × 20.1 cm, 1840, AGSA, 367D4.

Skipper, John M., 'Execution of Joseph Stagg, Adelaide, 18 November 1840, Pen and Brown Ink on Paper, 10.7 × 12.8 cm, 1840, AGSA, 367D5.

National Portrait Gallery of Australia (NPGA)

Kreitmayer, Maximilian L. 1880, 'Ned Kelly Death Mask', Plaster, 28.0 × 21.5 × 18.5 cm, NPGA, LOAN2000.39.

Public Record Office Victoria (PROV)

'Witnesses to Kelly's Execution, 11 October 1880', PROV, VPRS 4969/2/78.

Queensland State Archives (QSA)

'Circular from the Secretary of State for the Colonies, with Attached Plan and Section of the Gallows at Newgate Gaol, 28 December 1880', QSA, Series ID 12690, Item ID 1839168.

'Circular from the Secretary of State for the Colonies, Regarding a Memorandum on the Practice of Executing Criminals, 27 June 1880', QSA, Series ID 12690, Item ID 1839167.

'Circulars on Capital Punishment, 27 June 1880 to 28 December 1880', QSA, Series ID 12690.

'Memorandum upon the Execution of Prisoners by Hanging with a Long Drop, June 1880', QSA, Series ID 12690, Item ID 1139511.

State Library of South Australia (SLSA)

Cawthorne, William Anderson, 'Minutes of the Society for the Abolition of Capital Punishment, 26 September 1844–25 April 1845', in 'Rough Notes on the Manners and Customs of the Natives', SLSA, PRG 489/3.

Ponder, William David, 'Essays', SLSA Archival Collection, 1879, D 5218 T.

Skipper, John M., 'A Sketch of South Australia's First Execution by John M. Skipper, 1838', Pencil on Paper, 13 × 18 cm, 1838, SLSA Pictorial Collection, B 7797.

Taylor, John Fogg, 'Letter from John Fogg Taylor of Tundemunga, Near Adelaide, 1840, to "John" in Wigan, Lancashire, England, Dated September 1840', SLSA, D 7310.

State Library of Queensland (SLQ)

'Sketch of Ned Kelly at the Gallows, Melbourne Gaol, 11 November 1888', Copied and Digitised from an Image Appearing in the *Australiasian Sketcher*, 20 November 1880, p. 185, John Oxley Library, SLQ, record number: 187795.

State Library of Victoria (SLV)

Liardet, W.F.E., 'The First Execution', Watercolor, Pencil, Pen and Ink, 8.7 × 16.4 cm, 1875, SLV, H28250/14.

Macfarlane, J., 'The Executive Council Considering a Death Sentence, 1892', Print of a Wood Engraving, Melbourne: David Syme and Co., SLV.

State Records Authority of New South Wales (SRNSW)

'Woolloomooloo Gaol, Execution of John Knatchbull', SRNSW, Government Printing Office, Glass Negative 1–21799.

'New South Wales Charter of Justice, Letters Patent, 2 April 1787', SRNSW, SRNSW:X24.

State Records of South Australia (SRSA)

'Despatches Received from the Secretary of State, London, Later Governor General, 1892', SRSA, GRG2/1/52.

'Despatches Received from the Secretary of State, London, Later Governor General, 1905', SRSA, GRG2/1/70.

'Dispatches Received from the Secretary of State, London, Later Governor General, 27 June and 28 December, 1880', SRSA, GRG 2/1/40.

'Execution, Whippings and Commuted Death Sentence Register', SRSA, GRS 2625/1.

Tasmanian Archives (TA)

'Copies of Declaration by Witnesses and Doctors of the Execution of Convicted Persons, 1 January 1856 to 31 December 1946', TA, SC485/1/1.

Published Colonial Material

Books and Pamphlets (Including Reprints and New Editions)

Bannow, Waldemar, *The Colony of Victoria, Socially and Materially*, Melbourne: McCarron, Bird & Co., 1896.

Blackstone, William, *Commentaries on the Laws of England: Book the Fourth* [1769], W. Prest and R. Paley (eds), Oxford: Oxford University Press, 2016.

Brewer, Ebenezer Cobham, *Dictionary of Phrase and Fable: Giving the Derivation, Source, or Origin of Common Phrases, Allusions, and Words That Have a Tale to Tell* [1870], Cambridge: Cambridge University Press, 2014.

Burford, W.H., *Lecture on Capital Punishment, Viewed in Its Social, Political, and Scriptural Aspects*, Adelaide: William Kyffin Thomas Printer, 1864.

Calvert, Albert Frederick, *My Fourth Tour in Western Australia*, London: W. Heinemann, 1897.

Capper, Henry, *Capper's South Australia: Containing the History of the Rise, Progress and Present State of the Colony, Hints to Emigrants … Embellished with Three Maps Showing the Maritime Portion of the Located Districts, the … Districts of Adelaide and Encounter Bay, and the City of Adelaide*, third edition, London: H. Capper, 1839.

Castieau, John Buckley, *The Difficulties of My Position: The Diaries of Prison Governor John Buckley Castieau, 1855–1884*, M. Finnane (ed.), Canberra: National Library of Australia, 2004.

Clarke, Marcus, *For the Term of His Natural Life* [1870–1872], Adelaide: Rigby Limited, 1977.

Collins, David, *An Account of the English Colony in New South Wales, from Its First Settlement in January 1788, to August 1801: With Remarks on the Dispositions, Customs, Manners &c. of the Native Inhabitants of That Country*, second edition, London: T. Cadell and W. Davies, 1804.

Cunningham, Peter, *Two Years in New South Wales: Comprising Sketches of the Actual State of Society in That Colony, of Its Peculiar Advantages to Emigrants, of Its Topography, Natural History, &c. &c.*, vol. 2, London: Henry Colburn, 1827.

Finn, Edmund (pseudonym 'Garryowen'), *The Chronicles of Early Melbourne 1835 to 1852: Historical, Anecdotal and Personal* [1888], centennial edition, Melbourne: Heritage Publications, 1976.

Ford, John J., *Capital Punishment*, Melbourne: The Australian Catholic Truth Society, 18[-?].

G.H., *A Lecture on Capital Punishment, Delivered at the Court House, Orange, New South Wales by G.H., an Old Settler*, Orange: Printed at the 'Western Examiner' Office, 1871.

Grose, Francis, *1811 Dictionary of the Vulgar Tongue. A Dictionary of Buckish Slang, University Wit, and Pickpocket Eloquence* [1811], Adelaide: Bibliophile Books, 1981.

Hamilton, A.S., *Abstract of a Lecture on Criminal Legislation, Prison Discipline, and the Causes of Crime, and on Capital Punishments: With Delineations on the Characters of Alexander and Charles Ross*, Sydney: F. Cunningham, 1863.

Hill, W.R.O., *Forty-Five Years' Experiences in North Queensland, 1861 to 1905, with a Few Incidents in England, 1844 to 1861*, Brisbane: H. Pole & Col., Printers 1907.

Hotton, John Camden, *A Dictionary of Modern Slang, Cant, and Vulgar Words*, London: Antiquarian Bookseller, Piccadilly, 1859.

Hotton, John Camden, *The Slang Dictionary, Etymological, Historical and Anecdotal: A New Edition, Revised and Corrected, with Many Additions*, London: Chatto and Windus Publishers, 1874.

'Iota', *Crime: Its Causes: Is Death Punishment a Deterrent?* West Maitland: T. Dimmock, Printer and Publisher, High Street, 1880.

James, T. Horton, *Six Months in South Australia: With Some Account of Port Philip and Portland Bay, in Australia Felix: With Advice to Emigrants: To*

Which Is Added a Monthly Calendar of Gardening and Agriculture, Adapted to the Climate and Seasons [1838], Adelaide: Public Library of South Australia, 1962.

Kentish, Nathaniel Lipscomb, *Essay on Capital Punishment*, Hobart Town: S. A. Tegg, 1842.

Kingsley, Henry, *The Recollections of Geoffry Hamlyn*, New York: Longmans, Green & Co., 1899.

Lang, John Dunmore, *An Historical and Statistical Account of New South Wales, both as a Penal Settlement and as a British Colony*, vol. 2, second edition, London: A. J. Valpy, 1837.

Lee, Fredrick, *Abolition of Capital Punishment: A Lecture, Delivered in the School of Arts, Sydney, New South Wales, on Thursday, May 26, 1864*, Sydney: Hanson and Bennet Printers, 1864.

Marjoribanks, Alexander, *Travels in New South Wales*, London: Smith, Elder, and Co., 1847.

McLaren, David, *Lecture on the Abolition of Capital Punishments Delivered by David McLaren to the Literary and Scientific Association and Mechanic's Institute, at Adelaide, December 18, 1840*, Hobart Town: S.A. Tegg, 1842.

Molesworth, William, *Report from the Select Committee of the House of Commons on Transportation: Together with a Letter from the Archbishop of Dublin on the Same Subject: And Notes*, London: Henry Hooper, 1838.

Nayler, Benjamin Suggitt, *An Appeal from the Prejudices, to the Judgements, of the Inhabitants of Melbourne; on the Capital Punishment Question*, Melbourne: Robert Bell, Machine Printer, 1866.

'Officer', *An Authentic and Interresting [sic] Narrative of the Late Expedition to Botany Bay*, London: W. Bailey, 1789.

Paterson, G., *The History of New South Wales from Its First Discovery to the Present Time*, Newcastle-upon-Tyne: Mackenzie and Dent, 1811.

Petrie, Constance Campbell, *Tom Petrie's Reminiscences of Early Queensland*, Brisbane: Watson and Ferguson, 1904.

Taylor, Alfred Joseph, *Additional Notes on Capital Punishment*, Hobart Town: Printed at the 'Mercury' Steam Press Office, 1878.

Taylor, Alfred Joseph, *Capital Punishment: Reasons Why the Death Penalty Should Be Abolished; with Suggestions for an Efficient Substitute*, Hobart Town: Davies Bros., Printers 'Mercury' Steam Press Office, 1877.

Taylor, Alfred Joseph, *The Death Penalty: A Plea for the Abolition of Capital Punishment*, Hobart: Printed at The Daily Post, 1912.

Tench, Watkin, *A Narrative of the Expedition to Botany Bay, with an Account of New South Wales, Its Productions, Inhabitants, &c. To Which Is subjoined, A*

List of the Civil and Military Establishments at Port Jackson [1789], Sydney: Sydney University Library, 1998.

Todd, Alpheus, *Parliamentary Government in the British Colonies* [1880], 2nd edition, Clark: The Lawbook Exchange, 2006.

Tolmer, Alexander, *Reminiscences of an Adventurous and Chequered Career at Home and at the Antipodes, Volume 1* [1882], facsimile edition, London: Gilbert and Rivington Ltd., 1972.

Ullathorne, William, *The Autobiography of Archbishop Ullathorne with Selections from His Letters*, London: Burns & Oates Ltd., 1891.

Wardley, Edward (pseudonym 'Fiat Justitia'), *The Abolition of Capital Punishment Considered by 'Fiat Justitia'*, Sydney: Gibbs, Shallard, & Co., Machine Printers, 1869.

Weale, John Camille, *The Calvary of Superstition or the Downfall of the Scaffold: An Essay on Capital Punishment*, Brisbane: A. Keith, Leader Office, Albert Street, 1886.

West, John, *The History of Tasmania* [1852], A.G.L. Shaw (ed.), Sydney: Angus and Robertson, 1971.

Willmer, George, *The Draper in Australia: Being a Narrative of Three Years' Adventures and Experience at the Gold-Fields, in the Bush and in the Chief Cities of Victoria and New South Wales; with Information and Advice Adapted for the Intending Emigrant and Others*, London: W. Freeman, 1856.

Newspapers, Periodicals and Government Gazettes

New South Wales

Australian
Australian Star
Bathurst Free Press
Bathurst Free Press and Mining Journal
Bell's Life in Sydney and Sporting Reviewer
Daily Telegraph
Empire
Evening News
Freeman's Journal
Hebrew Standard of Australasia
Morning Chronicle
People's Advocate
Queanbeyan Age
Sydney Chronicle
Sydney Gazette

Sydney Punch
The Armidale Express and New England General Advertiser
The Atlas
The Bird O' Freedom
The Bulletin
The Dubbo Liberal and Macquarie Advocate
The Maitland Mercury
The Maitland Mercury and Hunter River General Advertiser
The Riverine Grazier
The Sydney Gazette and New South Wales Advertiser
The Sydney Herald
The Sydney Monitor
The Sydney Morning Herald
Wagga Wagga Express

Queensland
Darling Downs Gazette
Evening Observer
Maryborough Chronicle
Maryborough Chronicle, Wide Bay and Burnett Advertiser
Moreton Bay Free Press
Queensland Times, Ipswich Herald and General Advertiser
The Brisbane Courier
The Darling Downs and General Advertiser
The Moreton Bay Courier
The Week

South Australia
Adelaide Observer
Adelaide Times
Adelaide Weekly Chronicle
Evening Journal
Kapunda Herald
Recorder
South Australian Government Gazette
South Australian Register
The Advertiser
The South Australian Advertiser
Wallaroo Times

Tasmania

Colonial Times
Colonial Times and Tasmanian Advertiser
Hobart Town Gazette
Hobart Town Gazette and Van Diemen's Land Advertiser
Launceston Examiner
The Cornwall Chronicle
The Courier
The Hobart Town Courier
The Hobart Town Gazette and Southern Reporter
The Hobarton Mercury
The Mercury
Tribune

Victoria

Bendigo Advertiser
Geelong Advertiser
Melbourne Punch
Mercury and Weekly Courier
Mount Alexander Mail
Northam Advertiser
Ovens and Murray Advertiser
Port Phillip Herald
Portland Guardian and Normanby General Advertiser
The Age
The Argus
The Ballarat Star
The Free Lance
The Maffra Spectator
The Port Phillip Gazette
Victorian Government Gazette

Western Australia

Albany Advertiser
Inquirer
The Australian
The Herald
The Inquirer and Commercial News
The Perth Gazette and Independent Journal of Politics and News
The Perth Gazette and Western Australian Times
The West Australian

The Western Australian Times
Western Mail

International
Hawke's Bay Herald (New Zealand)
The Colonist (New Zealand)

Secondary Sources

Published Books, Book Chapters and Journal Articles

Adams, Simon, *The Unforgiving Rope: Murder and Hanging on Australia's Western Frontier*, Perth: UWA Publishing, 2009.

Anderson, Kay, *Race and the Crisis of Humanism*, London: Routledge, 2007.

Anderson, Margaret, 'Good Strong Girls: Colonial Women and Work', in K. Saunders and R. Evans (eds), *Gender Relations in Australia: Domination and Negotiation*, Sydney: Harcourt Brace Jovanovich Publishers, 1992, pp. 225–245.

Anderson, Steven, 'Nineteenth Century Dreams, Twentieth Century Realities: Reframing the Abolition of Capital Punishment in South Australia', in C. Collins and P. Sendziuk (eds), *Foundational Fictions in South Australian History*, Adelaide: Wakefield Press, 2018, pp. 165–176.

Anderson, Steven, 'Punishment as Pacification: The Role of Indigenous Executions on the South Australian Frontier, 1836–1862', *Aboriginal History*, vol. 39, 2015, pp. 3–26.

Anderson, Steven, and Paul Sendziuk, 'Hang the Convicts: Capital Punishment and the Reaffirmation of South Australia's Foundation Principles', *Journal of Australian Colonial History*, vol. 16, 2014, pp. 83–111.

Banner, Stuart, *The Death Penalty: An American History*, Cambridge, MA: Harvard University Press, 2002.

Barber, Ross, 'Rape as a Capital Offence in Nineteenth Century Queensland', *Australian Journal of Politics and History*, vol. 21, no. 1, 1975, pp. 31–41.

Barber, Ross, 'The Labor Party and the Abolition of Capital Punishment in Queensland, 1899–1922', *Queensland Heritage*, vol. 1, no. 9, 1968, pp. 3–10.

Barber, Ross, and P.R. Wilson, 'Deterrent Aspect of Capital Punishment and Its Effect on Conviction Rates: The Queensland Experience', *Australian and New Zealand Journal of Criminology*, vol. 2, 1968, pp. 100–108.

Barry, Judy E., *Executions at the Old Ararat Gaol*, Ararat: Judy E. Barry, 1990.

Beck, Deborah, *Hope in Hell: A History of Darlinghurst Gaol and the National Art School*, Sydney: Allen and Unwin, 2005.

Beckett, Ray, and Richard Beckett, *Hangman: The Life and Times of Alexander Green, Public Executioner to the Colony of New South Wales*, Melbourne: Thomas Nelson Australia, 1980.

Behan, H.F., *Mr. Justice J.W. Willis: With Particular Reference to His Period as First Resident Judge of Port Phillip 1841–1843*, Melbourne: Harold Frederick Behan, 1979.

Bennett, Rachel E., *Capital Punishment and the Criminal Corpse in Scotland, 1740–1834*, Basingstoke: Palgrave Macmillan, 2018.

Bessler, John D., *Death in the Dark: Midnight Executions in America*, Boston: Northeastern University Press, 1997.

Boyce, James, *Van Diemen's Land*, Melbourne: Black Inc., 2008.

Briggs, Asa, *The Age of Improvement, 1783–1867*, second edition, Harlow: Pearson Education Limited, 2000.

Briggs, Asa, *Victorian Cities*, Harmondsworth: Penguin Books, 1963.

Briggs, Asa, *Victorian People: A Reassessment of Persons and Themes, 1851–1867*, London: Penguin Books, 1954.

Briggs, John, Christopher Harrison, Angus McInnes, and David Vincent, *Crime and Punishment in England: An Introductory History*, London: UCL Press, 1996.

Brown, George, David Button, Elizabeth Mercer, Peter Mercer, and Brian Rieusset, *The Penitentiary Chapel Historic Site*, Hobart: National Trust of Australia, 2007.

Cannon, Michael, *The Woman as Murderer: Five Who Paid with Their Lives*, Mornington: Today's Australia Publishing Company, 1994.

Castle, Tim, 'Constructing Death: Newspaper Reports of Executions in Colonial New South Wales, 1826–1837', *Journal of Australian Colonial History*, vol. 9, 2007, pp. 51–68.

Castle, Tim, 'Watching Them Hang: Capital Punishment and Public Support in Colonial New South Wales, 1826–1836', *History Australia*, vol. 5, no. 2, 2008, pp. 43.1–43.15.

Castles, Alex, *An Australian Legal History*, Sydney: The Law Book Company Limited, 1982.

Chisholm, Hugh (ed.), *The Encyclopaedia Britannica*, 11th edition, New York: The Encyclopaedia Britannica Corporation, 1910.

Clark, Manning, *A History of Australia*, vol. 2, Melbourne: Melbourne University Press, 1968.

Clements, Nicholas, *The Black War: Fear, Sex and Resistance in Tasmania*, Brisbane: University of Queensland Press, 2014.

Clune, Frank, *The Norfolk Island Story*, Sydney: Angus & Robertson, 1967.

Cobley, John, *Sydney Cove 1788*, London: Camelot Press Ltd., 1962.

Connors, Libby, 'A Hanging, a Hostage Drama and Several Homicides: Why Sovereignty in 1859 Is Problematic', *Queensland History Journal*, vol. 20, no. 12, 2009, pp. 716–727.

Connors, Libby, 'Sentencing on a Colonial Frontier: Judge Therry's Decisions at Moreton Bay', *Legal History*, vol. 12, 2008, pp. 81–97.

Connors, Libby, 'The Theatre of Justice: Race Relations and Capital Punishment at Moreton Bay 1841–59', in R. Fisher (ed.), *Brisbane: The Aboriginal Presence 1824–1860*, Brisbane: Brisbane History Group, 1992, pp. 48–57.

Connors, Libby, 'Traditional Law and Indigenous Resistance at Moreton Bay 1842–1855, Part II', *Australian and New Zealand Law and History E-Journal*, 2006, pp. 1–14.

Connors, Libby, 'Traditional Law and Indigenous Resistance at Moreton Bay 1842–1855', *Australian and New Zealand Law and History E-Journal*, 2005, pp. 107–117.

Cooper, David D., *The Lesson of the Scaffold: The Public Execution Controversy in Victorian England*, London: Allen Lane, 1974.

Davies, Susanne, 'Aborigines, Murder and the Criminal Law in Early Port Phillip, 1841–1851', *Historical Studies*, vol. 22, no. 88, 1987, pp. 313–335.

Davis, Jennifer, 'Book Review: *A History of the English Criminal Law and Its Administration from 1750, Volume 5*', *The Cambridge Law Journal*, vol. 45, no. 3, 1986, pp. 521–523.

Davis, Richard, *The Tasmanian Gallows: A Study of Capital Punishment*, Hobart: Cat and Fiddle Press, 1974.

Davison, G., J. Hirst, and S. Macintyre (eds), *The Oxford Companion to Australian History*, revised edition, Melbourne: Oxford University Press, 2001.

Dawson, Christopher, *A Pit of Shame: The Executed Prisoners of Boggo Road*, second edition, Brisbane: Inside History, 2010.

Dawson, Christopher, *Dirty Dozen: Hanging and the Moreton Bay Convicts*, Brisbane: Inside History, 2007.

Dawson, Christopher, *No Ordinary Run of Men: The Queensland Executioners*, Brisbane: Inside History, 2010.

Dawson, Christopher, *Swinging in the Sixties: Hanging Around Colonial Queensland*, Brisbane: Inside History, 2011.

Dawson, Christopher, *That Gingerbread Structure: The Trials and Tribulations of the Queen Street Gaol*, Brisbane: Inside History, 2010.

Dawson, Christopher, 'The Dead Outside the Fence: Burying Executed Prisoners in Brisbane, 1830–1913', *Queensland History Journal*, vol. 20, no. 8, 2008, pp. 351–369.

Dawson, Christopher, *The Hanging at the Brisbane Windmill*, Brisbane: Inside History, 2009.

Dawson, Christopher, *The Prisoners of Toowong Cemetery: Life, Death and the Old Petrie Terrace Gaol*, Brisbane: Inside History, 2006.

Dixson, Miriam, *The Real Matilda: Women and Identity in Australia—1788 to the Present* [1976], fourth edition, Sydney: UNSW Press, 1999.

Donaldson, I., and T. Donaldson (eds), *Seeing the First Australians*, Sydney: Allen & Unwin, 1985.

Douglas, Heather, and Mark Finnane, *Indigenous Crime and Settler Law: White Sovereignty After Empire*, Basingstoke: Palgrave Macmillan, 2012.

Doyle, Helen, 'Batavia', in G. Davison, J. Hirst, and S. Macintyre (eds), *The Oxford Companion to Australian History*, revised edition, Melbourne: Oxford University Press, 2001, pp. 62–63.

Doyle, Helen, 'Mount Rennie Rape', in *The Oxford Companion to Australian History*, G. Davison et al. (eds), Melbourne: Oxford University Press, 1998, p. 441.

Duff, R. A., *Punishment, Communication, and Community*, Oxford: Oxford University Press, 2003.

Duff, Xavier, *Noose: True Stories of Australians Who Died at the Gallows*, Melbourne: The Five Mile Press, 2014.

Dunning, Eric, and Stephen Mennell, 'Elias on Germany, Nazism and the Holocaust: On the Balance Between "Civilizing" and "Decivilizing" Trends in the Social Development of Western Europe', *British Journal of Sociology*, vol. 49, no. 3, 1998, pp. 339–357.

Elias, Norbert, *The Civilizing Process* [1939], 2nd revised edition, E. Dunning, J. Goudsblom, and S. Mennell (eds), E. Jephcott (trans), Oxford: Blackwell, 2000.

Evans, Raymond, and Kay Saunders, 'No Place Like Home: The Evolution of the Australian Housewife', in K. Saunders and R. Evans (eds), *Gender Relations in Australia: Domination and Negotiation*, Sydney: Harcourt Brace Jovanovich Publishers, 1992, pp. 167–175.

Evans, Richard J., 'Justice Seen, Justice Done? Abolishing Public Executions in 19th-Century Germany', *History Today*, vol. 46, no. 4, 1996.

Evans, Richard J., *Rituals of Retribution: Capital Punishment in Germany, 1600–1987*, Oxford: Oxford University Press, 1996.

Finnane, Mark, *Punishment in Australian Society*, Melbourne: Oxford University Press, 1997.

Finnane, Mark, 'Settler Justice and Aboriginal Homicide in Late Colonial Australia', *Australian Historical Studies*, vol. 42, no. 2, 2011, pp. 244–259.

Finnane, Mark, and John McGuire, 'The Uses of Punishment and Exile: Aborigines in Colonial Australia', *Punishment and Society*, vol. 3, no. 2, 2001, pp. 279–298.

Finnane, Mark, and Jonathon Richards, 'Aboriginal Violence and State Responses: Histories, Policies and Legacies in Queensland, 1860–1940', *Australian and New Zealand Journal of Criminology*, vol. 43, 2010, pp. 238–261.

Foster, Robert, '"Don't Mention the War": Frontier Violence and the Language of Concealment', *History Australia*, vol. 6, no. 3, 2009, pp. 68.1–68.15.

Foster, Robert, Rick Hosking, and Amanda Nettelbeck, *Fatal Collisions: The South Australian Frontier and the Violence of Memory*, Adelaide: Wakefield Press, 2001.

Foucault, Michel, *Discipline and Punish: The Birth of the Prison* [1975], Alan Sheridan (trans), New York: Vintage Books, 1995.

Friedland, Paul, *Seeing Justice Done: The Age of Spectacular Capital Punishment in France*, Oxford: Oxford University Press, 2012.

Garkawe, Sam, 'The Reintroduction of the Death Penalty in Australia?—Political and Legal Considerations', *Criminal Law Journal*, vol. 24, no. 2, 2002, pp. 101–108.

Garland, David, 'A Culturalist Theory of Punishment? Review of Philip Smith, *Punishment and Culture*', *Punishment & Society*, vol. 11, no. 2, 2009, pp. 259–268.

Garland, David, 'Foucault's "Discipline and Punish"—An Exposition and Critique', *American Bar Foundation Research Journal*, vol. 11, no. 4, 1986, pp. 847–880.

Garland, David, *Peculiar Institution: America's Death Penalty in an Age of Abolition*, Oxford: Oxford University Press, 2010.

Garland, David, *Punishment and Modern Society: A Study in Social Theory*, Oxford: Clarendon Press, 1990.

Garland, David, *The Culture of Control: Crime and Social Order in Contemporary Society*, Oxford: Oxford University Press, 2001.

Gatrell, V.A.C., *The Hanging Tree: Execution and the English People 1770–1868*, Oxford: Oxford University Press, 1994.

Gilchrist, C., 'Space, Sexuality and Convict Resistance in Van Diemen's Land: The Limits of Repression?' *Eras Journal*, vol. 6, 2004.

Gleeson, K., 'From Centenary to the Olympics, Gang Rape in Sydney', *Current Issues in Criminal Justice*, vol. 16, no. 3, 2004, pp. 183–201.

Gregory, James, *Victorians Against the Gallows: Capital Punishment and the Abolitionist Movement in Nineteenth Century Britain*, London: I. B. Tauris, 2012.

Greig, Alastair, *The Australian Way of Life: A Sociological Introduction*, Melbourne: Palgrave Macmillan, 2013.

Griffiths, A.R.G., 'Capital Punishment in South Australia 1836–1964', *Australian & New Zealand Journal of Criminology*, vol. 3, no. 4, 1970, pp. 214–222.

Harris, Carmel, 'The Terror of the Law as Applied to Black Rapists in Colonial Queensland', *Hecate*, vol. 8, no. 2, 1982, pp. 22–48.

Harris, Steve, *Solomon's Noose: The True Story of Her Majesty's Hangman of Hobart*, Melbourne: Melbourne Books, 2015.

Hay, Douglas, Peter Linebaugh, John G. Rule, E.P. Thompson, and Cal Winslow, *Albion's Fatal Tree: Crime and Society in Eighteenth-Century England* [1975], revised edition, London: Verso, 2011.

Hobsbawm, Eric, *Bandits* [1969], revised edition, London: Abacus, 2001.

Hobsbawm, Eric, *Primitive Rebels*, Manchester: Manchester University Press, 1959.

Hornadge, Bill, *Old Dubbo Gaol*, Dubbo: Old Dubbo Gaol Restoration Committee, 1974.

Hughes, Robert, *The Fatal Shore: A History of Transportation of Convicts to Australia, 1787–1868*, London: Vintage Books, 1986.

Ignatieff, Michael, *A Just Measure of Pain: The Penitentiary in the Industrial Revolution, 1750–1850*, New York: Pantheon Books, 1978.

Ingleton, Geoffrey Chapman, *True Patriots All, or News from Early Australia*, Sydney: Angus and Robertson, 1952.

Johnston, Judith, and Monica Anderson, *Australia Imagined: Views from the British Periodical Press: 1800–1900*, Perth: University of Western Australia Press, 2005.

Jones, Barry (ed.), *The Penalty Is Death: Capital Punishment in the Twentieth Century, Retentionist and Abolitionist Arguments with Special Reference to Australia*, Melbourne: Sun Books, 1968.

Jones, Ian, *Ned Kelly: A Short Life*, Sydney: Hachette Australia, 2008.

Kaladelfos, A., 'The "Condemned Criminals": Sexual Violence, Race, and Manliness in Colonial Australia', *Women's History Review*, vol. 21, no. 5, 2012, pp. 697–714.

Kaladelfos, A., 'The Politics of Punishment: Rape and the Death Penalty in Colonial Australia, 1841–1901', *History Australia*, vol. 9, no. 1, 2012, pp. 155–175.

Kercher, Bruce, *An Unruly Child: A History of Law in Australia*, Sydney: Allen and Unwin, 1995.

Kirby, Michael, 'The Sodomy Offence: England's Least Lovely Criminal Law Export?', in C. Lennox and M. Waites, *Human Rights, Sexual Orientation and Gender Identity in the Commonwealth*, London: School of Advanced Study University of London, pp. 61–82.

Kociumbas, Jan, *Australian Childhood: A History*, Sydney: Allen and Unwin, 1997.

Kociumbas, Jan, *The Oxford History of Australia: Possessions, 1770–1860*, vol. 2, Melbourne: Oxford University Press, 1992.

Konishi, Shino, *The Aboriginal Male in the Enlightenment World*, London: Pickering & Chatto Publishers, 2012.

Langbein, John H., 'Albion's Fatal Flaws', *Past and Present*, no. 98, 1983, pp. 96–120.

Laqueur, Thomas W., 'Crowds, Carnival and the State in English Executions', in A.L. Beier, D. Cannadine, and J.M. Rosenheim, *The First Modern Society: Essays in English History in Honour of Lawrence Stone*, Cambridge: Cambridge University Press, 1989, pp. 305–355.

Laster, Kathy, 'Arbitrary Chivalry: Women and Capital Punishment in Victoria, 1842–1967', in D. Philips and S. Davies (eds), *A Nation of Rogues? Crime, Law and Punishment in Colonial Australia*, Melbourne: Melbourne University Press, 1994, pp. 166–186.

Laster, Kathy, 'Famous Last Words: Criminals on the Scaffold, Victoria, Australia, 1842–1967', *International Journal of the Sociology of Law*, vol. 22, 1994, pp. 1–18.

Laster, Kathy, and Kerry Alexander, 'Chivalry or Death: Women on the Gallows in Victoria, 1856–1975', *Criminology Australia*, vol. 4, no. 2, 1992, pp. 6–10.

Laster, Kathy, and R. Douglas, 'A Matter of Life and Death: The Victorian Executive and the Decision to Execute 1842–1967', *The Australian and New Zealand Journal of Criminology*, vol. 24, no. 2, 1991, pp. 144–160.

Lattas, Andrew, 'The Aesthetics of Terror and the Personification of Power: Public Executions and the Cultural Construction of Class Relations in

Colonial New South Wales, 1788–1830', *Social Analysis*, no. 19, 1986, pp. 3–21.

Lennan, Jo, and George Williams, 'The Death Penalty in Australian Law', *Sydney Law Review*, vol. 34, 2012, pp. 659–694.

Leyton-Brown, Ken, *The Practice of Execution in Canada*, Vancouver: UBC Press, 2010.

Liddy, Peter, *The Rainberd Murders: 1861*, Adelaide: Peacock Publications, 1993.

Linders, Annulla, 'The Execution Spectacle and State Legitimacy: The Changing Nature of the American Execution Audience, 1833–1937', *Law and Society Review*, vol. 36, no. 2, 2002, pp. 607–656.

Linebaugh, Peter, *The London Hanged: Crime and Civil Society in the Eighteenth Century*, London: Verso, 2003.

Linklater, Andrew, and Stephen Mennell, 'Norbert Elias, *The Civilizing Process: Sociogenetic and Psychogenetic Investigations*—An Overview and Assessment', *History and Theory*, vol. 49, 2010, pp. 384–411.

Lucy, Richard, 'The Division of Powers Between the British Empire and Its Australian Self-Governing Colonies, 1855–1900', *Australian Journal of Law and Society*, vol. 6, 1990, pp. 83–96.

Lukes, Steven, and Andrew Scull (eds), *Durkheim and the Law*, Oxford: Martin Robertson & Company, 1983.

MacDonald, Helen, *Human Remains: Dissection and Its Histories*, Melbourne: Melbourne University Press, 2005.

MacFarlane, Ian, *1842: The Public Executions at Melbourne*, Melbourne: Victorian Government Printing Office, 1984.

Mac Master, Hugh, *Mostly Murder*, North Rockhampton: Hugh Mac Master, 1999.

Main, Jim, *Hanged: Executions in Australia*, Melbourne: Bas Publishing, 2007.

Martschukat, Jürgen, 'A Horrifying Experience? Public Executions and the Emotional Spectator in the New Republic', in J.C.E. Gienow-Hecht (ed.), *Emotions in American History: An International Assessment*, New York: Berghahn Books, 2010, pp. 181–200.

Martschukat, Jürgen, 'Nineteenth-Century Executions as Performances of Law, Death, and Civilization', in Austin Sarat and Christian Boulanger (eds), *The Cultural Lives of Capital Punishment: Comparative Perspectives*, Stanford: Stanford University Press, 2005, pp. 49–68.

Masur, Louis P., *Rites of Execution: Capital Punishment and the Transformation of American Culture, 1776–1865*, Oxford: Oxford University Press, 1989.

Maxwell-Stewart, Hamish, *Closing Hells Gates: The Death of a Convict Station*, Sydney: Allen and Unwin, 2008.

McGowen, Randall, 'A Powerful Sympathy: Terror, the Prison, and Humanitarian Reform in Early Nineteenth-Century Britain', *Journal of British Studies*, vol. 25, no. 3, 1986, pp. 312–334.

McGowen, Randall, 'Civilizing Punishment: The End of the Public Execution in England', *Journal of British Studies*, vol. 33, no. 3, 1994, pp. 257–282.

McGowen, Randall, 'Cruel Inflictions and the Claims of Humanity in Early Nineteenth-Century England', in K.D. Watson (ed.), *Assaulting the Past: Violence and Civilization in History Context*, Newcastle: Cambridge Scholars Publishing, 2007, pp. 38–57.

McGowen, Randall, 'History, Culture and the Death Penalty: The British Debates, 1840–70', *Historical Reflections*, vol. 29, no. 2, 2003, pp. 229–249.

McGowen, Randall, 'Power and Humanity, or Foucault Among the Historians', in C. Jones and R. Porter (eds), *Reassessing Foucault: Power, Medicine and the Body*, London: Routledge, 1994, pp. 91–112.

McGowen, Randall, 'Punishing Violence, Sentencing Crime', in N. Armstrong and L. Tennenhouse (eds), *The Violence of Representation: Literature and the History of Violence*, London: Routledge, 1989, pp. 140–156.

McGowen, Randall, 'The Body and Punishment in Eighteenth-Century England', *The Journal of Modern History*, vol. 59, no. 4, 1987, pp. 651–679.

McGowen, Randall, 'The Image of Justice and Reform of the Criminal Law in Early Nineteenth-Century England', *Buffalo Law Review*, vol. 32, 1983, pp. 89–125.

McGregor, Russell, 'The Doomed Race: A Scientific Axiom of the Late Nineteenth Century', *Australian Journal of Politics and History*, vol. 39, no. 1, 1993, pp. 14–22.

McGuire, John, 'Judicial Violence and the "Civilizing Process": Race and the Transition from Public to Private Executions in Colonial Australia', *Australian Historical Studies*, vol. 29, no. 111, 1998, pp. 187–209.

McKenzie, Andrea, 'Martyrs in Low Life? Dying "Game" in Augustan England', *Journal of British Studies*, vol. 42, no. 2, 2003, pp. 167–205.

Melossi, Dario, 'The Penal Question in *Capital*', *Crime and Social Justice*, vol. 5, 1976, pp. 26–33.

Mennell, Stephen, 'Decivilising Processes: Theoretical Significance and Some Lines of Research', *International Sociology*, vol. 5, no. 2, 1990, pp. 205–223.

Mennell, Stephen, and Johan Goudsblom, 'Civilizing Processes—Myth or Reality? A Comment on Duerr's Critique of Elias', *Comparative Studies in Society and History*, vol. 39, no. 4, 1997, pp. 729–733.

Morgan, Kevin, *The Particulars of Executions 1894–1967: The Hidden Truth About Capital Punishment at the Old Melbourne Gaol and Pentridge Prison*, Melbourne: The Old Melbourne Gaol, 2004.

Mukherjee, Satyanshu K., John R. Walker, and Evelyn N. Jacobsen (eds), *Crime and Punishment in the Colonies: A Statistical Profile*, Historical Statistics Monograph no. 6, Sydney: History Project Inc., 1986.

Nadel, George, *Australia's Colonial Culture: Ideas, Men and Institutions in Mid-Nineteenth Century Eastern Australia*, Cambridge, MA: Harvard University Press, 1957.

National Trust of Australia, *The Old Melbourne Gaol*, Melbourne: National Trust of Australia, 1991.

Parkinson, Patrick, *Tradition and Change in Australian Law*, fifth edition, Sydney: Thomson Reuters (Professional) Australia Limited, 2013.

Peers, Juliet, 'The Tribe of Mary Jane Hicks: Imaging Women Through the Mount Rennie Rape Case 1886', *Australian Cultural History*, no. 12, 1993, pp. 127–144.

Philips, David, 'Sex, Race, Violence and the Criminal Law in Colonial Victoria: Anatomy of a Rape Case in 1888', in D. Philips and S. Davies (eds), *A Nation of Rogues? Crime, Law and Punishment in Colonial Australia*, Melbourne: Melbourne University Press, 1994, pp. 97–122.

Philips, David, 'Sex, Race, Violence and the Criminal Law in Colonial Victoria: Anatomy of a Rape Case in 1888', *Labour History*, no. 52, 1987, pp. 30–39.

Plater, David, and Jenny Crofts, 'Bushrangers, the Exercise of Mercy and the "Last Penalty of the Law" in New South Wales and Tasmania 1824–1856', *University of Tasmania Law Review*, vol. 32, no. 2, 2013, pp. 295–343.

Plater, David, Joanne Duncan, and Sue Milne, '"Innocent Victim of Circumstance" or "a Very Devil Incarnate"? The Trial and Execution of Elizabeth Woolcock in South Australia in 1873', *Flinders Law Journal*, vol. 15, 2013, pp. 315–380.

Plater, David, and Sue Milne, '"The Quality of Mercy Is Not Strained": The Norfolk Island Mutineers and the Exercise of the Death Penalty in Colonial Australia 1824–1860', *Australian and New Zealand Law and History Society e-Journal*, 2012, pp. 1–43.

Pope, Alan, *One Law for All? Aboriginal People and the Criminal Law in Early South Australia*, Canberra: Aboriginal Studies Press, 2011.

Porter, Trevor J., *Executions in the Colony and State of Victoria 1842–1967*, Adelaide: The Wednesday Press, 1999.

Porter, Trevor, *Seven Lengths of Rope*, Adelaide: The Wednesday Press, 1995.

Pratt, John, 'Elias, Punishment, and Decivilization', in J. Pratt, D. Brown, M. Brown, S. Hallsworth, and W. Morrison (eds), *The New Punitiveness: Trends, Theories, Perspectives*, Abingdon, Devon: Willan Publishing, 2005, pp. 256–271.

Pratt, John, *Punishment and Civilization: Penal Tolerance and Intolerance in Modern Society*, London: Sage, 2002.

Pratt, John, *Punishment in a Perfect Society: The New Zealand Penal System, 1840–1939*, Wellington: Victoria University Press, 1992.

Prior, Tom, and John Brosnan, *A Knockabout Priest: The Story of Father John Brosnan*, Melbourne: Hargreen Publishing Company, 1985.

Purdue, Brain, *Legal Executions in Western Australia*, Perth: Foundation Press, 1993.

Radzinowicz, Leon, *A History of the English Criminal Law and its Administration from 1750*, vols. 1–4, London: Stevens and Sons Limited, 1948–1968.

Radzinowicz, Leon, and P.H. Winfield, 'Some Sources of Modern English Criminal Legislation', *The Cambridge Law Journal*, vol. 8, no. 2, 1943, pp. 180–194.

Radzinowicz, Leon, and Roger Hood, *A History of the English Criminal Law and Its Administration from 1750*, vol. 5, London: Stevens and Sons Limited, 1986.

Reece, Bob, 'Tell 'Em I Died Game: The Legend of Ned Kelly—Book Review', *Journal of Australian Studies*, no. 82, 2004, pp. 159–160.

Richards, Mike, 'Ronald Ryan and Ned Kelly', *The Sydney Papers*, vol. 14, no. 2, 2002, pp. 30–40.

Richards, Mike, *The Hanged Man: The Life and Death of Ronald Ryan*, Melbourne: Scribe, 2002.

Rickard, John, *Australia: A Cultural History*, second edition, New York: Addison Wesley Longman Limited, 1996.

Roderick, Colin, *John Knatchbull: From Quarterdeck to Gallows*, Sydney: Angus & Robertson, 1963.

Roe, Michael, *The Quest for Authority in Eastern Australia, 1835–1851*, Melbourne: Melbourne University Press, 1965.

Roginski, Alexandra, *The Hanged Man and the Body Thief: Finding Lives in a Museum Mystery*, Melbourne: Monash University Press, 2015.

Rorty, Richard, *Contingency, Irony, Solidarity*, Cambridge: Cambridge University Press, 1989.

Rusche, Georg, 'Labor Market and Penal Sanction' [1933], *Crime and Social Justice*, vol. 10, 1978, pp. 2–8.

Rusche, Georg, 'Prison Revolts or Social Policy: Lessons from America' [1930], *Crime and Social Justice*, vol. 13, 1980, pp. 41–44.

Rusche, Georg, and Otto Kirchheimer, *Punishment and Social Structure* [1939], New Brunswick: Transaction Publishers, 2003.

Russ, Andrew, and Bianca Zanatta, 'The Application and Eventual Abolition of the Death Penalty in South Australia', South Australian Parliamentary Research Library, 2017.

Russell, Penny, *Savage or Civilised? Manners in Colonial Australia*, Sydney: The University of New South Wales Press, 2010.

Sarat, Austin, and Christian Boulanger, *The Cultural Lives of Capital Punishment: Comparative Perspectives*, Stanford: Stanford University Press, 2005.

Seal, Graham, *Tell 'Em I Died Game: The Legend of Ned Kelly*, second edition, Sydney: Hyland House Publishing, 2002.

Sendziuk, Paul, 'No Convicts Here: Reconsidering South Australia's Foundation Myth', in R. Foster and P. Sendziuk (eds), *Turning Points: Chapters in South Australian History*, Adelaide: Wakefield Press, 2012, pp. 33–47.

Shoemaker, R.S., 'Streets of Shame? The Crowd and Public Punishments in London, 1700–1820', in S. Devereaux and P. Griffiths (eds), *Penal Practice and Culture, 1500–1900: Punishing the English*, New York: Palgrave Macmillan, 2004, pp. 232–257.

Simon, Jonathan, and Richard Sparks (eds), *The Sage Handbook of Punishment and Society*, London: Sage, 2013.

Smith, Greg T., 'Civilized People Don't Want to See That Kind of Thing: The Decline of Public Physical Punishment in London, 1760–1840', in C. Strange (ed.), *Qualities of Mercy: Justice, Punishment, and Discretion*, Vancouver: University of British Columbia Press, 1996, pp. 21–51.

Smith, Philip, *Punishment and Culture*, Chicago: University of Chicago Press, 2008.

Smith, Philip, and Alexander Riley, *Cultural Theory: An Introduction*, second edition, Oxford: Blackwell, 2009.

Smith, Phillip Thurmond, 'Book Review: *A History of the English Criminal Law and Its Administration from 1750, Volume 5*', *The American Historical Review*, vol. 92, no. 3, 1987, pp. 660–661.

Spierenburg, Pieter, *The Spectacle of Suffering: Executions and the Evolution of Repression; From a Preindustrial Metropolis to the European Experience*, Cambridge: Cambridge University Press, 1984.

Strange, Carolyn, 'Capital Punishment', in *The Oxford Companion to Canadian History*, G. Hallowell (ed.), Oxford: Oxford University Press, 2004.

Strange, Carolyn, 'Discretionary Justice: Political Culture and the Death Penalty in New South Wales and Ontario, 1890–1920', in C. Strange (ed.), *Qualities of Mercy: Justice, Punishment, and Discretion*, Vancouver: UBC Press, 1996, pp. 130–165.

Strange, Carolyn, 'Masculinities, Intimate Femicide and the Death Penalty in Australia, 1890–1920', *British Journal of Criminology*, vol. 43, 2003, pp. 310–339.

Strange, Carolyn, 'The Undercurrents of Penal Culture: Punishment of the Body in Mid-Twentieth Century Canada', *Law and History Review*, vol. 19, no. 2, 2001, pp. 343–385.

Sturma, Michael, 'Death and Ritual on the Gallows: Public Executions in the Australian Penal Colonies', *Omega*, vol. 17, no. 1, 1987, pp. 89–100.

Sturma, Michael, 'Public Executions and the Ritual of Death, 1838', *Push from the Bush*, no. 15, 1983, pp. 3–11.

Summers, Anne, *Damned Whores and God's Police: Women's Lives in Australia*, second revised edition, Melbourne: Penguin Books, 1975.

Tait, H.C., 'Convictism to Codification: The Prerogative of Mercy in Colonial Queensland', *Australian Bar Review*, vol. 38, no. 3, 2014, pp. 319–331.

Thompson, E.P., *Whigs and Hunters: The Origin of the Black Act*, London: Allen Lane, 1975.

Thornton, Harold, 'Executive Councils and Their Place in Australian Westminster Systems', *Legislative Studies*, vol. 10, no. 1, 1995, pp. 65–80.

Towler, David J., and Trevor J. Porter, *The Hempen Collar: Executions in South Australia, 1838–1964, A Collection of Eyewitness Accounts*, Adelaide: The Wednesday Press, 1990.

Walker, David, 'Youth on Trial: The Mt Rennie Case', *Labour History*, no. 50, 1986, pp. 28–41.

Ward, Ross, *The Office of the Sheriff: A Millennium of Tradition*, Sydney: Department of Courts Administration, 1992.

Ward, Russel, *The Australian Legend*, Melbourne: Oxford University Press, 1958.

Watson, Frederick (ed.), *Historical Records of Australia*, series 1, vol. 12, Sydney: The Library Committee of the Commonwealth Parliament, 1919.

Watson, Frederick (ed.), *Historical Records of Australia*, series 3, vol. 3, Sydney: The Library Committee of the Commonwealth Parliament, 1921.

White, Matthew, 'Rogues of the Meaner Sort? Old Bailey Executions and the Crowd in the Early Nineteenth Century', *The London Journal*, vol. 33, no. 2, 2008, pp. 135–153.

Wiener, Martin J., 'The March of Penal Progress?', *Journal of British Studies*, vol. 26, no. 1, 1987, pp. 83–96.
Wilson, Dean, 'Explaining the "Criminal": Kelly's Death Mask', *The La Trobe Journal*, no. 69, 2002, pp. 51–58.
Wilson, Jan, 'An Irresistible Impulse of Mind: Crime and the Legal Defense of Moral Insanity in Nineteenth Century Australia', *Australian Journal of Law and Society*, vol. 11, 1995, pp. 137–168.
Woods, Gregory D., *A History of Criminal Law in New South Wales: The Colonial Period, 1788–1900*, Sydney: The Federation Press, 2002.
Young, Sherwood, *Guilty on the Gallows: Famous Capital Crimes of New Zealand*, Wellington: Grantham House, 1998.

Unpublished Theses

Barber, Ross, 'Capital Punishment in Queensland', unpublished B.A. (Hons) thesis, The University of Queensland, 1967.
Coates, Peter Ralph, 'Cape Colonial Parliamentary Publications, 1854–1910, with Special Reference to Documents in the Dutch Language', unpublished Information Science M.A. Thesis, University of South Africa, 2009.
Mattingley, Neil, 'The Abolition of Capital Punishment in Western Australia, 1960–1984', unpublished B.A. (Hons) thesis, Murdoch University, 1990.
McGuire, John, 'Punishment and Colonial Society: A History of Penal Change in Queensland, 1859–1930s', unpublished PhD thesis, The University of Queensland, 2002.
Phillips, Patricia K., 'John McEncroe', unpublished M.A. thesis, The University of Sydney, 1965.
Tait, H.C., 'Law's Objects: Execution and Reprieve in Queensland, 1859–1900', unpublished B.A. (Hons) thesis, University of Queensland, 2013.
Thompson, Zachary, 'Destroying Sodom in the South Pacific: How the Terror of Sodomy Was Invoked to End Convict Transportation to New South Wales c.1837', unpublished B.A. (Hons) thesis, The University of Sydney, 2013.
White, Matthew Trevor, 'Ordering the Mob: London's Public Punishments, c.1783–1868', unpublished PhD thesis, The University of Hertfordshire, 2009.
Wintle, Arthur L. 'The Abolition of Public Executions in New South Wales', unpublished B.A. (Hons) thesis, La Trobe University, 1973.

Online Sources

Baker, D.W.A., 'Lang, John Dunmore (1799–1878)', *Australian Dictionary of Biography* 1967, http://adb.anu.edu.au/biography/lang-john-dunmore-2326, viewed 10 July 2015.

Barry, John V., 'Kelly, Edward (Ned) (1855–1880)', *The Australian Dictionary of Biography* 1974, http://adb.anu.edu.au/biography/kelly-edward-ned-3933, viewed 12 November 2013.

'Bedford, William (1781–1852)', *Australian Dictionary of Biography* 1966, http://adb.anu.edu.au/biography/bedford-william-1760, viewed on 28 October 2013.

Bergman, G.F.J., 'Davis, Edward (1816–1841)', *Australian Dictionary of Biography* 1966, http://adb.anu.edu.au/biography/davis-edward-1964, viewed 15 March 2015.

Blake, L.J., 'Kentish, Nathaniel Lipscomb (1797–1867)', *Australian Dictionary of Biography* 1967, http://adb.anu.edu.au/biography/kentish-nathaniel-lipscomb-2302, viewed 5 January 2015.

Borchardt, D.H., 'Tenison-Woods, Julian Edmund (1832–1889)', *Australian Dictionary of Biography* 1976, http://adb.anu.edu.au/biography/tenison-woods-julian-edmund-4700, viewed 10 October 2019.

Currey, C.H., 'Wardell, Robert (1793–1834)', *Australian Dictionary of Biography* 1967, http://adb.anu.edu.au/biography/wardell-robert-2773, viewed 3 October 2013.

'Dr Henry Grattan DOUGLASS (1790–1865)', *The Parliament of New South Wales* 2008, http://www.parliament.nsw.gov.au/prod/parlment/members.nsf/1fb6ebed995667c2ca256ea100825164/8a28df421cb43794ca256e69000968aa?OpenDocument, viewed 20 August 2013.

Eddy, J., 'Therry, John Joseph (1790–1864), *Australian Dictionary of Biography* 1967, http://adb.anu.edu.au/biography/therry-john-joseph-2722, viewed 11 October 2019.

Finnane, Mark, and Chris Leppard, 'The Hanging Years: Research Brief 30', *The Prosecution Project* 2018, https://prosecutionproject.griffith.edu.au/the-hanging-years/, viewed 5 October 2019.

Fitzhardinge, L.F., 'Cunningham, Peter Miller (1789–1864)', *Australian Dictionary of Biography* 1966, http://adb.anu.edu.au/biography/cunningham-peter-miller-1942, viewed 6 March 2015.

Hill, Kate, 'Friday Rewind: The Hangman of Old Mount Gambier Gaol', *ABC South East SA* 2015, http://www.abc.net.au/local/photos/2015/08/21/4297622.htm, viewed 16 November 2015.

'Jerry Koci and John Novotny', *National Archives of Australia* 2019, http://guides.naa.gov.au/records-about-northern-territory/part2/chapter16/16.11.aspx, viewed 20 November 2019.

Jones, Barry, 'Deeming, Frederick Bailey (1853–1892)', *Australian Dictionary of Biography* 1981, http://adb.anu.edu.au/biography/deeming-frederick-bailey-5940, viewed 12 December 2019.

'Knatchbull, John (1782–1844)', *Australian Dictionary of Biography* 1967, http://adb.anu.edu.au/biography/knatchbull-john-2313, viewed 5 January 2015.

Laster, Kathy, 'Capital Punishment', *eMelbourne—The Encyclopedia of Melbourne* 2008, http://www.emelbourne.net.au/biogs/EM00290b.htm, viewed 1 August 2015.

Laugesen, Amanda, 'As Game as Ned Kelly', *Ozwords: A Blog from the Australian National Dictionary Centre* 2012, http://ozwords.org/?p=3014, viewed 12 November 2013.

Laurence, Patrick, 'Twenty-One Hanged in Seventy-Two Hours', *Mail and Guardian*, 11 December 1987, https://mg.co.za/article/1987-12-11-00-twenty-one-hanged-in-seventy-two-hours, viewed 15 November 2019.

MacDonald, Helen, 'Public Executions', *The Companion to Tasmanian History* 2006, http://www.utas.edu.au/library/companion_to_tasmanian_history/P/Public%20executions.htm, viewed 14 June 2011.

Macnab, K., T. Castle, and A. Kaladelfos, 'NSW Capital Convictions Database, 1788–1954', *Frances Forbes Society for Australian Legal History* 2013, http://research.forbessociety.org.au/, viewed 13 August 2015.

Noad, K.B., 'Douglass, Henry Grattan (1790–1865)', *Australian Dictionary of Biography* 1966, http://adb.anu.edu.au/biography/douglass-henry-grattan-1987, viewed 20 August 2013.

Norden, Peter, 'Ned Kelly: Hero or Hell Raiser?', *Australian Geographic Magazine* 2014, http://www.australiangeographic.com.au/topics/history-culture/2014/06/ned-kelly-hero-or-hell-raiser/, viewed 8 February 2015.

'Our History', *Supreme Court of Victoria* 2019, https://www.supremecourt.vic.gov.au/about-the-court/our-history, viewed 15 December 2019.

Parliament of New South Wales, 'Mr John Haynes (1850–1917)', *Parliament of New South Wales Website* 2019, https://www.parliament.nsw.gov.au/members/formermembers/Pages/former-member-details.aspx?pk=931, viewed 20 October 2019.

Parliament of New South Wales, 'Mr Thomas Waddell (1854–1940)', *Parliament of New South Wales Website* 2019, https://www.parliament.nsw.gov.

au/members/formermembers/Pages/former-member-details.aspx?pk=975, viewed 20 October 2019.

Parliament of New South Wales, 'Sir Albert John Gould (1849–1936)', *Parliament of New South Wales Website* 2019, https://www.parliament.nsw.gov.au/members/formermembers/Pages/former-member-details.aspx?pk=897, viewed 23 October 2019.

Parliament of New South Wales, 'The Hon. Henry Copeland (1839–1904)', *Parliament of New South Wales Website* 2019, https://www.parliament.nsw.gov.au/members/formermembers/Pages/former-member-details.aspx?pk=751, viewed 24 October 2019.

Phillips, A.A., 'Kingsley, Henry (1830–1876)', *Australian Dictionary of Biography* 1974, http://adb.anu.edu.au/biography/kingsley-henry-396, viewed 4 April 2015.

'Queensland Courts', *The Prosecution Project* 2019, https://prosecutionproject.griffith.edu.au/other-resources/queensland-courts/, viewed 12 December 2019.

Radi, Heather, 'Haynes, John (1850–1917)', *Australian Dictionary of Biography* 1972, http://adb.anu.edu.au/biography/haynes-john-3738, viewed 14 October 2019

Reynolds, John, 'West, John (1809–1873)', *Australian Dictionary of Biography Online* 1967, http://adb.anu.edu.au/biography/west-john-2784, viewed 1 July 2015.

'Robert "Nosey Bob" Howard (1832–1906)', *Waverley Council* 2009, http://www.waverley.nsw.gov.au/__data/assets/pdf_file/0020/8732/Hangman_Waverleys_First.pdf, viewed 11 November 2014.

Roe, Michael, 'Taylor, Alfred Joseph (1849–1921)', *Australian Dictionary of Biography* 1976, http://adb.anu.edu.au/biography/taylor-alfred-joseph-4691, viewed 10 October 2019.

Ryan, Lyndall et al. 'Colonial Frontier Massacres, Australia: 1780–1930', *The University of Newcastle Website*, https://c21ch.newcastle.edu.au/colonialmassacres/map.php, viewed 18 October 2019.

Serle, Geoffrey, 'Wilson, Edward (1813–1878)', *Australian Dictionary of Biography Online* 1976, http://adb.anu.edu.au/biography/wilson-edward-4866, viewed 14 July 2015.

'South Australian Courts', *The Prosecution Project* 2019, https://prosecutionproject.griffith.edu.au/other-resources/south-australian-courts/, viewed 2 December 2019.

Suttor, T.L., 'Ullathorne, William Bernard (1806–1889)', *Australian Dictionary of Biography* 1967, http://adb.anu.edu.au/biography/ullathorne-william-bernard-2750, viewed 6 May 2015.

'Tasmanian Courts', *The Prosecution Project* 2019, https://prosecutionproject.griffith.edu.au/other-resources/tasmanian-courts/, viewed 2 December 2019.

'Western Australian Courts', *The Prosecution Project* 2019, https://prosecutionproject.griffith.edu.au/other-resources/western-australian-courts/, viewed 12 December 2019.

Index

S. Anderson, *A History of Capital Punishment in the Australian Colonies, 1788 to 1900*, Palgrave Histories of Policing, Punishment and Justice
https://doi.org/10.1007/978-3-030-53767-8

The manufacturer's authorised representative in the EU is Springer Nature Customer Service Centre GmbH, Europaplatz 3, 69115 Heidelberg, Germany. If you have any concerns regarding our products, please contact ProductSafety@springernature.com

Printed and bound by CPI Group (UK) Ltd, Croydon, CR0 4YY

30/09/2026

02225502-0008